'Whether you are new to the sector or an FE veteran, *The Coming of Age for FE?* is essential reading. No minister should be allowed to preside over the FE sector before reading and answering questions about this book. I finished reading with a much better appreciation of the sector and how its leaders have responded to ever-changing and often contradictory Government policy. Despite the complexity of the sector and its recent history, the book's essays paint a fascinating picture. If only all policy analysis was as engaging as this.'

Matthew Taylor, Chief Executive, Royal Society of Arts

'Here, at last, is a text to help comprehend what happened to further education colleges after they became formally independent institutions in the 1990s. It is a story of gains, retreats, survivals and renewals. Reflecting on these years are expert commentators from within the college system and its professional and academic communities. The accounts are illuminating and the judgements telling, not least for the policy learning that did not happen and the autonomies still to be won.'

Gareth Parry, Professor of Education, University of Sheffield

'This important and stimulating collection goes a long way to showing the FE sector coming of age – with key actors analysing a wide range of dimensions of the over-regulated, under-valued work of colleges since 1993, and opening rich agendas for future debate.'

Alan Tuckett, Professor of Education, University of Wolverhampton

'This is a really timely and important book. It not only sets out the recent history of FE colleges, and their evolution under successive governments, but also a plausible and compelling vision for their future as central players in a decentralized English state, in which policy goals for adult learning and skills development are pursued by democratic institutions, rather than bureaucracies or markets.'

Nick Pearce, Director, Institute for Public Policy Research

D0415219

KIDDERMINSTER COLLEGE

057138

The Coming of Age for FE?

Reflections on the past and future role of further education colleges in England

Edited by Ann Hodgson

The LRC
@
KIDDERMINSTER
COLLEGE

Institute of Education Press

First published in 2015 by the Institute of Education Press,
University College London, 20 Bedford Way, London WC1H 0AL

ioepress.co.uk

© Ann Hodgson 2015

British Library Cataloguing in Publication Data:
A catalogue record for this publication is available from the British Library

ISBNs
978-1-78277-123-4 (paperback)
978-1-78277-124-1 (PDF eBook)
978-1-78277-125-8 (ePub eBook)
978-1-78277-126-5 (Kindle eBook)

All rights reserved. No part of this publication may be reproduced, stored in a retrieval system, or transmitted in any form or by any means, electronic, mechanical, photocopying, recording, or otherwise, without the prior permission of the copyright owner.

Every effort has been made to trace copyright holders and to obtain their permission for the use of copyright material. The publisher apologizes for any errors or omissions and would be grateful if notified of any corrections that should be incorporated in future reprints or editions of this book.

The opinions expressed in this publication are those of the author and do not necessarily reflect the views of the UCL Institute of Education, University College London.

Typeset by Quadrant Infotech (India) Pvt Ltd
Printed by CPI Group (UK) Ltd, Croydon CR0 4YY

Cover images, top to bottom: ©iStock.com/bowdenimages; ©iStock.com/Geber86; ©iStock.com/bjones27; ©iStock.com/vm

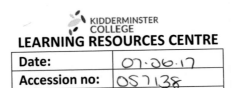
KIDDERMINSTER COLLEGE
LEARNING RESOURCES CENTRE

Date:	07.06.17
Accession no:	OS7138
Classification:	374.47 HOD

Contents

Acknowledgements

This book was conceived at a seminar held on 5 June 2014 at UCL Institute of Education in London, which was attended by a large number of people who have worked within the further education sector for many years, who generously shared their ideas and expertise on life after FE incorporation in 1993. Thanks are due to Paul Grainger and the Centre for Post-14 Research and Innovation for organizing that fascinating event and to RCU Ltd, 157 Group, and *FE Week* for their sponsorship. I am very grateful to Professor Lorna Unwin, OBE, who has spent her professional life studying and writing about further education colleges and vocational education, for writing the Foreword to this book. I would particularly like to thank Mick Fletcher, Paul Grainger, Sue Jones, Norman Lucas, Ian Nash, and Dan Taubman who acted as the Editorial Board for the book and, of course, all the chapter authors who worked to a very tight schedule. In addition, I am grateful to Julian Gravatt for his expert comments on the book. However, I take full responsibility for final decisions on editing and any inaccuracies that might have ensued as a result.

About the contributors

Bill Bailey is a Visiting Fellow at UCL Institute of Education.

Norman Crowther is National Official for Post-16 Education, Association of Teachers and Lecturers.

Peter Davies is an independent researcher and consultant with over 35 years' experience in the further education system, including work on educational marketing, student participation, retention, progression, and achievement.

Mick Fletcher is an education consultant, a director of RCU Ltd, and a Visiting Research Fellow at UCL Institute of Education.

Paul Grainger is Co-Director of the Post-14 Centre for Research and Innovation, and coordinator for FE@IOE at UCL Institute of Education.

Julian Gravatt is Assistant Chief Executive of the Association of Colleges.

John Graystone is now an education consultant having been Chief Executive of ColegauCymru/CollegesWales for 13 years.

Ann Hodgson is Professor of Post-Compulsory Education and Co-Director of the Centre for Post-14 Research and Innovation at UCL Institute of Education.

Sue Jones is a freelance journalist, writer, and former teacher at a Hertfordshire comprehensive school where she was head of history and humanities.

Tom Jupp was the first principal of the newly created City and Islington College (1993–2001). Subsequently, he has undertaken a wide range of work across further and adult education.

Norman Lucas is Reader of Further and Adult Education at the UCL Institute of Education.

Andrew Morris works in a freelance capacity on the use of evidence in education and was formerly a manager at the Learning and Skills Development Agency and a director at City and Islington College.

Ian Nash is a freelance journalist, writer, and former Assistant Editor (Further Education) of the *Times Educational Supplement.*

Judith Norrington, formerly a Group Director of Policy, Research, and Regulation at City & Guilds and a Director of Curriculum and Quality at the Association of Colleges, is now an Education and Skills Consultant.

Kevin Orr is Reader in Work and Learning at the University of Huddersfield.

Adrian Perry was a college principal for 15 years in Sheffield and London, then worked as a consultant on further education policy and practice and was appointed OBE in the 2003 New Year Honours.

Tony Pitcher worked in further education from 1968 to 2014; as a teacher, then as the principal of three colleges and subsequently as a non-executive board member of three colleges, including holding chair and vice-chair positions.

David Sherlock is the former Chief Inspector of the Adult Learning Inspectorate and a director of the consultancy 'Beyond Standards'.

Ken Spours is Professor of Post-Compulsory Education and Co-Director of the Centre for Post-14 Research and Innovation at UCL Institute of Education.

Geoff Stanton is an independent consultant and visiting fellow at the UCL Institute of Education, having previously worked in four colleges and been Director of the Further Education Unit.

Dan Taubman retired from his position as UCU Senior National Education Official at the end of 2013. Since then he has been working as an education consultant. He is a visiting research associate at the UCL Institute of Education.

Lorna Unwin, OBE, is Professor Emerita Vocational Education at the UCL Institute of Education.

Joanna van Heyningen co-founded van Heyningen and Haward Architects in 1982 and retired in 2012. She is now an active participant in further education.

Chris Wilderspin is a partner at van Heyningen and Haward Architects where he has focused on education building projects.

Rob Wye was formerly Chief Executive of the Learning and Skills Improvement Service and Council for Awards in Care, Health and Education. He is now a Research Fellow at UCL Institute of Education.

List of figures and tables

List of figures and tables

Foreword

When I became a university lecturer in 1987, after teaching in further education (FE), one of my new colleagues, a professor of education, said to me: 'Ah. Further education. That's where hairdressers go to get qualifications isn't it? If I were you, I'd forget about that and do research on proper education.' This encounter introduced me to a widespread and ignorant view of FE within higher education and among some parts of the civil service and the media. That such a view existed came as a shock, but in writing this Foreword some 28 years later, I am sorry to say that I still come across people who are woefully ill-informed about this major part of the UK's education system. Two key reasons are often cited for this: (1) social class – 'proper education' means staying in school to take A levels or Highers, then going straight to university; and (2) complexity – the work of FE colleges covers a vast range of academic, vocational, and leisure courses from entry to degree level involving students from age 14 through to post-retirement. And then there is the double whammy of FE colleges providing vocational education – for my professor of education, trying to associate hairdressers (or indeed any form of occupational expertise not deemed to be a 'profession') with anything educational was unthinkable. It is to the great credit of everyone who works in, studies in, and supports FE colleges that the ignoramuses continue to be outflanked.

Like all complex and dynamic organizations engaged in public service, colleges do, of course, require rigorous scrutiny. As well as making a much-needed contribution to the general understanding of the role of FE colleges, this book should also act as a guide for those who inspect, fund, and research them. FE colleges have survived through a remarkable capacity for adaptation – to changes in national policies, to the demands of employers, to the impact of economic bubbles and recessions, and to the needs of students. This book provides a highly readable, yet meticulously detailed, account of how the FE colleges we see today have been shaped and the challenges they continue to face. It celebrates FE by offering a critical appraisal of its strengths and weaknesses and, hence, provides a valuable and robust resource for current and future researchers, FE teachers and managers, and others who work in and with colleges.

Lorna Unwin
Professor Emerita Vocational Education
UCL Institute of Education

Chapter 1

What is FE?
Ann Hodgson, Bill Bailey, and Norman Lucas

An important but invisible sector

Everyone knows what schools and universities are and what they do. We all go to school and an increasing proportion of the population experiences higher education at first hand. Most people have heard of apprenticeships too, even if their perception of what an apprenticeship is may be outdated. Far fewer will know what a general further education or sixth form college is and this will drop sharply again when it comes to independent training providers. Yet in 2012/13 these latter organizations, together with a range of others described later and known collectively as further education (FE), engaged with over 4 million learners and were allocated over £8 billion of public funding across the UK (see Table 1.1). Furthermore, in England almost twice as many 16 to 18-year olds – 846,000 studied in colleges than in the much better-known maintained school and academy sixth forms – 441,000 (Association of Colleges, 2014). These learners were mainly on vocational education programmes or building their skills for employment although, as Chapter 4 indicates, the FE curriculum is both broad and diverse.

Why is such an important part of the education system in this country so invisible? Part of the answer to this question lies in the fact that FE has a low political profile when compared with schools and universities, because it, like vocational education and training, is seen as 'for other people's children' (Galley, 2014). However, there is also undoubtedly a severe lack of knowledge about the nature of this complex, amorphous, and ever-changing sector, as well as the part that it plays in lifelong learning. While its role in the provision of vocational education and training is perhaps best known, the FE sector, squeezed like the 'middle child' (Foster, 2005) between its two bigger siblings, arguably also caters for all those whom the schools and universities cannot or will not serve. This, together with the fact that it is tied to fluctuations in employment and the labour market, often taking on the role that workplaces and employers play in other countries, such as Germany, Austria, and Switzerland, make its identity and purpose somewhat opaque. If you add to the mix the constant bombardment of national policy emanating from a bewildering range of ministries, government agencies, and regulatory bodies directed at the FE sector since colleges became incorporated organizations in 1993 (see, for example, Green and Lucas, 1999; Coffield *et al.*, 2008), perhaps it is not surprising that few understand its parameters and mission.

A major purpose of this book, therefore, is, in its own modest way, to tackle the issue of FE invisibility by increasing the knowledge base about the sector and, in particular, to examine the changes that have taken place since further education incorporation. The contributors to this book see it as important both to raise the profile of those who work in, study within, use, or research the sector and to make sure that FE takes its rightful place on the education map of this country. However, while we begin by setting out some of the key facts and figures about the FE sector as a whole in the UK in order to indicate its size, variety, and complexity, our primary focus will be on England and on a specific subset of FE – General Further Education Colleges (GFEs). We also include tertiary colleges in this discussion because of their similarity to GFEs and because they are considered as a single entity by Ofsted.

A brief overview of FE across the UK

Cross-national studies of education and training tend to consider the UK as a single unit for the purposes of comparison and UK GFEs are often seen as similar to Australian Technical and Further Education (TAFE) Colleges/Institutes or Community Colleges in the United States. Like the former, they cater primarily for young people and adults wanting vocational education and training, but, like both types of institutions, they also offer a range of courses for those who want to progress to higher education. As Table 1.1 indicates, in some cases GFEs also offer their own degrees. This is less common among TAFE Colleges/Institutes and, in the case of Community Colleges, it is the two-year Associate Degree that is the most common higher education provision.

But in order to understand the nature and role of GFEs in England, it is necessary first to locate them within the broader UK FE sector. Then, because the education and training systems of the four countries of the UK have been increasingly diverging since the establishment of the Scottish Parliament and the National Assembly for Wales in 1999 and of the Northern Ireland Assembly in 2007, it is important to distinguish them from GFEs in those three countries.

GFEs take the lion's share of the further education and skills budgets in the UK (see Table 1.1), but they are by no means the only providers of publicly funded further education nor the most numerous. According to Ofsted (2014), in England alone, alongside the 235 GFEs there are 432 publicly funded Independent Learning Providers offering a wide range of training and learning experiences for young people and adults, including apprenticeships and traineeships; 247 community learning and skills providers; 93 sixth form colleges providing a wide range of general and a smaller number of vocational qualifications mainly for 16–19-year olds; 51 independent specialist colleges that specialize in areas such as land-based industries and provision for students with disabilities; further education programmes in prisons (122); armed forces training (48); Dance and Drama Award schemes (19); and FE provision in higher education (HE) institutions (26). The other three countries of the UK have similar provision, with Scotland, like England, also supporting Group Training Associations that organize and deliver apprenticeships for groups of employers usually within a single sector, and Wales supporting 15 Adult and Community Learning Partnerships. In all four countries, school sixth forms, like GFEs, also offer academic and, to a lesser extent, vocational qualifications to 16–19-year olds and, of course, universities, like some GFEs, provide higher education.

GFEs, therefore, have to decide on their role and take their place within this complex territory, which will vary by locality and region and will be affected by demography, geography, the local economy, and the transport infrastructure as well as by the degree to which others in the local ecology are prepared to collaborate or compete. This means that GFEs vary significantly in terms of their size; the nature and level of provision they offer; the degree to which they specialize and the sectors in which they specialize; the age and previous educational experience of the students they serve; the proportion of full-time to part-time learners; and their relationships with other key social partners such as local employers, the local authority, and the other providers in the area. The only thing that characterizes all UK GFEs is that they are primarily concerned with vocational education and training and that they cater for all ages from 14 upwards.

Table 1.1 FE across the UK

Feature	England	Scotland	Wales	Northern Ireland
Number of FE colleges	235 GFE and tertiary colleges and 93 SixthFCs[1]	27 colleges (25 of which form 10 regional colleges)[2]	13 colleges + 2 specialist colleges)[3]	6 regional colleges[4]
Other major publicly funded FE providers	51 ISCs; 432 ILPs; 247 CLSP; 122 Prisons; 48 AFT sites; 19 DADA schemes; 26 FE in HEIs[5]	Private training providers and Group Training Associations represented by the Scottish Training Federation	24 lead WBL providers; 15 ACL partnerships[6]	Non-statutory providers (e.g. Apprenticeship Northern Ireland and Training for Success providers)[7]
Students	4.2m; more female than male[8] (3 million in colleges, of which 66% are 19+)	236.5k; more female than male[9] (230k in FE colleges, of which 89% are 16+)[10]	211.3k; more female than male[11] (195.9 in FE colleges, of which 68% are 19+)[12]	141.7k; equal male and female[13] (90k in FE colleges)[14]
Provision	Primarily VET but 28% of A Level students study in colleges[15] and 8% of HE students[19]	Overwhelmingly VET – 71% part-time; FE provision 82%; HE provision 18%[16]	Learning aims primarily VET quals (71.5%), 4% A Level, and 1.4% HE level[17]	Mainly VET, professional, and technical but also 18% of NI HE)[18]

Feature	England	Scotland	Wales	Northern Ireland
Funding (recurrent)	DfE (£3.78bn)[20], for 16–19 in colleges; SFA (£2bn)[21] for 19+	SFC (£521.7m)[22]	Welsh Government (£305.1m)[23]	Department for Employment and learning (£356.1m)[24]
Inspection	Ofsted	Education Scotland (more focused on development than inspection.	Estyn	Education and Training Inspectorate
Governance	Incorporated status since 1993	Incorporated status since 1993; 10 regional colleges have board of management	Incorporated status since 1993	Incorporated status since 1998

Notes: [1] Ofsted, 2014; [2] Colleges Scotland, 2014; [3] Colleges Wales, 2014. (It should be noted that the two specialist colleges are planning to merge in summer 2015); [4] Colleges Northern Ireland, 2014; [5] Ofsted, 2014; [6] Estyn, 2014; [7] DELNI, 2013; [8] Department for Education, 2014; [9] Department for Education, 2014; [10] Colleges Scotland, 2014; [11] Department for Education, 2014; [12] National Assembly for Wales, 2013; [13] Department for Education, 2014; [14] Colleges Northern Ireland, 2014; [15] Association of Colleges, 2014; [16] Department for Business, Innovation and Skills, 2012; [17] Colleges Scotland, 2014; [18] National Assembly for Wales, 2013; [19] Colleges Northern Ireland, 2014; [20] Education Funding Agency, 2014; [21] Skills Funding Agency, 2014; [22] Scottish Funding Council, 2013; [23] National Assembly for Wales, 2013; [24] Department for Employment and Learning Northern Ireland, 2013.

Key to abbreviations

AFT = Armed forces training

CLSP = Community learning and skills providers

DADA = Dance and Drama Award

DfE = Department for Education

GFE = General further education college

ILP = Independent learning provider

ISC = Independent specialist college

SFA = Skills Funding Agency

SFC = Scottish Funding Council
SixthFC = Sixth form college
VET = Vocational education and training
WEA = Workers' Education Association
YMCA = Young Men's Christian Association

However, while GFEs in all four countries of the UK gained incorporated status in the 1990s and thus work as autonomous organizations in terms of deciding their own mission and priorities, their main funding still comes from their national governments. National policies, particularly around funding and inspection, thus play a major role in shaping their behavior, as Chapter 8 points out.

It is here that the divergence between the four countries of the UK begins to become apparent and as Table 1.1 illustrates, there are differences beginning to emerge between England, Scotland, Wales, and Northern Ireland that are to do with more than just the significant differences in the size of their populations – 54 million; 5 million; 3 million and just under 2 million respectively. These include:

- *Organization* – In Wales, Scotland, and Northern Ireland, GFEs have been encouraged to regionalize by their governments in order to rationalize provision and provide economies of scale, but also to align them more closely with the local and regional economies. (In the case of Wales, colleges were given a choice. This was not the case in the other two countries.) In England, the decision about whether to merge or go it alone has largely been left up to individual colleges to decide within what has become an education marketplace, although some political administrations have pushed more strongly for merger than others. Within this, however, the idea of a regional approach has not found favour in England under the current Conservative–Liberal Democrat Coalition government, possibly because it has been associated to some degree with the policies of the previous Labour administration.
- *Gender* – Only in Northern Ireland is there a similar number of male and female students in GFEs. In the other three countries, females predominate.
- *HE provision* – HE is a more important part of GFE provision in Scotland and Northern Ireland than it is in England and Wales, and in both countries one organization funds both types of provision (the Scottish Funding Council and the Department for Employment and Learning respectively).

- *Funding* – FE funding is the responsibility of a single department in all countries except England, where it is split between two ministries.
- *Collaboration and competition* – There appears to be a greater division of labour between schools and colleges in Scotland, Wales, and Northern Ireland than in England, which allows for greater partnership working between the two in relation to provision for 14–19-year olds (Hodgson *et al.*, 2011). In Scotland, for example, schools and colleges collaborate over the new Skills for Work courses that are part of the Curriculum for Excellence reforms (see Education Scotland, 2014), although, according to recent interviews with policymakers in Scotland, this is becoming more difficult to sustain because of the reductions in funding to GFEs (Hodgson and Spours, 2014). Similarly, in Northern Ireland schools and colleges have been active partners in Area Learning Communities that have been set up to support the delivery of the 14–19 Entitlement Framework, which is intended to ensure that all young people have access to a range of vocational as well as general qualifications during their upper secondary phase (see Department for Education Northern Ireland, 2012a). In Wales, colleges have been seen as important partners in the 14–19 Pathways (Welsh Government, 2004) and Welsh Baccalaureate reforms (Welsh Baccalaureate, 2015), particularly in relation to NEETs (those young people not in employment, education, or training). In England, on the other hand, while there is a limited amount of collaboration between schools and colleges in relation to provision for 14–19-year olds, competition, particularly between the new academy sixth forms, SFCs, and GFEs can be intense. Moreover, the financial support for collaboration that was available under the previous Labour government was removed in 2010 by the incoming Conservative–Liberal Democrat Coalition administration, which has actively promoted the twin concepts of a market in education and training, and student choice.
- *Inspection* – Inspection appears to be more adversarial under the Ofsted regime in England, compared to the more developmental approach taken by Education Scotland in Scotland, Estyn in Wales, and the Education and Training Inspectorate in Northern Ireland.
- *The policy process* – Finally, partly as a result of the smaller size of Scotland, Wales, and Northern Ireland, but also because of their social democratic politics, the ability of education professionals, including those in GFEs, to contribute to local and national policymaking in those countries is, and has been, much greater than has recently been the case in England (Hodgson *et al.*, 2011; Hodgson and

Spours, 2014). Recent examples include the consultation processes surrounding Curriculum for Excellence in Scotland, the Review of Qualifications for 14- to 19-year olds in Wales, which is chaired by an ex-college principal (see Welsh Government, 2014), and the reviews of the National Curriculum (Department of Education Northern Ireland, 2005) and GCSEs and A Levels (Department of Education Northern Ireland, 2012b) in Northern Ireland. All of these consultations have included a large number of face-to-face and online discussion forums, rather than being the closed question paper exercises that predominate in England; can be characterized as open and evidence-based rather than being ideologically driven; and, crucially, have taken place over a reasonable period of time in order to encourage participation and consensus-building rather than being rushed through to a political deadline.

In conclusion, while those outside the UK may still see considerable similarities between FE in the four countries, when compared with the very different systems in continental Europe, for example, devolution and divergence are making their mark within the UK. England is increasingly becoming an outlier as the effects of several years of neo-liberal policies shape the development of its GFEs and increase the natural differences that occur because of differences in population size.

To understand how and why GFEs in England have taken their current form, we now turn to a brief historical account of their development both prior to and following incorporation in 1993.

The history of FE colleges – before incorporation

The wide range of work of English further education institutions has been their distinctive characteristic from the early 1900s, when they were first recognized as part of the education service (see Bailey, 2002). Indeed it is this wide range that has led to the frustration of policymakers who look for a clear role and purpose. In this section we outline the provision made by colleges with the important caution that, as mentioned above, GFEs vary in their size and in the courses they offer. No two colleges are alike and any generalization has to be qualified with the phrase 'but, on the other hand ...'

From the beginning, GFEs' core work was providing technical and commercial courses, usually related to local industries and employment, and leading to the certificates awarded by one of the examining bodies (see Bailey and Unwin, 2014). Hence the common reference to 'the tech'. The best known of these examining bodies was the City & Guilds of London

Institute but for much of the twentieth century there were others, including the Royal Society of Arts, the London Chamber of Commerce and Industry, and a number of regional bodies. The industries served differed from one region to another: textiles in West Yorkshire and Lancashire, and printing in London, for example, with engineering, building, and branches of business subjects featuring in most places. The vast majority of students attended on their own initiative in the evening, the successful completion of technical and commercial courses requiring attendance on two or three evenings a week for two or three years (see Abbot, 1933; Venables, 1955). Evening-only attendance was reduced to a considerable extent after 1945 when many employers – particularly in the public sectors of industry and administration – released employees, with pay, to attend their courses during the day (Cantor and Roberts, 1969). Some of these were on formal apprenticeships.

Although for decades their work was referred to as 'technical education', an examination of the courses offered in colleges shows that they offered more opportunities than would be included in the category of 'technical and commercial'. So, at a time when many working class young people and adults had received an inadequate elementary education, there was considerable demand for classes in the basics of English language and mathematics. Students could be acquiring these skills in order to use them in life generally, to improve their job prospects, or to be able to go on to obtain technical qualifications. As well as instruction at this elementary level, colleges could also provide classes leading to examinations in academic subjects that could lead to entry to degree courses or advanced level technical courses. These were typically the academic qualifications taken by secondary-school leavers; before 1951 the School Certificate, then the General Certificate of Education (GCE) Ordinary (O) and Advanced (A) levels, later the General Certificate of Secondary Education (GCSE), Advanced Subsidiary (AS), and A levels. From 2001, the 'Skills for Life' literacy, numeracy, and English for speakers of other languages (ESOL) courses became the contemporary form of post-school basic education (Department for Education and Skills, 2001).

As well as assisting students to obtain qualifications for entry to higher education, it was possible for some colleges themselves to offer degree courses through the use of University of London external degrees. This was the case in some of the polytechnics established in London in the 1890s – for example, full-time science and engineering courses were offered at Battersea Polytechnic. The growth of this work led to some colleges being raised to university status in the 1960s (when Battersea Polytechnic became the University of Surrey), so confirming a recurrent theme in further education of supplying 'new' institutions to the university sector. The 'new polytechnics' formed after 1966 joined the university sector after 1992. Today when colleges offer higher education courses it is normally done under arrangements with universities.

As well as their stake in higher education, many colleges have also been involved in secondary education. It became increasingly common during the first half of the twentieth century for colleges to establish full-time junior technical schools for young people aged between 13 and 15 or 16 years (Bailey, 1990). These prepared their students, almost all ex-elementary school pupils, for entry to employment in local industry and possibly an apprenticeship. They were located in the technical college and provided teaching during the day for staff whose main work was in the evening, and made use of specialist accommodation and equipment. These schools were the working/practical models for the secondary technical schools in the selective secondary system after the Second World War. Their numbers were small and in turn they were absorbed into comprehensive schools, but in the 1980s the Conservative Government introduced the Technical and Vocational Education Initiative (TVEI), which often involved colleges' cooperation with secondary schools. Since September 2013, young people aged 14–16 have been funded to enrol in certain GFE colleges in order to complete their compulsory schooling (Department for Education, 2013).

In some places, in addition to their courses related to skilled occupations, the technical colleges offered provision for groups of young workers in unskilled jobs for which no technical training or qualification was required. Such provision originated in concern for the young worker who had left school for work at 13, 14, 15, or 16 as the school-leaving age was raised during the twentieth century. As adolescents they were still immature and were likely to have had less successful school careers. These college courses were experimental, with curricula that lacked a skilled occupation as their organizing focus. Since the 1970s, when changes in the labour market increased the difficulties of young people finding employment, GFEs have been involved in programmes for these young people and for unemployed adults.

A final aspect of the work of many colleges as they developed in the twentieth century was adult education. GFEs provided opportunities for adults to participate in studies and activities not necessarily connected to their work; for example, history or economics, or practical and leisure activities such as ballroom dancing, bridge, and radio mechanics; more recently computing and Pilates. After incorporation the numbers of students on these courses fell as the funding system focused mainly upon students obtaining qualifications. However, since 2003 a small annual allocation for adult and community learning (£210 million in 2012/13), frozen in real terms, has been available to try to protect some of this work.

Criticisms and reform

Colleges, almost all maintained by the county or borough council as the local education authority (LEA), developed this variety of provision by meeting demand from individuals and employers in their local area. Until after the Second World War the law allowed LEAs to provide further and technical education but did not require that they did so. This meant that the opportunities for further education differed among LEA areas, reflecting political will and interest, other priorities in education and other services, and the resources available. For these reasons the availability of further education in 1939 was patchy, with colleges established in some cities (such as London, Leicester, and Manchester), while in others (such as Leeds and Sheffield) there was no college, and students attended evening classes that were held in the classrooms of elementary and secondary schools.

The legal basis of further education was changed by the 1944 Education Act, which made it a duty of the LEA to provide an 'adequate' service of further education, described as vocational and non-vocational provision for young people and adults in full-time or part-time attendance. In the post-war period further education had a lower priority than housing and primary and secondary schools, and when resources were available there were again variations in the expanding provision made by different LEAs. There was no national plan or policy for further education and no definition of what comprised an adequate service.

The resulting local variations can be seen to lie at the basis of the criticisms of GFEs from the 1970s (Central Policy Review Staff, 1980). They were taken to exemplify the inefficiency and lack of responsiveness to economic needs of the unreformed public sector. The differences between colleges made it difficult for officials at the national level to grasp and assess the overall role of colleges. The colleges' multiple functions – their contribution to the education and training of employees, their commitment to young people on GCSE and GCE A level courses, their involvement in higher education and in adult education – all these varied locally and regionally to the extent that it was difficult to assess how they might play their part in national policies aimed at addressing national economic needs. Attention was also directed at evidence about the 'performance' of colleges and the inefficiencies of the administration of the LEAs. A report by the Audit Commission in 1985 concluded that LEAs could save £50 million a year through better management and organization. More effective use of existing staff would make it possible to teach 75,000 additional students at no extra cost (Audit Commission, 1985).

Considerations of this sort were taken to be evidence of LEAs' failure to run GFEs in the national interest and led the Conservative Government to include the 'local management of colleges' in the 1988 Education Act, giving the governing bodies of GFEs a limited amount of financial discretion, along with a duty to improve their colleges' efficiency and focus on the market. This change was only partly implemented at the time of the publication of the 1991 White Paper and the passing of the Further and Higher Education Act in 1992. The terms of the latter granted statutory independence from the LEAs to the GFEs by making them independent corporations responsible for finances, staffing, and premises. Their governing bodies – 'corporations' – were reduced in size and the representation of business and industry increased. Responsibility for their funding and inspection was given to the Further Education Funding Council for England.

Incorporation and its aftermath

In trying to understand incorporation it is important to distinguish between its governance and funding dimensions. In terms of governance, incorporation was a particular form of public ownership and control set up by the 1992 Act. Quite separate from the Act is the funding method, the overall level or quantum of funding, and the funding-led political priorities of government and policymakers. The combination of these factors gave incorporation its particular form. We unravel these dimensions of incorporation through six different stages of its development since its inception 21 years ago.

Stage one (1993–4) The 'salad days'? Freedom from local education authority (LEA) control

In the first year or so of incorporation, colleges enjoyed independence from LEAs without significant variations in expenditure or a funding regime controlling their activities. It would seem that the majority of college principals were well disposed towards incorporation in 1993 (Further Education Funding Council, 1993; Lucas, 2004), believing that colleges would be freed from local control and cuts in resources, with FE achieving a higher national profile – perhaps even being seen as a national sector. It was during this first stage of incorporation that the Further Education Funding Council (FEFC), which was established in 1992, developed an approach that would determine the form that incorporation took.

The FEFC approach was influenced in particular by three publications. The first was *Obtaining Better Value from FE* (Audit Commission, 1985);

the second was the White Paper *Education and Training for the 21st Century* (Department for Education and Science/Employment Department/ Welsh Office, 1991). Both pointed to the poor financial management of FE colleges and proposed improvements in the level of student participation by placing the colleges in a competitive market situation and expecting them to use management practices adopted from the private sector, both aspects of the general Conservative approach to public services (Newman and Clark, 1994). The third, and possibly the most important, document influencing the newly formed FEFC was the seminal report, *Unfinished Business* (Audit Commission/Ofsted, 1993). This document focused on 16–19-year olds studying in both schools and FE colleges. Its major findings centred on poor student retention and success rates, concluding that between 30 and 40 per cent of 16–19-year olds who started a course did not succeed. Not only did this have a damaging effect on learners, the report argued, it also represented a massive waste of public money. Furthermore, it highlighted a wide variation in cost per student, ranging from just over £1,000 to almost £7,000 for those following the same course. Even more damning, the report found no link between cost per student and examination results.

Influenced by these reports, the FEFC consulted on a number of funding options (Further Education Funding Council, 1992). Each option was examined and critiqued, with option 'E' being strongly recommended. This option was finally supported by 95 per cent of college principals and became the system that is described below (Further Education Funding Council, 1993). According to one principal, the supporters of option 'E' entered a 'Faustian bargain' with the FEFC and 'leaped smiling over the cliff' (Perry, 1997: 3).

Stage two (1994–6) The FEFC model of incorporation: Convergence, change, and upheaval.

It has been argued that the FEFC introduced a number of new concepts with its funding methodology. Three key concepts underpinned the approach. The first was the introduction of a new funding currency, the 'unit of activity' (the unit), replacing the earlier 'student full-time equivalent'. The unit was used to allow the funding to follow the student, so that if the student left the programme the funding would cease. The second concept was that the unit of funding was based upon a three-stage programme – 'entry', 'on programme', and 'achievement' (with additional units earned for such things as fee remission, and additional learning support). The third key concept was that of 'convergence' based upon expanding student numbers. Colleges were funded on 90 per cent of the previous year's budget, with the other 10 per cent based upon units funded at the national average and tied to student growth: this was known as the demand led element (DLE). Therefore colleges with high average levels of funding (ALF) had to increase student numbers just to maintain their budgets. As the process was repeated year after year the ALF would get lower, approaching the convergence figure.

These ingenious concepts, tied into the funding mechanism, addressed the uneven funding between colleges, and poor student retention and achievement, and satisfied the government's policy of greater 'efficiency' that was being applied right across the public sector. At the same time a new FEFC inspectorate was created, along with a strict auditing regime in which colleges competed in an education and training market (Gleeson, 1996).

The effect of the FEFC model was greater centralized control through funding and regulations (Atkinson, 1995; Lucas, 2004). During this period all colleges went through rapid change but their experience varied depending upon their average level of funding. One report found college principals divided between low-ALF colleges, who wanted convergence speeded up, and high-ALF colleges (often in the inner city), who wanted it slowed down and reconsidered (Education and Employment Committee, 1998).

During this period of incorporation considerable improvements were made in terms of service to students and participation rates. Colleges found different ways of delivering learning programmes and became more flexible and responsive organizations (Levacic and Glatter, 1997). However, there were also problems, the severity of which varied between colleges. These included cuts in course hours, the increasing use of part-time staff, and a long and damaging dispute with lecturers over changes to their conditions of service (see Chapter 5 for more detail).

Did the FEFC create a national FE sector? Not in any real sense. There was a national funding mechanism, inspection, and auditing controls, yet as colleges competed to attract more students and 'maximize units', they also reflected the heterogeneous and diverse nature of local and regional needs and remained, as described above, organizations with no clear national strategic role.

Stage three (1997–2001) Continuity and change: The demand-led funding crisis and the demise of the FEFC

By 1997 'efficiency savings' were causing financial problems in many colleges and the FEFC's efforts to provide a measure of stability were undermined by constant adjustments to the funding and regulatory criteria. In the first five years of incorporation there had been an 8 per cent increase in full-time student numbers and a 42 per cent increase in part-time students (Melville and Macleod, 2000; Ainley and Bailey, 1997). There were also improvements made for students across the board, including colleges developing better tracking and information systems. For a government bent on cutting public expenditure this was a big success.

Yet there was growing criticism of the bureaucratic rigidities and data collection systems required to satisfy the demands of the FEFC. There was also some evidence of colleges manipulating or maximizing units by 'tariff farming', 'nesting', or 'additionality' (Lucas, 1999), all of which were a means of increasing units without increasing student numbers. One college increased its unit total by 100 per cent while actually reducing student numbers (Perry, 1997). Other colleges registered dramatic growth, lowering their ALF by franchising courses and training that already existed in the private sector, such as scuba diving and St John Ambulance first aid training (Gravatt and Silver, 2000).

It was against this backdrop that in early 1997 the Treasury refused to provide additional money based on growth to the FEFC. This became known as the 'DLE crisis', which marked the end of the second period of incorporation, based upon competition and an unplanned dash for growth (Lumby and Tomlinson, 2000). The crisis coincided with the election of a Labour Government in 1997 as well as important reports calling for widening participation and a clearer strategic role for FE colleges both nationally and locally (Kennedy, 1997; Fryer, 1997). The first clear signal of Labour's policy changes came with the White Papers, *The Learning Age* (Department for Education and Employment, 1998) and *Learning to Succeed* (Department for Education and Employment, 1999). These heralded fundamental change, not of incorporation itself, but in the funding regime and strategic direction of the FE sector (Lucas, 2004).

Stage four (2001–5) Enter the Learning and Skills Council: Growth, targets, and strategic planning.

The Learning and Skills Council (LSC) replaced the FEFC in April 2001, taking over responsibility for all post-16 education and training, including work-based training, in England (excluding higher education). The FEFC inspectorate was replaced by Ofsted, which had its responsibility extended from only inspecting schools to include 16–19-year olds in colleges. A new Adult Learning Inspectorate (ALI) was established to inspect all adult learning provision.

A feature worth noting is that FE colleges were now part of what government agencies called the 'learning and skills sector' (LSS), with an LSC to plan its provision. At the same time Individual Learning Accounts (ILAs) were introduced to give individual learners more choice, although these were shut down in 2001, only eighteen months after their establishment, following reports of fraud and poor provision. The failure of ILAs not only demonstrated the difficulty of regulating choice-based markets, it also influenced the Department for Education and Skills' (DfES) approach to the LSCs, which was one of increasing centralization.

The Learning and Skills Act 2000 and *Success for All* (Department for Education and Skills, 2002) brought about a number of fundamental changes. Firstly, they allowed the LSC to fund a much wider range of institutions to encourage more strategic planning and cooperation between providers in the LSS. Secondly, the LSC scrapped units of resource and replaced them with cash payments based on full-time equivalents. Thirdly, the new sector was to some degree influenced by employers and employer-led bodies, such as the emerging Sector Skills Councils (SSCs). The government claimed at the time that by putting employers in the 'driving seat' the sector would become consumer driven, which in turn would lead to finding new solutions for the learning needs of businesses (Hook, 2003).

Another fundamental drive was the desire to raise standards across the sector, led by the new Standards Unit, which would work with practitioners and social partners to identify and disseminate effective practice, to develop new teaching and learning frameworks to support teachers, and to improve the provision of training, including the introduction of compulsory teacher training, as discussed in Chapter 5.

During this period there was an increased focus on planning (rather than pure market-led policies), which led to the introduction of Strategic Area Reviews (StARs), led by the local LSCs, with colleges gaining increased expenditure linked to their production of agreed three-year plans.

However, in less than three years StARs were dropped because of a reluctance on the part of government to give the local LSCs the funding and power needed to plan provision locally (Panchania, 2013). Control was pulled back to the DfES, with generous funding tied to centrally set targets. It has been suggested that this move towards centralization was part of a broader government policy that did not just apply to the LSS (Coffield *et al.*, 2008).

Stage five (2005–10) From supply-led planning to a demand-led system: The demise of the LSC

During this stage of incorporation, FE colleges and the LSS generally enjoyed increases to their funding tied to targets – the beginning of a business model led by the LSC emerged. One example was Train to Gain, a government-funded employer-led scheme launched in 2006 after three years of piloting, which provided free work-based training to adults. In many respects the role of the LSC was changing from being a planning and funding body to being a 'market maker' (Lanning and Lawton, 2012).

Stage four described how competition and unplanned growth was replaced by an emphasis on planning and collaboration. In stage five local planning was abandoned in favour of central control. Two government reports influenced this change. The Foster Review (2005) concluded that the sector was over-regulated and placed undue emphasis on qualifications. It recommended a realignment towards skills and employability. In 2006 the Leitch Review suggested moving to a system where funding was routed through employer-led schemes, advocating a 'demand-led system' responsive to the needs of employers and individuals, with quality defined according to the degree to which provision met the needs of employers and the labour market.

While the LSC was ready to implement the new performance-based system outlined in *Framework for Excellence* (2006), there was growing criticism of its inefficiencies. In 2010, alongside changes to the national ministries responsible for education and training, the LSC itself was replaced by two new bodies, the Skills Funding Agency (19+), an agency of the Department for Business, Innovation and Skills, and the Young People's Learning Agency (16–19), a non-departmental public body overseen by the Department for Education (DfE). Dividing the funding between 16–19-year olds and 19+ reversed the previous policy emphasis on coherence and integration through a single LSS (Panchania, 2013).

During the LSC period there were a number of notable achievements, such as an increase in the participation of 16–19-year olds, a new focus on adult basic skills, the establishment of Centres of Vocational Excellence, substantially increased FE success rates, and major investment in GFE buildings (Coffield *et al.*, 2008). On the other hand, FE colleges had been micromanaged by the government and the LSC and, arguably, were still perceived as not meeting employer needs or adequately tackling the high proportion of young people not in any form of education, employment, or training (NEETs).

Stage six (2010–) Austerity and deregulation

The Conservative–Liberal Democrat Coalition Government, which came to power in 2010, pledged to cut public expenditure drastically and to have a 'bonfire of the quangos'. Almost immediately Train to Gain was closed, funding was withdrawn for 14–19 Diplomas and school–college collaboration and the Education Maintenance Allowance was abolished in England. Furthermore, the Coalition closed the Young People's Learning

Agency (YPLA) and established in its place a new DfE-managed Education Funding Agency (EFA) with an extended remit for 3–19-year olds.

For education and training outside of the school sector, the reforms seem to be somewhat contradictory. The Coalition Government funded students in FE colleges based upon enrolment and qualifications passed in the previous year, thereby removing central planning in favour of demand-led and outcome-led funding. Furthermore, the Education Act 2011 allowed FE colleges to borrow money without permission from central government and to change the nature of their governance. At the same time, the government ring-fenced money to pay for 2 million apprenticeships over five years, which has echoes of past central planning and supply-led funding.

Adult provision has been cut across the board as part of the public spending cuts. Individuals over the age of 24 are now expected to take out loans to pay for education and training, much like the higher education funding model. It is hoped that introducing a greater role for market forces will empower individuals to make better choices according to the costs and the benefits to their employment. This change pushes funding for training away from colleges and towards employers, reinforcing the previous government's shift from supply-led to demand-led funding.

The closing down of quangos, such as Lifelong Learning UK (LLUK) and the Learning and Skills Improvement Service (LSIS) reinforced deregulation. A good example of this is the removal of the requirement to be teacher trained in FE (Lingfield, 2012). Policies aiming to reduce the public spending deficit continue at the time of writing and the sector is uncertain of future budget savings. The depth of the present funding reductions is considerable. The overall reduction in the predicted budget for the Department for Business, Innovation and Skills (BIS) between 2010 and 2018 is some 43 per cent (Keep, 2014). Given this level of reduction, colleges may no longer be able to rely on central state funding, which may lead to an increasingly deregulated sector.

The chapters in the book: Piecing together the jigsaw

Given this history, and the scenario described under stage six, a number of key questions face GFEs in the future. These can be grouped under four main themes:

1. What have been the effects of FE incorporation over the last two decades – what has changed for GFEs in England and what remains constant?
2. To what extent can the changes that have taken place in GFEs be attributed to incorporation and what might better be understood as part of wider societal, economic, and political trends?

3. What is the future role for GFEs and where do they fit within the broader national, regional, and local education and training landscape in England?
4. Who should GFEs serve and what kind of governance and accountability arrangements do they require?

Each of the chapters that follow contributes to addressing these questions by commenting in depth on a particular piece of what might be seen as a giant jigsaw.

In Chapter 2, Ian Nash and Sue Jones, long-standing commentators on FE, focus on politicians and their perceptions of, and role in shaping, GFEs in England.

Chapter 3 is dedicated to the students in FE. Adrian Perry and Peter Davies, who have worked in the FE sector for most of their working lives, examine patterns of participation in FE over time and note some of the changes that have taken place in the period since FE incorporation.

In Chapter 4, Geoff Stanton, Andrew Morris, and Judith Norrington, who have worked in FE as practitioners, researchers, and policymakers over several decades, use their experience to survey key trends and themes in curriculum and qualifications over the period 1993 to 2014 and identify the particular features and strengths of FE provision.

Mick Fletcher, Norman Lucas, Norman Crowther, and Dan Taubman follow this with a focus in chapter 5 on the multifaceted workforce in GFEs. They use the expertise they have gained through their involvement in initial and continuing teacher education, researching the sector, and teacher unions to comment on how and why the workforce has changed over the period since FE incorporation.

An important piece of the FE jigsaw is the space and place within which GFEs function. Paul Grainger and Tony Pitcher, from their perspectives as ex-principals of FE colleges, and Joanna van Hennigan and Chris Wilderspin, as practising architects, consider this often neglected aspect of the FE landscape in Chapter 6.

John Graystone, Kevin Orr, and Rob Wye, representing between them FE researchers, policymakers, and practitioners, fill in some of the background of the jigsaw by looking at the governance of the sector in Chapter 7. They focus on accountability and the role of college governors, exploring how things have changed since incorporation.

Chapter 8 expands on this big-picture approach as Mick Fletcher, Julian Gravatt, and David Sherlock, highly experienced and long-standing

FE policymakers and commentators, describe the role of key policy levers and accountability mechanisms on GFE decision-making and behaviour.

We slot the final piece into the jigsaw with Chapter 9, in which Tom Jupp, who has managed and led GFEs over many years, considers the part that leadership plays in these organizations. The chapter draws on a number of interviews with past and present college leaders and policymakers who reflect on how their roles have evolved over the past 21 years.

In the final chapter of the book, Ann Hodgson and Ken Spours, researchers of upper secondary and lifelong learning systems, stand back to make sense of the jigsaw as a whole. They summarize the key arguments contained in earlier chapters and suggest that a new post-incorporation model is needed in which GFEs play a leadership role locally and regionally with less dependence on national steering.

References

Abbot, A. (1933) *Education for Industry and Commerce in England*. Oxford: Oxford University Press.

Ainley, P., and Bailey, B. (1997) *The Business of Learning*. London: Cassell.

Association of Colleges (AoC) (2014) *College Key Facts 2013/14*. Online. www.aoc.co.uk/sites/default/files/AoC_College_Key_Facts_2013_14.pdf (accessed 27 August 2014).

Atkinson, D. (1995) *The Dan Quayle Guide to FEFC Recurrent Funding*. Bristol: Coombe Lodge Report.

Audit Commission (1985) *Obtaining Better Value from Further Education*. London: HMSO.

Audit Commission/Ofsted (1993) *Unfinished Business: Full-time education courses for 16–19 year olds*. London: HMSO.

Bailey, B. (1987) 'The development of technical education 1934–1939'. *History of Education*, 16 (1), 49–65.

— (1990) 'Technical education and secondary schooling 1905–1945'. In Summerfield, P., and Evans, E.J. (eds) *Technical Education and the State Since 1850: Historical and contemporary perspectives*. Manchester: Manchester University Press, 97–119.

— (2002) 'Further education'. In Aldrich, R. (ed.) *A Century of Education*. London: RoutledgeFalmer, 54–74.

Bailey, B., and Unwin, L. (2014) 'Continuity and change in English further education: A century of voluntarism and permissive adaptability'. *British Journal of Educational Studies*, 62 (4), 449–64.

Cantor, L.M., and Roberts, I.F. (1969) *Further Education in England and Wales*. London: Routledge and Kegan Paul.

Central Policy Review Staff (1980) *Education, Training and Industrial Performance*. London: HMSO.

Coffield, F., Edward, S., Finlay, I., Hodgson, A., Spours, K., and Steer, R. (2008) *Improving Learning, Skills and Inclusion: The impact of policy on post-compulsory education*. London: Routledge.

Colleges Northern Ireland (2014) 'About Colleges NI'. Online. www.anic.ac.uk/About-Colleges-NI.aspx (accessed 27 August 2014).

Colleges Scotland (2014) 'Colleges Scotland Keyfacts 2014'. Online. www.collegesscotland.ac.uk/download-document/5555-colleges-scotland-keyfacts-2014 (accessed 10 March 2015).

Colleges Wales (2014) 'Home page'. Online. www.collegeswales.ac.uk/en-GB/wales_colleges-42.aspx (accessed 27 August 2014).

Department for Business, Innovation and Skills (BIS) (2012) *Understanding Higher Education in Further Education Colleges*. Online. www.gov.uk/government/uploads/system/uploads/attachment_data/file/32425/12-905-understanding-higher-education-in-further-education-colleges.pdf (accessed 28 August 2014).

Department for Education (DfE) (2013) *Enrolment of 14- to 16-year-olds in full-time further education*. Online. www.gov.uk/government/publications/enrolment-of-14-to-16-year-olds-in-full-time-further-education (accessed 19 March 2015).

— (2014) *Education and Training Statistics for the United Kingdom: 2013*. Online. www.gov.uk/government/uploads/system/uploads/attachment_data/file/255083/v01-2013.pdf (accessed 28 August 2014).

Department for Education and Science/Employment Department/Welsh Office (1991) *Education and Training for the 21st Century*. London: HMSO.

Department for Education and Skills (2001) *Skills for Life: The national strategy for improving adult literacy and numeracy skills*. London: DfES.

Department for Employment and Learning Northern Ireland (DELNI) (2013) *Resource Accounts for the Year Ended 31 March 2013*. Online. www.delni.gov.uk/del-resource-accounts-for-the-year-ended-31-march-2013.pdf (accessed 28 August 2014).

Department for Education and Employment (DfEE) (1998) *The Learning Age: A renaissance for a new Britain*. London: The Stationery Office.

— (1999) *Learning to Succeed: A new framework for post-16 learning*. (White Paper). London: The Stationery Office.

Department for Education and Skills (DfES) (2002) *Success for All: Reforming further education and training. Discussion document – June 2002*. Online. www.education.gov.uk/consultations/downloadableDocs/189_1.pdf (accessed 10 March 2015).

Department of Education Northern Ireland (2005) 'The Northern Ireland curriculum'. Online. www.deni.gov.uk/the_northern__ireland__curriculum_-_amended_05-2.pdf (accessed 25 March 2015).

— (2012a) 'Entitlement framework'. Online. www.deni.gov.uk/entitlement-framework.htm (accessed 25 March 2015).

— (2012b) 'Consultation on the fundamental review of GCSEs and A levels'. Online. www.deni.gov.uk/fundamental-review-of-gcses-and-a-levels (accessed 25 March 2015).

Education and Employment Committee (1998) *Hodge Report: Sixth report of the House of Commons Education and Employment Committee*. Vol. 1 and 2. 19 May. London: The Stationery Office.

Education Funding Agency (EFA) (2014) *EFA Annual Report and Financial Statement for the Period 1 April 2012 to 31 March 2013*. Online. www.gov.uk/government/uploads/system/uploads/attachment_data/file/271353/EFA_Annual_Report_and_Accounts_2012-13.pdf (accessed 28 August 2014).

Education Scotland (2014) 'Skills for work'. Online. www.educationscotland.gov. uk/nationalqualifications//about/skillsforwork.asp (accessed 25 March 2015).

Estyn (2014) *Annual Report of Her Majesty's Chief Inspector of Education and Training in Wales 2012–13*. Online. www.estyn.gov.uk/english/annual-report/ annual-report-2012-2013/ (accessed 28 August 2014).

Further Education Funding Council for England (FEFC) (1992) *Funding Learning*. Coventry: Further Education Funding Council.

— (1993) *Further Consultation on Funding Learning*. London: Further Education Funding Council.

Foster, A. (2005) *Realising the Potential: A review of the future role for further education colleges*. London: DfES.

Fryer, R.H. (1997) *Learning for the 21st Century: First report of the national advisory group for continuing education and lifelong learning*. London: NAGCELL.

Galley, H. (2014) 'An ode to other people's children'. Online. www.aoc.co.uk/blog/ ode-other-people's-children (accessed 27 August 2014).

Gleeson, D. (1996) 'Post-compulsory education in a post-industrial and post-modern age'. In Avis, J., Bloomer, M., Esland, G., and Hodgkinson, P. (eds) *Knowledge and Nationhood: Education, politics and work*. London: Cassell, 83–104.

Gravatt, J., and Silver, R. (2000) 'Partnerships with the community'. In Smithers, A., and Robinson, P. (eds) *Further Education Re-formed*. London: Falmer Press, 111–23.

Green, A., and Lucas, N. (eds) (1999) *FE and Lifelong Learning: Realigning the sector for the twenty-first century* (Bedford Way Papers). London: Institute of Education Publications.

Hodgson, A., and Spours, K. (2014) 'Upper secondary education across the countries of the UK: Possibilities for expansive policy learning'. Paper presented at the ECER conference, Porto, 2 September.

Hodgson, A., Spours, K., and Waring, M. (eds) (2011) *Post-compulsory Education and Lifelong Learning Across the United Kingdom: Policy, organization, and governance*. London: Institute of Education Publications.

Hook, S. (2003) 'Seats on "shadow board" agreed'. *THES (FE Focus)*, 10 Oct. Online. www.tes.co.uk/article.aspx?storycode=385067 (accessed 16 March 2015).

Keep, E. (2014) *What Does Skills Policy Look Like Now the Money has Run Out?* London: SKOPE, Association of Colleges.

Kennedy, H. (1997) *Learning Works: Widening participation in further education*. Coventry: Further Education Funding Council.

Lanning, T., and Lawton, K. (2012) *No Train No Gain: Beyond free-market and state-led skills policy*. London: Institute for Public Policy Research.

Leitch, S. (2006) *Prosperity for All in the Global Economy: World-class skills*. London: The Stationery Office.

Lingfield, R. (2012) *Professionalism in Further Education: Final report of the independent review panel established by the Minister of State for Further Education, Skills and Lifelong Learning*. Online.www.bis.gov.uk/assets/biscore/ further-education-skills/docs/p/12-1198-professionalism-in-further-education-final (accessed 3 March 2015).

Levacic, R., and Glatter, R. (eds) (1997) *Managing Change in Further Education.* London: FEDA.

Lucas, N. (1999) 'Incorporated colleges: Beyond the Further Education Funding Council's model'. In Green, A., and Lucas, N. (eds) *FE and Lifelong Learning: Realigning the sector for the twenty-first century* (Bedford Way Papers). London: Institute of Education Publications, 42–68.

— (2004) *Teaching in Further Education: New perspectives for a changing context* (Bedford Way Papers). London: Institute of Education Publications.

Lumby. J., and Tomlinson. H. (2000) 'Principals speaking: Managerialism and leadership in further education'. *Research in Post-compulsory Education*, 5 (2), 139–52.

Melville, D., and Macleod D. (2000) 'The present picture'. In Smithers, A., and Robinson, P. (eds) *Further Education Re-formed*. London: Falmer Press, 24–34.

National Assembly for Wales (2013) *Further Education Structure in Wales.* Online. www.assemblywales.org/13-025.pdf (accessed 28 August 2014).

Newman, J., and Clarke, J. (1994) 'Going about our business? The managerialism of public services'. In Clarke, J., Cochrane, A., and McLaughlin, E. (eds) *Managing Social Policy*. London: Sage, 13–31.

Office for Standards in Education, Children's Services and Skills (Ofsted) (2014) *HM Chief Inspector's Annual Report on Further Education and Skills 2013/14.* Online. www.gov.uk/government/publications/ofsted-annual-report-201314-further-education-and-skills-report (accessed 15 December 2014).

Panchania, N. (2013) *Choice and Competition in Further Education*. London: Institute for Government.

Perry, A. (1997) *A Pencil Instead: Why we need a new funding system for further education*. London: Lambeth College.

Scottish Funding Council (SFC) (2013) *Annual Audit Report 2012–13*. Online. www.audit-scotland.gov.uk/docs/central/2013/fa_1213_scottish_funding_council.pdf (accessed 28 August 2014).

Skills Funding Agency (SFA) (2014a) *SFA Annual Report and Accounts 2012–2013*. Online. www.gov.uk/government/uploads/system/uploads/attachment_data/file/229128/0237.pdf (accessed 28 August 2014).

— (2014b) *SFA Annual Report and Accounts 2013–14*. Online. www.gov.uk/government/uploads/system/uploads/attachment_data/file/322531/SFA_Annual_Report_2013_to_2014.pdf (accessed 29 September 2014).

Venables, P.F.R. (1955) *Technical Education: Its aims, organisation and future development*. London: Bell.

Welsh Government (2004) 'Learning pathways 14–19 guidance'. Online. http://wales.gov.uk/topics/educationandskills/publications/circulars/learning_pathways_14_19?lang=en (accessed 25 March 2015).

— (2014) 'Review of qualifications 14–19'. Online. http://gov.wales/topics/educationandskills/qualificationsinwales/revofqualen/?lang=en (accessed 25 March 2015).

Welsh Baccalaureate (2015) 'Welcome to the Welsh Baccalaureate website'. Online. www.welshbaccalaureate.org.uk/Welsh-Baccalaureate-Home-Page (accessed 25 March 2015).

Chapter 2

The politicians' tale
Ian Nash and Sue Jones

Introduction

This chapter addresses the political imperatives that drove incorporation and subsequent developments affecting colleges – the rising influence of the marketplace as a means of addressing UK skills shortages and the impact of changing political priorities on the wider issues of accountability, participation, and learning. We do not deal with issues such as funding, sector organization, management, recruitment, and other factors, which are analysed in detail elsewhere in the book. Nor do we attempt a full political analysis in the limited space available.

Instead, we explore the underlying political pressures, the ideas that drove politicians, what they said and documented at the time and – through 30- to 40-minute telephone and face-to-face interviews with eight former Secretaries of State and their ministers in 2014 – we point to what was won and lost along the way. Equally importantly, we look at positive pointers towards the future. For example, there is a cross-party consensus emerging over the desire to see a revival of some form of Individual Learning Accounts (ILAs) as a mechanism for a fairer, more rational, and balanced means of sharing the costs of learning in the medium to long term. There is also widespread regret among politicians over the knee-jerk rejection of proposals in the 2004 Tomlinson report on 14–19 qualifications reform and the introduction of an overarching diploma. (Despite the widest consensus to date for radical reform, Tony Blair pre-empted an announcement by Ruth Kelly, Education Secretary, by telling the 2004 Confederation of British Industry (CBI) annual conference that A levels were here to stay. For detailed analysis see Baker, 2005.) In fact, failed efforts by successive governments to reform post-14 assessment and accreditation, for the sake of short-term political expediency, are seen by those we interviewed as a serious impediment to academic and vocational curriculum development.

We also address the question of whether cross-party agreements affecting colleges amount to a broad consensus, akin to that arising from the 1944 Education Act, or whether they merely allow governments to tinker with policy in a way most advantageous to the politics of the day, irrespective of the longer-term consequences.

Department for Education			
Kenneth Baker	1986–89		
John McGregor	1989–90		
Kenneth Clarke	1990–92		
John Patten	1992–94	Min – Lord Boswell	1992–95
Gillian Shephard	1994–95	Min – James Paice 1994 (Employment) –97	
Department for Education and Employment			
Gillian Shephard	1995–97		
		P Us -Kim Howells	1997–98
David Blunkett	1997–2001	Min – Tessa Blackstone	1997–1999
		Min – Malcolm Wicks	1999–2001
Department for Education and Skills			
Estelle Morris	2001–02	P Us – Ivan Lewis	2001–05
		Min – Margaret Hodge	2001–02
Charles Clarke	2002–04	Min – Alan Johnson	2003–04
		Min – Kim Howells	2005–05
Ruth Kelly	2004–06	Min – Bill Rammell	2005–08
		Min – Andrew Adonis	2005
Alan Johnson	2006–07		
Ed Balls	2007–10		
Department for Innovation, Universities and Skills			
SoS – John Denham	2007–09	PUs – David Lammy	2007–09
		PUs – Sion Simon	2008–09
Department for Business, Innovation and Skills			
SoS – Lord Mandelson	2009–10	Min – Kevin Brennan	2009–10
SoS – Vince Cable	2010–	Min David Laws	2012–
Department for Education			
Michael Gove	2010–14	Min – John Hayes	2010–12
		Min – Matthew Hancock	2012–14
		Min – Nick Boles	2014–
Nicky Morgan	2014–		
Key			
Min – Minister of State			
PUs – Permanent Under-Secretary of State			
SoS – Secretary of State			

Figure 2.1: Secretaries of State and ministers with responsibility for FE 1986–2014

The promise of freedom

Kenneth Baker started the ball rolling with the 1988 Education Reform Act (ERA), which gave colleges greater power over finance, staffing, and courses – the first steps towards freedom from local education authorities (LEAs). 'I gave them freedom and they really showed their potential commercially, proving most innovative', he said. It was in the post-school arena, however, that he saw the greatest potential for colleges; industry-sponsored city technology colleges and, later, university technical colleges (UTCs) were his 'beacons of vocational excellence' for school-age pupils, a theme to which we return later in this chapter.

If the ERA represented a file for divorce between colleges and local authorities, incorporation was the decree nisi. Kenneth Clarke, Baker's successor, who oversaw the 1992 Further and Higher Education (FHE) Act, says the reason that colleges were incorporated was to send them down the same road that polytechnics had taken earlier, to help achieve mass participation in further and higher education: 'For this, I had to free them from the burden of unnecessary regulation that persisted under LEAs.' His vision was more all-encompassing than Baker's and, when the Act was passed, he said: 'Let 100 flowers bloom.' He nevertheless envisaged a new era of cooperation between education and industry. The opposition, however, smelled a rat. Baroness Blackstone, for Labour in the House of Lords, said: 'It has been introduced to reduce educational spending at the local level by £2 billion in order to help the Government out of their poll tax quagmire' (Hansard, 1991a). Whether or not this was the prime motive, further opposition warnings from Shadow Education Secretary Jack Straw that the Act amounted to 'enforced transfer to centralised control from Whitehall' (Hansard, 1991b), were borne out to a greater extent than Clarke had indicated, as the creation of the Further Education Funding Council (FEFC) brought with it greater central control through funding regulations. For example, Clarke told the Commons: 'Schedule 2 [of the Act] sets out, for the first time, a list of the courses which we want to see available all over the country and for which we propose national funding' (Hansard, 1992a).

It fell to Clarke's successor, John Patten, however, to deal with the accusations of centralized control and the replacement of local democracy with non-governmental agencies to drive consumer choice, in what was disparagingly called a 'quangocracy'. The media were swift to round on quangos as an attack on democracy. On the eve of incorporation, the BBC broadcaster Jonathan Dimbleby, in the *On the Record* programme, challenged Patten, saying: 'you've taken a vast new panoply of powers upon yourself which allows you to ride roughshod over contrary opinion and simply heed those who are compliant to your own assumptions and attitudes.' Patten's response was bullish: 'It's to take powers to the centre so we can then redistribute power back to the rim of the wheel from the hub, to borrow a phrase of Ken Baker's and a very good phrase', he said (Dimbleby, 1993).

For colleges, this redistribution of power and new freedom to enter the marketplace would, however, soon lead to further headaches for the government, as a small number of colleges abused the system. Ministers from the period point to three issues that were to undermine the concept of greater freedom: weak or out-of-control governing boards; abuse of franchise programmes, where public subsidies went from colleges to businesses for training those for whom companies were already providing; and misappropriation of funds. The most high-profile case of misappropriation was in 1994, at Derby Wilmorton College, prefiguring a series of scandals at Bilston, Halton, Stoke-on-Trent, and Wirral Metropolitan, and triggering a government-commissioned official inquiry by Professor Michael Shattock, registrar at the University of Warwick.

Tim (now Lord) Boswell, who was minister of state for FE from 1992 to 1994, says such issues were blown out of proportion, both at the time and subsequently, resulting in undue curtailment of freedom. 'We were trying through self-governance and arms-length funding to put more emphasis on FE', he said. 'There is always a dilemma; you want to get the benefits of enterprise and independent decision-making but when you give people the chance, some have the habit of exploiting it. If you are running 450 ships, 2 or 3 will have engine trouble at any one time.'

From the government's viewpoint, gains were certainly considerable, not least on student recruitment, which surpassed the 25 per cent expansion target while spending increased by just 16 per cent. But there were other concerns: about under-performing Training and Enterprise Councils (TECs); about an increasingly fractious relationship between the government's education and employment departments, which failed to cooperate fully on skills training; and about inadequate controls over college spending, which would lead to a Treasury block on any additional funding in 1997.

In 1994, a fixer would succeed Patten in the shape of Gillian Shephard, who shared Clarke's vision and merged departments to create the Department for Education and Employment, aimed at ending the turf wars. At the time she said: 'There will be no effort wasted defining departmental differentials. We can get rid of all that and get on with the job' (*TES*, 1995). But there would soon be other developments to worry her. The Shattock report on Derby Wilmorton College, published under her stewardship, listed a damning catalogue of errors and mismanagement by a 'small inner group' of governors backing the principal, Andrew Stromberg, and millionaire chair of governors, Stuart Webb, while the governing body as a whole had 'inadequate financial control', Shattock said. They had spent £10 million on outlandish ventures, including the purchase of the town-centre nightclub, Oscars, with no cost-benefit analysis (Shattock, 1994). In his effort to reassure ministers that such abuses were being dealt with, Lord Lucas signalled that a crackdown would affect every college, not just Derby. He told the House of Lords: 'She [Gillian Shephard] will also wish to consider, in consultation with the Further Education Funding Council and others involved, what action should be taken to apply any lessons arising from these reports more generally across the further education sector' (Hansard, 1994).

Post incorporation, colleges became richer and more diverse. Many had taken over adult education, which was contracted out by local authorities, and were growing fast. But it was soon evident that defeat was looming for the Conservatives in the May 1997 general election and, in consequence, constraints on freedom would go much further.

A new era of planning

The arrival of the New Labour Government brought about a radical shift from freedom in the marketplace to an era of planning, goals, and target-setting. David Blunkett was a visionary, seeking a broad entitlement to lifelong learning. He says now that he regrets Labour's failure to fulfil its pre-election pledge to ensure an entitlement to education to everyone over 50. While it never became a manifesto commitment, however, the notion is implicit in the consultation paper, *The Learning Age* (Department for Education and Employment, 1998) and the White Paper, *Learning to Succeed* (Department for Education and Employment, 1999). Indeed, Blunkett today sees *The Learning Age* as a high point in his political career: '*The Learning Age* is the best thing that I ever wrote and I have not done anything better since. We clearly need to take account of how we use new technology more meaningfully but that said, the roots of everything we believe in and our values are there already.'

The Learning and Skills Act 2000 would be a culmination of the consultations and series of inquiries including *Learning Works* (Kennedy, 1997), the major report on widening participation by the high-profile barrister Helena (now Baroness) Kennedy, and *A Fresh Start: Improving literacy and numeracy* (Moser, 1999), by Sir Claus Moser, chair of the Basic Skills Agency, which suggested that one in five adults were functionally illiterate, with even higher levels of poor numeracy. On the one hand, Blunkett saw the Act as an instrument of social justice and second-chance education. Kennedy had summed up the imperative to encourage adults returning to learn with the memorable phrase: 'If at first you don't succeed, you don't succeed' (Kennedy, 1997: 21). Blunkett says: 'We did everything we could to consign that to history.' On the other hand, he preached 'zero tolerance', calling for more college mergers to cut waste, greater cooperation, and big improvements in staff training. In 1997, at the Association of Colleges' (AoC) annual conference in Birmingham (*TES*, 1997), he had warned college leaders: 'We will be as tough on failing colleges as we have been on failing schools.' Colleges would also be set targets for a massive reduction in drop-out rates: 'We need a concerted drive to raise standards – just as in schools. Further education is too important to our economy and society for us to tolerate poor standards or a lack of accountability. Too many students drop out and too many fail to get their qualifications.'

Blunkett was also concerned about the behaviour and performance of TECs: 'There was disquiet about the operations of TECs – they had taken on a freebooting culture, and there was a disconnect with the FEFC – it soon became clear it had to be joined up.' In 2001, therefore, the TECs were abolished with the creation of the Learning and Skills Council (LSC), with its 47 local councils replacing the FEFC. *The Learning Age* Green Paper had proposed a set of actions, crafted over five years in opposition and now enshrined in the Act, plans, and budgets: the University for Industry (UfI): leading edge technology to make learning available at work, in learning centres, in the community, and at home; making opportunities easier to access through a new freephone helpline called learndirect; all 16- and 17-year olds in jobs, education, or training; a legal right to undertake education and training to National Vocational Qualification (NVQ) Level 2; and expansion of Modern Apprenticeships. For adults there would be Individual Learning Accounts (ILAs) to encourage people to save to learn (£150 million to kick-start it with the first 1 million learners); a huge expansion in basic literacy and numeracy skills programmes through colleges; the New Deal and help for unemployed people; and other education and training routes to involve over 500,000 adults a year. More than £2 billion would be invested in two stages over five years from 1998, for everything from capital spending to student support. Alan Johnson, Minister for Lifelong Learning in 2003, says: 'The year before we came into government capital expenditure was zilch and it was quite clear that FE needed it. Student numbers had gone up 29 per cent under the Tories but by the end there was a drop of 27 per cent in full-time equivalent funding.'

Blunkett asked a high price: an increase in student numbers of 700,000. Also, he wanted to encourage private sector initiative and asked: 'How do we gel the public/private operations without ending up with the franchising mess that has bedevilled the work of a couple of colleges, and without sweeping it all away?' (*Times Higher Education*, 1999). Labour would attempt this in part through a series of measures including ILAs (a scheme supporting adult learning through employer tax incentives and £150 cash contributions to individuals) and later Train to Gain (a government-funded initiative reimbursing employer costs of training staff in basic skills to a full Level 2 qualification, equivalent to five GCSEs at A*–C). These would fall foul of the same abuses and accusations of deadweight funding that bedevilled Tory initiatives. The collapse of ILAs in particular was a major embarrassment and one that Blunkett's successor, Estelle Morris, had to deal with. What began with a promise to remove barriers faltered when unscrupulous providers abused it to make money. At the time, she insisted: 'the rapid growth of the scheme has exceeded all expectations, causing us to think again about how best to target public funds in this area and secure value for money' (Hansard, 2001). More recently in interview, however, she said that Treasury insistence that ILAs should not be over-regulated left the initiative open to abuse and exposed Labour to the very criticisms they had levelled at the Tories – the scheme was flawed and lacked robust quality assurance, opening doors to inexperienced and inadequate providers.

When Morris took office, there was a police inquiry into ILAs, 'and there were already stories of people at Victoria station giving out leaflets and discs at inflated prices,' she said. The National Audit Office (NAO) estimated that £67 million of the £196 million funding was lost to fraud (House of Commons Committee of Public Accounts, 2003). Morris said: 'Once we got knocked back on that it was difficult to get adult learning going again; we really got our fingers burned. Had the ILAs been successful, adult learning and skills would have built on that.'

The problem for colleges was that, since Blunkett had recast ILAs as part of a wider learning and skills sector, they were led to expect considerable business from individual account holders that never transpired.

Despite all this, there is a cross-party consensus among former ministers interviewed, including Baker, Blunkett, Boswell, Charles Clarke, and Morris, for better-regulated ILAs to be revived. Boswell sees them offering unique flexibility: 'In many ways losing ILAs was a huge disadvantage,' he commented. Blunkett said that there was still considerable potential 'with better management and oversight'.

The arrival of Charles Clarke to succeed Morris in 2002 signalled the start of a firmer push towards the skills agenda. Six out of ten colleges inspected in the previous year were judged inadequate or required reinspection. Relations with business were at a new low. Clarke introduced a three-year development plan funded with a record £1.2 billion tied to goals agreed between each college and the LSC. However, his aim, to get colleges and employers working more cooperatively, was only 'marginally successful', he says, because of the level of distrust between them. It was, in part, an age-old problem: 'Many in colleges did not think it their job to prepare people for work, while people in work thought colleges were not giving the right education and training. Sector Skills Councils (SSCs) were about getting employers engaged; we were looking to them and colleges to get models of work and education into the local economy.' Clarke was becoming more firmly fixed in the view that problems stemmed from a supply-led approach. The record-level spending would, therefore, bring more specific and tougher targets in what proved to be a somewhat vain hope that skills levels would be boosted significantly.

Refocusing on a demand-led approach

In 2002, Clarke wrote in *The Guardian*: 'Businesses will not accept what FE has to offer unless they can see skills being developed that will be of material benefit to them, whether in the private or public sector' (Clarke, 2002a). And he told the AoC annual conference: 'the real route to growth and success in the further education sector is not direct core funding alone, important though that is. Real growth and success comes from finding new markets for the education and training products that you have to offer, and so opening new streams of income for the expertise which you possess' (Clarke, 2002b).

A number of reports would help shape a new agenda along demand-led lines and lead to the creation in 2008 of Train to Gain, aimed at reimbursing costs to employers who provide basic skills training for staff. Exhortations in the Foster Review (Foster, 2005), commissioned by Clarke; directives from the Treasury-commissioned Leitch Reviews (Leitch, 2005; Leitch, 2006) on UK skills; and performance targets arising from Framework for Excellence (Learning and Skills Council, 2006) would all put pressure on colleges to focus more on skills training and employability needs.

Bill Rammell, Minister for Lifelong Learning under Ruth Kelly, Clarke's successor, not only consolidated the skills approach but oversaw cuts to wider adult learning, including a contentious reduction in English for speakers of other languages (ESOL). He says now that he was a reluctant cutter, particularly where it affected groups such as asylum seekers: 'We argued that where the Home Office failed to process a decision within eight weeks, it should pay for the ESOL until a decision is made.' But the Home Office refused; only adults on income support would qualify for state funding.

When Alan Johnson succeeded Kelly as Secretary for Employment and Skills in 2006 he drove the message further home. Speaking at the first national conference of the Quality Improvement Agency in Birmingham, he said: 'We must rebalance taxpayers' money towards the subjects where there is greatest need – so more plumbing, less Pilates; subsidized precision engineering, not over-subsidized flower arranging, except of course where flower arranging is necessary for a vocational purpose' (MacLeod, 2006).

In a recent interview, he insisted this was not to denigrate 'other' adult learning but to emphasize the need for plumbers over graduates. But the policy direction was set government-wide and within two years there would be a decline of more than 1 million adult learners.

Labour made a last stab at reviving general adult learning with the arrival of John Denham, Secretary of State at the Department for Innovation, Universities and Skills (DIUS) in 2007, and publication of the White Paper *The Learning Revolution* (Department for Innovation, Universities and Skills, 2009). With no new money to be had, this would focus on information technology and informal learning in the community. It was an acceptance that a decade of 'general', 'other', and 'extramural' learning had to be rethought. Denham says: 'Sadly, that approach did not succeed in delivering the results we wanted for people who needed the sorts of skills and qualifications that enable them to succeed at work, and so we are right to have focused attention on vocational qualifications.'

On the skills front, however, the government would soon find itself in trouble with both the NAO and the House of Commons Public Accounts Committee over poor financial management of its £1 billion Train to Gain workforce training programme. In a last attempt to define the skills agenda more sharply, the Department for Business, Innovation and Skills (BIS) was created to succeed DIUS. The Apprenticeships, Skills, Children and Learning Act 2009 led to a renewed push on apprenticeship training and the creation of the Skills Funding Agency (SFA), all focusing on, in the words of Charles Clarke 'key priorities of economic growth and education to promote trade'.

Return to the freedoms of incorporation

The Conservative–Liberal Democrat Coalition Government came to power in 2010 with Vince Cable and John Hayes at the helm of BIS. Hayes, as FE and Skills Minister, was responsible for colleges. In *New Challenges; New Chances*, (Department for Business Innovation and Skills, 2011a) he set the agenda for skills for business, personal growth, and mobility. He wanted a combined effort with colleges, training providers, employers, voluntary organizations, and community working together.

Changes Hayes began making included: the introduction of Level 3 and 4 loans; greater FE college freedom; more flexibility for all providers; simplified funding; reform of vocational qualifications; and the creation of an FE Guild (which would become the Education and Training Foundation – ETF). He criticized the previous government for being 'too top-down, too bureaucratic and insufficiently responsive to employers and learners'. It was a return to the idea of the market, with minimal external scrutiny and intervention. Centrally imposed targets were removed and a single adult skills budget was introduced with less emphasis on detailed auditing – streamlining and simplifying the administrative system.

In order to 'inform' employers and learners about which colleges provided high quality, Matthew Hancock, Coalition Government Minister of Business, Innovation and Skills, introduced Chartered Status and the FE Guild (later ETF), an FE Commissioner to take swift action against failing colleges, and better information for employers and learners to help them more confidently choose qualifications and providers. Local Enterprise Partnerships (LEPs), which had been created in 2011 to encourage local responsiveness and to stimulate economic growth, assumed new responsibilities in 2013. It was expected that they would be represented on all college governing bodies, with college representatives also on the LEP boards.

With an expectation that loans will cover most adult education and training needs, the direction for young people is to simplify training for work into apprenticeships, with traineeships for those not yet ready for apprenticeships. At the launch of National Apprenticeship Week in March 2013, David Cameron said: 'I want it to be the new norm for young people to either go to university or into an apprenticeship.'

Perennial issues

Politicians are still chasing the same issues they did at the outset following incorporation in 1992. They are trying to:

- improve the nation's skills for employment
- reform the 14–19 curriculum, relating it more closely to the workplace
- encourage more adults into learning
- develop social cohesion and well-being.

Incorporation was supposed to open up colleges to two markets: employers and learners. Most of the difficulties have arisen because those two markets have either failed to buy sufficient learning from colleges or, in the judgement of politicians, they have purchased the wrong learning.

The 14–19 curriculum and assessment is properly the business of politicians because it deals with young people of school age. But when it comes to adult engagement, given that the employers did not buy everything that the government wanted, the government has tried to enter the market itself, either by paying from the public purse for training it thinks the employers want and the country needs (for example, courses under Schedule 2 of the Further and Higher Education Act 1992, which identified courses fundable in the FE sector by the FEFC) or by supplementing employers' spending on training (Train to Gain).

The TECs, Sector Skills Councils (SSCs), and LEPs were/are all different mechanisms to bring employers into the process by getting them to define the training they need – and basically it has not worked well enough, as the former minsters interviewed largely agree. Nobody says it has been a success. Matthew Hancock tried to gain cash up front to fund apprenticeships by cracking the whip at employers. In interviews with the media at the 2014 annual conference of the Association for Employment and Learning Providers, he insisted that 'employers value what they pay for and pay for what they value' (Policy Consortium, 2014). But Nick Boles, his successor, slapped down the idea soon after his appointment: 'We ... are not going to be introducing any reforms that are off-putting to employers who currently don't provide apprenticeships, let alone people who already do' (Whittaker, 2014).

There is always a tension between asking employers and telling them. Sandy (now Lord) Leitch in his 2006 Treasury-commissioned review of UK skills to the year 2020 (Leitch, 2006), told the Chancellor, Gordon

Brown, that if by 2010 employers failed voluntarily to implement proposed skills training reforms, there should be the threat of compulsion – as in Germany and Switzerland. Hancock tried, but the Coalition Government soon sounded the retreat.

The other market is the learners. There are areas where the government tried to encourage co-investment, such as ILAs and loans; and others where they have accepted there are certain types of education and training that people cannot be expected to pay for themselves – for example, low-skilled and unemployed people needing basic skills training to get back into work. Where there is a social need, politicians have wanted to pay but as was seen in the retrenchment post-2003, provision such as ESOL and general adult learning soon suffer deep cuts in hard times.

Repeated attempts to increase the participation of employers and learners have led to ever more initiatives and changes in the machinery of government as ministers attempt to re-engineer the politicians' levers of influence (see Chapter 8). The problem for colleges is that FE is relevant to so many different areas of government concern that, as ministers explain below, there is no obvious single place to put it. But this has led to greater confusion since no reforms have lasted long enough to bed in, as the report *Sense and Instability: Three decades of skills and employment policy* (City & Guilds, 2014) shows. Many of the proposals being put forward now by ministers are very similar to those pursued in the 1980s but no one recalls or remembers them: there has been a costly loss of policy memory.

Key developments

14–19 reforms

Repeated efforts to reform the 14–19 school and college curriculum around an overarching diploma or baccalaureate have ended in failure as politicians disagree over the worth of vocational studies and retention of A Levels as the gold standard (see Chapter 4). There is now a growing cross-party consensus that this was a wasted opportunity that needs addressing with urgency.

Lord Boswell described this particular holy grail as 'something that was rigorous, and fit for purpose, and held in credibility by employers and the media, and was usable to those who had to participate', thus neatly demonstrating the diverse range of demands to be satisfied. He sees a 'false polarity' in assuming that a qualification must be either academic or practical. Regarding the commonly held 'default position' that vocational qualifications cannot, by definition, be as good as academic ones, his aim was to 'be able to say that they are as good as A Levels and you get a bit extra'. He described how John Patten was 'embattled' by a 'rearguard action from some MPs and the press', who think that 'the only thing that matters are A Levels', that led to a revision of General National Vocational Qualifications (GNVQs). Patten proposed a new A* grade for the top 5 per cent of those taking A Levels, but was told by his curriculum chief, Sir Ron Dearing, chair of the School Curriculum and Assessment Authority (SCAA), that it would not work, and by John Marks, a traditionalist on the SCAA, 'A Level doesn't have a credibility problem, but the GNVQ does. I have always said that would be my first priority.'

Gillian Shephard began a new drive to bridge the academic–vocational divide in 1994 when she commissioned the Dearing Review of 16–19 qualifications. She promised a new curriculum and qualifications framework to address the divide and a focus on skills that would equal the rigour of A Levels. However, the exercise fell well short of expectations because academic A levels would still rule supreme. In her letter of response to Sir Ron Dearing of 10 April 1995, Shepherd wrote: 'Our key priorities remain to ensure that the rigour and standards of GCE A Levels are maintained.' The overarching diploma never happened and any chance of parity of esteem seemed as remote as ever.

New Labour tried to address this in 2002 when Estelle Morris published the Green Paper, *14–19 Education: Extending Opportunities, Raising Standards* (Department for Education and Skills, 2002), which proposed a matriculation diploma at Intermediate, Advanced, and Higher levels. But Cabinet refusal to interfere with A Levels scuppered the move. To this day Morris thinks they took the wrong decision: 'What value should you put on vocational qualifications? Do you justify them on their own or equate them to the academic? We took the second view and I think we were wrong. We encouraged them in schools by equating them with the academic, but this never became joined up.'

Also in 2002, Labour commissioned a wholesale 14–19 review by Mike Tomlinson, ex-chief inspector for Ofsted, which completed its final report in 2004, and again the results proved unpalatable. Following the lead of Tony Blair, who signalled his discontent in a speech to the Confederation of British Industry (CBI) (Hodgson and Spours, 2008), Ruth Kelly said: 'We don't transform opportunities by abolishing what is good'. In 2005 she told the BBC's *Breakfast with Frost* programme: 'To have credibility and robustness going forward we have got to build on GCSEs and A levels, which after all are recognized as very important and good exams out there by the general public and by employers.'" Labour finally agreed to introduce 14–19 Diplomas (in the form of broad vocational qualifications that were intended to cover 14 occupational sectors) alongside GCSEs and A Levels, but it was effectively a dual system – vocational Diplomas or A Levels – and, while Diplomas had a good report from Ofsted for 'continuing to widen opportunities and meet the needs of young people', these qualifications were first watered down by Labour then killed off by the Coalition Government when Michael Gove ended all funding support for Diploma development.

There is currently some cross-party agreement that Tomlinson was a missed opportunity. Charles Clarke's view now is that 'a key failure of the Labour Government was not to implement the Tomlinson report. If we had agreed Tomlinson and taken that through, it would have led to a strong curriculum and a basis for funding and structural changes.' Lord Baker said: 'I'm not making a party political point, but Labour bottled out of Tomlinson because Blair was worried it would undermine A Levels.'

The situation was reviewed again in 2011 by Professor Alison Wolf, who concluded that young people were being badly served by a plethora of poor-quality vocational qualifications that were not recognized by employers and did not lead to employment or progression in education (Wolf, 2011). Large numbers of vocational awards were duly struck off the list of qualifications and not recognized in school performance tables, a reaction described by Lord Baker as 'throwing the baby out with the bath water' by getting rid of 'useful experiences as well as unsuitable qualifications'.

Charles Clarke concurs: 'The problem was, we had too many reorganizations. We never got the definition of educational phases right; 14–19 never got a comprehensive, coherent approach. It was all sticking plaster opportunities to get coherent 14–19. Transformation would take too long and would pull up so much. The chief failure of the Labour Government was that we should have agreed Tomlinson; then we would have had a curriculum basis for funding and structural changes.'

Since then the Coalition Government has introduced the concept of a Technical Baccalaureate through a new performance measure with this name, comprising tech levels, a mathematics qualification, and an extended project, and this is now being piloted in five FE colleges. Whether this will prove successful, the politicians reserve judgement.

Employer engagement and apprenticeships

Successive governments have failed to secure sufficient employer engagement and participation or have seen initiatives founder due to inadequate regulation and oversight. Also, in the view of several ex-ministers, the agencies and non-governmental organizations created to nurture closer employer links with colleges and ensure that the mechanisms were in place to deliver more robust skills development have not measured up.

There is concern too that much of the spending on skills and related policy development was about the failure of the market, in particular employers, to come forward and buy what they wanted. The employers accept in principle that they must pay for industry-specific training but the question is what counts as specific, especially in relation to functional skills. Charles Clarke said: 'Either they did not want it or they thought the state should pay.'

Alan Johnson questions whether any government over the past two decades has been explicit enough in spelling out what is expected of employers. For example, on the sponsorship of UTCs he says: 'It would have to be made clear that they have to stay with it for the sake of their reputation; maybe there has been too much carrot and not enough stick.'

Nowhere is this dilemma more obvious than in the area of apprenticeships. Ever since Kenneth Clarke announced Modern Apprenticeships in 1993, efforts to bring employers on board have proved problematic. Successive ministers have made claims about record growth in numbers and improved quality, but these have too often turned out to refer to older workers who are already employed, leading to accusations of deadweight funding.

The details of apprenticeship reform are dealt with in Chapter 4. For politicians, apprenticeships have been a way of dealing with two quite separate issues; technician-level skills gaps and youth unemployment. The subject has grown in importance in recent years, or as Martin Doel, chief executive of the AoC, observed to the Association's 2014 national conference: 'the answer to everything is an apprenticeship'; they can appeal to both Left and Right as a symbol of lost stability and prosperity.

The dual aim was neatly described by Skills Minister John Hayes in a speech to the CBI on 6 September 2011 (Department for Business, Innovation and Skills, 2011b): 'Our Government is facing two profound domestic policy challenges. First, promoting renewed economic growth and prosperity for British businesses. And second, giving renewed hope and purpose to British people, especially the young, whose disaffection with things as they are was shown so graphically recently. Building an Apprenticeships programme that delivers to its maximum potential is highly relevant to increasing the chances of meeting both challenges successfully.' Current policy is that every young person on leaving school should either go to university or take up an apprenticeship.

The role of colleges, along with training providers, has been to provide the off-site elements of the apprenticeship frameworks and to go out and encourage local employers to take on apprentices. Politicians of all parties have concentrated on recruiting employers by promising them control of the programmes and access to public funding.

Where employers have not come forward, colleges have often taken up the slack with government funding for pre-apprenticeship training, such as National Traineeships and Foundation Modern Apprenticeships, or schemes for unemployed young people such as Entry to Employment (E2E).

The respective roles of government and employers in apprenticeships have yet to be clearly decided. Conservative, and then Coalition, instincts have always been that they should be 'employer led' and that employers should be 'in the driving seat', but this leaves the government with few levers to pull to expand the programme or control funding. Labour politicians now take a more pessimistic view of employer involvement. Alan Johnson regrets that 'SSCs didn't seem to meet their remit. Employers complained about being told what was good for them, but when they were given the chance, they didn't take it.' For Bill Rammell the problem is deep rooted: 'There's too much of a culture within British industry that you don't invest in your own workforce in case they leave and an attitude that if times are tough you cut back on funding for training.'

Charles Clarke remains pessimistic about the future involvement of business: 'The chance of getting employers to really engage is very low; it all comes back to engagement for what – is it part of HR strategy or part of their local corporate responsibility strategy? Schools won't be good at getting relationships with employers; somebody has to understand what employers are really looking for and FE can do that.'

Engagement policies revisited

The latest push to promote employer engagement and make colleges more business orientated came in November 2014 with Vince Cable's announcement of employer-led National Colleges (Department for Business, Innovation and Skills, 2014) to develop advanced manufacturing, digital, wind energy, and creative skills – with the promise of more. But how different are these to the old Inner London Education Authority requirement for all colleges to specialize (e.g. catering at Westminster College)? Then there were National Skills Centres, followed by Centres of Vocational Excellence (COVEs). Each in turn was expected by successive governments to play to the same tune, identifying and working with the best-established providers and industry regionally or nationally. There are also echoes of a lament, voiced by virtually all ministers in interview for this book, over the demise of the polytechnics.

Then, when it comes to school-age provision, there's the question of the UTCs, invented by Labour and boosted by the Coalition. Kenneth Baker sees them as successors to CTCs and the fulfilment of a failed promise in the 1944 Act to create technical schools with a transfer age of 13 or 14. To promote UTCs, he and Sir Ron Dearing created the Baker Dearing Educational Trust, now jointly chaired cross-party by Baker and Lord Adonis. 'They said (after the '44 Act) you couldn't start then (age 13–14) because 1,400 grammar schools started at 11; they determined everything. Now there are only 163, we need a radical rethink of the curriculum 14–18.' Party differences over UTCs amount to fine-tuning; while Labour sees them as an option alongside FE, the Tories say UTCs should have the upper hand. Baker says: 'Colleges sponsor UTCs but they should see them as faculties or institutions distinct from post-19 provision.' Fourteen-year olds should not even be in FE, he insists, since they must follow the national curriculum as well as work-related studies. They would also advance to the TechBac or A Levels at the UTC – or at a National College.

This suggests, therefore, an emergent split in FE, whichever political party is in power. The occupational/adult side would resemble HE and the old polytechnics, subject to market forces, with little intervention from government. The other would offer an alternative secondary education 14–19. Both would be skills-driven at the behest of business and industry. But where, in the view of any government, would this leave the once significant realm of other adult, extramural, and return-to-learn opportunities?

One repeated criticism from former ministers interviewed for this book was the constant reshuffling of government departments, administrative reorganization, and redefinition of the role of colleges – substantially as part of an effort to improve employer engagement and address skills shortages. The constant flux, often revisiting failed departmental policies and changing the machinery of government (as illustrated in the changing list of ministerial roles and departments at the start of this chapter), has created instability and uncertainty and has undoubtedly impaired performance, they say. Charles Clarke said: 'Reform at times is necessary but it should be kept to a minimum for the sake of stability.'

Protecting adult participation

Adult education was a political football from the start, with MPs from both sides of the House arguing that local LEA provision would be destroyed and that Schedule 2 of the Further and Higher Education Act would whittle college provision down to the narrowest of vocational and skills-based courses.

During the final reading of the FHE Bill in 1992, Kenneth Clarke was, however, adamant that 'the 50 per cent [of adult education] that will continue to be provided locally will not be affected by the Bill' (Hansard, 1992a). That aspect of provision would not change, he said, and he decried campaigns that had been organized in defence of what were described as leisure courses: 'The case made in regard to the so-called leisure courses was entirely misconceived – and remains misconceived, where it continues to be made' (Hansard, 1992a).

Lord Boswell argues today that Schedule 2 was actually a boon, without which adult education would have been severely hit: 'Schedule 2 was a defensive option to stop the whole thing being kicked out. Now the issue is about holding the ring for general adult education. We must leave people with the motivation and the opportunity to do it.'

In the event, many LEAs contracted out their services to colleges, which also used Schedule 2 creatively to fit otherwise marginal programmes into the funding regime. Adult education grew overall: annual National Institute for Adult and Continuing Education (NIACE) surveys (e.g. Sargant, 1997) of people who said they were engaged in learning, support Boswell's contention. The surveys suggest that numbers rose slowly but steadily from 36 per cent in 1991 to 40 per cent in 1996 and rose further to 46 per cent under New Labour before slipping back (NIACE, 2010).

An overall rise of 25 per cent across the sector appeared to have been achieved by Clarke and his successors, John Patten and Gillian Shephard. However, figures from the House of Commons Library suggest that any estimates are unreliable. 'Since then [1993] the number of learners has been highly erratic. Most of the underlying increase since 1994, and the erratic figures for certain years, has been down to large changes in the number of part-time and evening learners and changes to the funding of further education' (Bolton, 2012).

The big rise would come in response to the Kennedy and Moser reports, and the investment of £1.5 billion in colleges, particularly for basic numeracy and literacy, in Labour's first term, with global participation topping 6 million. By 2001, colleges provided well over 80 per cent of adult learning (including ESOL) to students taking qualifications at Levels 1 and 2. There was a decline, however, post-2003, with a swing away from 'other' learning to skills and the move to employer-led training. By 2005, the entire political focus had narrowed to *Skills for Life* (Department for

Education and Skills, 2002), adult literacy, ESOL, and numeracy skills courses. In the event, participation in general adult learning and basic vocational skills training for older people plummeted. LSC data for 2006/7 showed sharp declines in participation for every cohort over age 25, with a peak of a 30 per cent fall in over-50s on safeguarded courses. But by 2007/8, with the global economy heading for a crisis, there was no question of new money for FE.

Small but significant gains in this period include the securing by Ivan Lewis, minister for young people and learning, of the safeguarded Adult and Community Learning Fund, set at 3 per cent of the LSC budget (£300 million). This Treasury guarantee would even survive the Coalition Government austerity cuts. In the words of former Labour minister Bill Rammell: 'I protected the (now £210 million) adult and community learning fund but to be blunt, skills had to come first. I think that the priority has to be more for an adult at work without GCSE Level 2 qualifications than someone in retirement and wanting to do art for leisure.' And, despite Coalition minister John Hayes's success in protecting the fund and an attempt by Labour to revive participation with the White Paper, *The Learning Revolution* (Department for Innovation, Universities and Skills, 2009), adult participation would continue to decline throughout the life of the Coalition Government.

Conclusion

As the Coalition's term of office is drawing to a close, problems in implementing consistent policies are becoming all too apparent, as had repeatedly been the case, first with the Tories soon after incorporation and then with New Labour. After almost a quarter of a century, politicians of all parties are still pursuing the same goals of parity of esteem for vocational qualifications and a further education and training system that is responsive to local employers and learners.

There are, however, very positive developments including an emerging political consensus on the value of reintroducing some form of ILAs and for the development of a broadly balanced practical and academic 14–19 diploma that ensures progression to employment and/or higher education. All former secretaries of state and ministers interviewed also agreed that the FE sector urgently needs stability and an end to constant reforms, changes in the machinery of government, and administrative reorganization.

While such stability is desirable there is, nevertheless, a deeper set of issues for colleges. The emerging consensus around ILAs, diplomas, and other issues such as the future of UTCs leaves FE at a fork in the road.

One way lies a split system with adult provision in vocational colleges and alternative, also skills-driven, 14–19 provision within the school system. Where does this leave the wider adult 'other', extramural, remedial, and return-to-learn opportunities, currently out of vogue and inaccessible to the poorest and most in need?

There are four problems that must be tackled with urgency if progress is to be achieved:

- first, is the 14–19 problem – that is, parity between academic and vocational routes, that has proved unreachable while academic A Levels are fixed in the minds of politicians as the only gold standard
- second, is the contradiction between maintaining the policy and strategy drivers at the centre while expecting colleges and other providers to be locally responsive
- third, is the constant exhortation to employers to get involved in the design and funding of vocational education and training while failing to identify exactly how this can be achieved
- fourth, is the supply, or not, of money and the increasing need when there is not enough money to choose between 14–19-year olds and adults.

References

Baker, M. (2005) 'Why Tomlinson was turned down', Online. http://news.bbc.co.uk/1/hi/education/4299151.stm (accessed 31 March 2015).

Blunkett, D. (1998) 'The lifelong learning revolution starts here'. *The Independent*, 26 February. Online. www.independent.co.uk/news/education/education-news/the-lifelong-learning-revolution-starts-here-1146923.html (accessed 3 March 2015).

Bolton, P. (2012) *Education: Historical statistics standard note SN/SG/4252* (Social and General Statistics). House of Commons Library.

City & Guilds (2014) *Sense & Instability: Three decades of skills and employment policy*. Online. http://tinyurl.com/ph38q8n (accessed 22 December 2014).

Clarke, C. (2002a) 'Reap what you sow'. *The Guardian*, 26 November. Online. www.theguardian.com/education/2002/nov/26/furthereducation.uk3 (accessed 22 March 2015).

— (2002b) 'Clarke promises £1.2bn to FE'. *The Guardian*, 19 November. Online. www.theguardian.com/education/2002/nov/19/furthereducation.lecturerspay (accessed 22 March 2015).

Department for Business, Innovation and Skills (BIS) (2011a) *New Challenges, New Chances: Further education and skills system reform plan: Building a world class skills system*. Online. www.gov.uk/government/uploads/system/uploads/attachment_data/file/145452/11-1380-further-education-skills-system-reform-plan.pdf (accessed 21 December 2014).

— (2011b) 'Cutting apprenticeship red tape for employers'. Speech by John Hayes to CBI annual conference, 6 September. Online. www.gov.uk/government/speeches/cutting-apprenticeship-red-tape-for-employers (accessed 22 December 2014).

— (2014) 'Cable: New generation of National Colleges will lead revolution in hi-tech skills'. Press release on Vince Cable's National College speech. Online. www.gov.uk/government/news/cable-new-generation-of-national-colleges-will-lead-revolution-in-hi-tech-skills (accessed 22 December 2014).

Department for Education and Employment (DfEE) (1998) *The Learning Age: A renaissance for a new Britain*. London: DfEE.

— (1999) *Learning to Succeed: A new framework for post-16 learning*. White Paper. London: DfEE.

Department for Education and Skills (DfES) (2002) *14–19: Extending opportunities, raising standards: Consultation document*. London: DfES.

Department for Innovation, Universities and Skills (DIUS) (2009) *The Learning Revolution*. Online. http://dera.ioe.ac.uk/8762/1/7555.pdf (accessed 22 December 2014).

Dimbleby, J. (1993) BBC *On the Record* transcript. Online. www.bbc.co.uk/otr/intext92-93/Patten28.2.93.html (accessed 22 December 2014).

Foster, A. (2005) *Realising the Potential: A review of the future role of further education colleges*. London: DfES.

Hansard (1991a) Online. http://hansard.millbanksystems.com/lords/1991/may/20/further-and-higher-education (accessed 22 March 2015).

— (1991b) Online. www.publications.parliament.uk/pa/cm199091/cmhansrd/1991-05-20/Debate-1.html (accessed 22 March 2015).

— (1992a) Online. www.publications.parliament.uk/pa/cm199192/cmhansrd/1992-03-03/Debate-4.html (accessed 22 March 2015).

— (1992b) Online. http://hansard.millbanksystems.com/commons/1992/mar/03/report-on-provision-for-adult-education (accessed 22 December 2014).

— (1994) Online. www.publications.parliament.uk/pa/ld199495/ldhansrd/vo941117/text/41117w01.htm (accessed 22 March 2015).

— (2001). Online. www.publications.parliament.uk/pa/cm200102/cmhansrd/vo011025/text/11025w05.htm (accessed 22 December 2014).

Hodgson, A., and Spours, K. (2008) *Education and Training 14–19: Curriculum, qualifications and organisation*. London: Sage.

House of Commons Committee of Public Accounts (2003) *Tenth Report of Session 2002–2003: Individual Learning Accounts*. Online. www.publications.parliament.uk/pa/cm200203/cmselect/cmpubacc/544/544.pdf (accessed 22 March 2015).

Kennedy, H. (1997) *Learning Works: Widening participation in further education colleges*. Online. http://core.ac.uk/download/pdf/9063796.pdf (accessed 22 March 2015).

Learning and Skills Council (LSC) (2006) *Framework for Excellence: A comprehensive performance assessment framework for the further education system.* Online. http://dera.ioe.ac.uk/12955/1/nat-frameworkforexcellenceaco mprehensiveperformanceassessmentframework-pu-july2006.pdf (accessed 22 December 2014).

Leitch, S. (2005) *Future Skills Needs in the UK.* London: The Stationery Office.

— (2006) *Prosperity for All in the Global Economy: World-class skills.* London: The Stationery Office.

MacLeod, D. (2006) 'Johnson: Fund more plumbing and less Pilates'. *The Guardian*, 7 June. Online. www.theguardian.com/education/2006/jun/07/ furthereducation.uk1 (accessed 22 Match 2015).

Moser, C. (1999) *A Fresh Start: Improving literacy and numeracy.* London: DfEE.

NIACE (2010) 'Adult participation in learning surveys 1996–2006'. Online. www.niace.org.uk/niace-adult-participation-in-learning-surveys (accessed 22 December 2014).

Policy Consortium (2014) 'Ambitious apprenticeship plans are yet to convince employers'. Online.http://policyconsortium.co.uk/ambitious-apprenticeship-plans-are-yet-to-convince-employers/ (accessed 22 March 2015).

Sargant, N., Field, J., Francis, H., Schuller, T., and Tuckett, A. (1997) *The Learning Divide.* Leicester: NIACE.

Shattock, M. (1994) *Derby College: Wilmorton. Report of an enquiry into the governance and management of the college.* Coventry: FEFC. TES (1995) 'Shephard bridges the divide'. 7 July. Online. www.tes.co.uk/article. aspx?storycode=299966 (accessed 22 March 2015).

— (1997) 'Blunkett gets tough on raising standards'. 21 November. Online. www. tes.co.uk/teaching-resource/Blunkett-gets-tough-on-raising-standards-73349/ AoC (accessed 22 December 2014).

Times Higher Education (1999) 'End of the road for franchising'. 31 May. Online. www.timeshighereducation.co.uk/news/end-of-the-road-for-franchising/146546. article (accessed 22 March 2015).

Whittaker, F. (2014) 'Skills Minister hints at scrapping cash contributions plan'. *FE Week*, 2 October. Online. http://feweek.co.uk/2014/10/02/exclusive-skills-minister-hints-at-scrapping-cash-contributions-plan/ (accessed 22 March 2015).

Wolf, A. (2011) *Review of Vocational Education: The Wolf Report.* London: DfE.

Chapter 3

Students count
Adrian Perry and Peter Davies

Introduction

A recurring phrase from ministerial speeches to the assembled audiences at professional conferences is that 'what matters most are the students'. This may be a cliché, but like all clichés it has a core of truth. This chapter is an attempt to see what happened to students under incorporation – adult and young, full-time and part-time. Did the promised freedoms of incorporation make a difference – or did student experience just reflect the trends observed from previous regimes or wider society?

However poorly specified were the objectives of incorporation – John Major's autobiography (Major, 1999), for example, makes no reference to the 1992 Act, apart from some fanciful remarks about reforming vocational qualifications and introducing training credits for post-16 education – they clearly included a desire for an increase in the number of qualified people. 'A coherent and strategic drive towards a comprehensive nation-wide system of educational targets began to emerge in the UK from the end of the 1980s and the setting of the National Targets for Education and Training (NTETs). The NTETs were first suggested in the 1989 CBI document *Towards a Skills Revolution*, which focused on reversing the perceived characteristics of the British workforce as "under-educated, under-trained and under qualified"' (Gorard *et al.*, 2000). The desire for expansion was expressed in the first letter of guidance from the Secretary of State for Education in 1992 (Further Education Funding Council, 1992), which sought growth in student numbers, greater participation, and greater efficiency. By the early 1990s, the Confederation of British Industry (CBI) was bringing forward the idea of national targets for education and training, endorsed by the government in 1995 'to improve the skills of the existing workforce as well as develop the potential of young people [which] is at the heart of the Government's strategy for achieving a world-class workforce' (Department for Education and Skills, 1995: 1). From the early 1980s the UK government had expressed concerns about FE's contribution to Britain's international competitive position (NEDO/MSC, 1984). The expansion of the polytechnics following their move from local education authority (LEA) control was felt to show the likely gains from granting greater independence to the further education sector.

The student body: Who are they?

The newly independent colleges had a broad client base from which to seek expansion. Compared with school sixth forms, sixth form colleges (SFCs), and universities, general FE colleges (GFEs) cater for a wider ability range, and have a higher proportion of learners from deprived backgrounds. They are also more ethnically mixed, especially in the younger age group. The sector welcomes both mature and younger students. This diversity is related to the wide range and type of courses and qualifications typically provided. When considering the experiences of learners at college, it is helpful to consider their rationale for being there:

- For entry to employment and/or progression to and study for advanced education, both in FE and at university – in the main involving younger learners, but also significant numbers of 'second chance' adults.
- For re-entry to employment – by the unemployed or, for example, by women seeking to return to work after childrearing.
- Students with learning difficulties developing skills for living.
- For career updating and progression – by adults in employment, both employer-sponsored and those attending in their own time and at their own expense. There can be an interesting distinction between these two cohorts. Employers tend to fund employees to do their existing job better; those financing their own education tend to aim at promotion, or even a new career move altogether.
- For personal interest and development – by adults as a 'leisure' activity, some being retired from paid employment.
- For community regeneration and neighbourhood renewal – by adults seeking to engage their communities in self-help activities.

We should therefore be careful with generalizations about the student experience of FE. Although these categories can overlap – as one holiday language student found when his firm was taken over by a Spanish enterprise – broadly speaking, different learners have different needs and expectations. The role of certification, for example, differs between vocational and leisure learners. Nonetheless, FE can lay genuine claims to catering successfully for the widely differing types of student that are enrolled.

EXAMPLES OF FE STUDENTS

Mandy left college with good A levels and a BTEC travel and tourism qualification. She now works for Virgin Airlines: 'I try not to forget I have so much to thank the tutors on the tourism and leisure course at my college. I can't praise them enough. They gave me the confidence to succeed. The course made me feel comfortable with the jargon of the aviation industry.'

Jenny*, a middle-aged female student: 'I used to be an office administrator before I had my children. When I started to think about returning to work I decided I'd love to work with children, and realized I'd need to gain some qualifications to help me achieve this. A friend recommended college to me, and I enrolled for Introduction to Childcare with English followed by English Levels 1 and 2. I'm currently studying Support Work in Schools Level 2 and ICT and maths classes. I've really enjoyed my time at the college – the staff and students are all really friendly and supportive. I have regained the confidence I lost from being a stay-at-home mum. I felt I'd forgotten how to communicate with adults in a professional manner, but the courses have helped me get that back.'

Darren is a young male student with learning difficulties: 'I am currently attending a Skills for Independent Living Bricklaying class, which I am really enjoying. I am being taught in a friendly, supportive, relaxed, professional, and welcoming environment and our tutor and support worker are really knowledgeable. I have been learning about the basic aspects of bricklaying and different bond types. I am improving each week and my confidence is growing with every class. People do not realize that when you are laying bricks that you are actually using numeracy skills as well. I have noticed that I am counting, measuring, levelling, and generally having to use basic numeracy skills when laying bricks, which helps sharpen these essential skills. After this course I would really like to learn about cooking.'

*All names have been changed to preserve anonymity.

Peter, studying at a college in the London area, is currently completing a Level 2 National Vocational Qualification (NVQ) Certificate in Team Leading course. He works at Metroline, which provides bus services that are under contract to London Buses. Ultimately he plans to move into management and become an engineering director. In the meantime, he is able to complete his course in the workplace. The company has a close relationship with its local college and a number of their engineering and operation staff have had the opportunity to benefit from its training.

Age

One of the distinctive features of further education is the mix of ages. In the main this reflects different modes of study – evening and part-time classes are largely populated by adult students, and full-time day classes by the 16–19 age group. Similarly, Access to HE courses are aimed at mature students who did not meet higher education matriculation requirements when younger (see Chapter 4). Having said this, colleges typically run a number of mixed-age classes, most commonly for those studying towards A levels, GCSEs, and NVQs. The main reason for the existence of mixed-age groups in FE has been economic – that is, there are insufficient numbers of learners to make separate groups viable. Indeed, one well-regarded college reported to one of the authors a decline in enrolments following the implementation of age-segregation, as it became more difficult to reach critical class sizes. Nonetheless, some 45 per cent of learners who experienced mixed-age learning preferred it to age segregation, and only 10 per cent took the opposite view. Staff overwhelmingly preferred mixed-age groups, finding them easier to teach and motivate. (Data in this paragraph are drawn from McNair and Parry, 2004.)

In the 2000s, government policy sought to promote separate learning for 16–19-year olds as being more likely to lead to a focus on their distinctive needs, and thereby to ensure high standards. This led to a number of colleges creating 'sixth form centres' (Morris *et al.*, 1999) – by the end of 2001, 58 out of 270 GFE colleges had done so (Department for Education and Skills, 2002; quoted in Burns, 2007). Hard evidence of the superiority of separate classes has however proved elusive. Neither does there seem to be any general justification for the frequently made assertion that school sixth forms provide better pastoral care than FE colleges.

Gender

Hall (1990) reported that males were the main customer for further education in the 1980s. Now the position has been reversed. By the time of the Foster Report in 2005, 60 per cent of the student body was made up of women, and 56.3 per cent of adult further education students in 2012 were women (Foster, 2005). There are well-known gender differences in the take-up of different courses – for example, those in construction and building are overwhelmingly chosen by males, and those in health and social care, and hairdressing and beauty therapy, largely by females. The growth in female enrolment can therefore be seen to reflect trends in the wider economy, as engineering and construction enrolments are overtaken by business, IT, and social care.

Ethnicity

Further education has generally provided for more students from black and minority ethnic populations than their proportion within the general population. In 2012/13, 19.2 per cent of adult learners were from black and minority ethnic groups. This compares with 14.6 per cent of England's population in the 2011 census (Skills Funding Agency, 2014). Some adults from minority groups are, however, under-represented in FE – particularly those from the Bangladeshi and Pakistani communities – which raises issues about how well colleges are geared to serving their needs.

Disadvantage

Compared to other educational sectors, FE colleges work with a disadvantaged student group. The appendix to the Foster Report (Foster, 2005: 83) tells us that 29 per cent of FE learners come from 'Widening Participation postcodes', compared to 25 per cent of the population. The figures quoted for school sixth forms and universities are 19 per cent and 20 per cent respectively, leading to the surprising conclusion that sixth forms, in fact, are more socially exclusive than universities. Foster noted the conclusion of the Youth Cohort Study for 2002 that 56 per cent of young people in full-time learning in colleges came from the bottom three socio-economic classes, compared to 41 per cent in state schools.

Further education makes a substantial commitment to students with learning difficulties and disabilities. Many of these students gain support to achieve success on mainstream programmes, but for others, specially designed programmes are delivered. Foundation programmes for challenged students – whether those with learning needs, or returners to study – now form a considerable part of the college workload. This is important in a world where school sixth forms are overwhelmingly academically selective. Whatever its other drawbacks, the Further Education Funding Council (FEFC) funding system that came in with incorporation (see Chapters 1 and 8) was widely praised for its ability to support such learners with Additional Learning Support.

Given the socio-economic profile of students who attend FE colleges, it is not surprising that it is commonplace for their experience to be affected by deprivation or financial hardship. The first major study of student income and expenditure in relation to their participation in FE found that over half experienced financial hardship, two-thirds had no savings and two-thirds were in debt (Callender, 1999). The most financially vulnerable were those who were:

- from the lower socio-economic groups
- aged over 19
- lone parents or
- couples with children.

Over two-thirds of students experienced difficulties meeting the costs associated with attending college – such as travel and books. Another study indicated that 39 per cent of full-time, and 16 per cent of part-time, learners in FE were finding it difficult to cope financially (IFF Research Ltd, 2003). Further research agreed that financial hardship was widespread among some groups of students; and that some were deterred from even thinking about FE because of the fear of the cost – which could be substantial, since it included loss of earnings as well as additional expenditure (Davies *et al.*, 2008).

Concerns about the effect of poverty on student participation led to a system of Education Maintenance Allowances (EMA) being trialled across 15 LEAs in 1999 and rolled out nationally from 2004. An EMA granted £30 a week to students from lower income families, and was conditional on attendance and progress. By 2007/8, more than half a million young learners were receiving EMAs (Hubble, 2008). Research from the Institute for Fiscal Studies suggested that EMAs raised participation rates for eligible 16-year olds from 65 to 69 per cent, and for 17-year olds from 54 to 61 per cent (Chowdury and Emerson, 2010). Nevertheless, the Conservative–Liberal Democrat Coalition Government announced their abolition as part of the 2010 spending review. They were replaced by a more modest bursary scheme; the bursaries are paid to the educational establishment rather than the student, making it difficult to know the level of support before enrolment. The ending of EMAs was described by Alan Milburn as 'a very bad mistake' (Wintour, 2012), and the shadow Education Secretary Tristram Hunt moved to promise a restoration were Labour to win the 2015 election (Eaton, 2013).

The engagement of 16–19-year olds in paid employment alongside (supposedly) full-time study is very common, with two-thirds working for ten hours or more per week: the amount of time worked does not vary significantly according to relative deprivation. Young people in FE tend to mix paid employment and study to a greater extent than their counterparts at school, as do those enrolled on vocational courses compared to others following the academic route. Some combination of paid employment and full-time study is viewed positively, both by young people and by their teachers; indeed, many colleges shape their timetables to allow students to take on part-time jobs. This has been made easier by the substantial reduction in teaching hours that accompanied incorporation – courses that had involved more than 25 hours per week shrank to 15 or so. Mixing full-time education and part-time employment does not seem to be correlated with early withdrawal to any great extent; indeed, a mixing of full-time education and modest amounts of part-time employment seems to have a positive effect on student retention (Davies, 1999a; Hodgson and Spours, 2001). However, when the hours of employment involved exceed ten per week, there appears to be a marked and progressive negative impact on students' achievement.

What do they study?

As Chapter 1 notes, English further education started as a support for the industries of the industrial revolution. Even in 1980, engineering was the most popular vocational subject (Hall, 1990). This was overtaken by business studies in the following years, then through the middle years of incorporation the growing and ultimately largest single area of study was computing and IT. This was a result not just of students aiming for a career in that industry, but also reflected a strong demand from adults to get 'up-to-speed' with the new digital world, shown in the popularity of short IT courses, often offered on an outreach basis. Once this backlog was cleared, health and public services became the largest vocational area (see Figure 3.2). These trends had nothing to do with governance arrangements in the colleges, but reflected the de-industrialization process and the coming of a digital world.

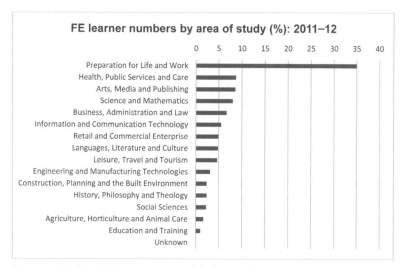

Figure 3.2: What FE learners studied in 2011–12

This is an important point. Colleges are only paid for actual enrolments, and these reflect student demand. Any institution that offered courses in what it felt students ought to do, rather than what they wanted to do, would soon go out of business. Nevertheless, there have been calls throughout the period of incorporation for greater direction of studies. In answer to a question at the 1996 Association of Colleges (AoC) conference James Paice, a junior minister in the Department of Education from 1994 to 1997, said that there were too many media studies programmes - 'in-vogue courses that appear to lead to no job at all' – and not enough engineering (*Times Higher Education*, 1996). (Depressingly, the proposals for regional control of FE that followed the Scottish referendum nearly twenty years later also featured a desire to have less hairdressing and more engineering to meet the perceived real needs of the economy – see Pidd, 2014.) It is difficult to remember a more ineffectual ministerial intervention: evidence to the Foster Report showed that enrolments for engineering subsequently fell nearly 50 per cent between 1998 and 2003 (Foster, 2005).

Another influence on FE enrolment, separate from incorporation, has been the development of greater autonomy for schools, and particularly the opening of new sixth forms. The consequence in some areas has been a de facto split, with academic work going on in schools and vocational work in colleges. A number of FE colleges closed their general education departments, some of which had been large and consciously established as part of tertiary reform in the 1970s and 1980s.

Both before and after incorporation, further education institutions provided a substantial amount of higher education, often linked to a vocational specialism and offering a pull-through opportunity. (Here, as elsewhere, we enter a statistical fog. Some higher education is described as NVQ Levels 4 and 5, some as degree level, some simply 'HE'.) Melville and Macleod reported the 'astonishing fact' that by 1996/7 'the number of higher education students in FE colleges now exceeds the total number of students studying in HE at the time of the Robbins Report in 1963' (Smithers and Robinson, 2000: 33). This may not have been all that astonishing. University-provided higher education had itself expanded rapidly throughout the period, but this growth was not replicated in HE in FE – where the numbers were broadly the same after twenty years of 'freedom'. As a result, there is now a smaller proportion of HE delivered in FE than at the time of incorporation.

Problems of counting

We have seen that one driver for incorporation was the desire for growth. Was the sector successful in this ambition? This may seem to be an easy matter to resolve, because further education in 1992 was a mature sector. Many colleges had been open for more than a century, a fact reflected too often in their capital stock. Data on student numbers were, however, unreliable. Though each college was required to return a Further Education Student Record, its collection and accuracy was not a management priority, and it was rarely audited. Computerized management systems came late to the sector, and even by 1992 few colleges possessed the ability to build up their FE student return from individual student enrolment entries.

Student number calculations had become increasingly important, though, with the coming of the 1988 Education Reform Act. This linked budgets with student numbers, creating a need for more accurate and timely information. The coming of incorporation four years later greatly sharpened this process. The FEFC's Individual Student Record (ISR), which morphed into the Individual Learner Record (ILR), was used as the basis not only of cash allocations, but also well-publicized judgements about retention and pass rates. The sector was slow to meet all of the FEFC's statistical demands. In the early 1990s, a college that returned a validated ILR on time was a rare beast indeed – the *TES* reported that only one college in nine had been able to make a timely return for the 1994/5 academic year (*TES*, 2008). But by the turn of the century, informed commentators felt that the statistical base of the sector was a substantial achievement and one of its main strengths. Some felt, however, that it might also be a weakness. It has been argued, for example, that the problem of student wastage in colleges received more severe scrutiny than that in school sixth forms and universities simply because it was better evidenced by the rich ILR dataset.

Linking student information with budgets may have brought a sense of priority – and audit – to individual institutional data collection, but actually did little to create a clear national view of learner numbers. It is striking that a national picture of enrolment information is difficult to find, even in the age of Google. For example, figures in Smithers and Robinson on something as crucial and simple as full-time and part-time enrolments refer to 'unpublished data from the FEFC' (Smithers and Robinson, 2000: 28–9).

The big picture

Bearing in mind these reservations about the figures, Table 3.1 shows the authors' calculations of student recruitment. It does not go all the way back to 1992. Smithers and Robinson tell us that college enrolments grew by 8 per cent in the five years after incorporation (see Chapter 3 of Wolf, 2011), made up of an increase of 15 per cent in FEFC-funded students but a decline of 21 per cent in those funded from other sources. The Fryer Report spoke of a surge of a third in the volume of FE participation to four million between 1992 and 1996 (Fryer, 1997). The subsequent publication of the reports *Inclusive Learning* (Further Education Funding Council, 1996) and *Learning Works* (Further Education Funding Council, 1997), led to a continued increase in budget, but not a significant increase in volume of participants.

Table 3.1 FE sector (colleges and external institutions) learner numbers (000s) 1996/7–2011/12

	96/97	97/98	98/99	99/00	00/01	01/02
Below 19	676.0	672.0	646.0	634.0	625.0	647.0
19+	2698.0	2722.0	2630.0	2575.0	2737.0	3187.0
Full-time	717.0	690.0	670.0	667.0	638.0	636.0
Part-time	2497.0	2510.0	2413.0	2374.0	2552.0	2986.0
Total	3214.0	3200.0	3083.0	3041.0	3190.0	3622.0

	02/03	03/04	04/05	05/06	06/07	07/08
Below 19	687.0	698.0	747.9	741.7	754.1	780.0
19+	3483.0	3319.8	3452.5	2860.2	2055.3	1900.3
Full-time	691.0	703.4	726.8	748.3	784.9	806.9
Part-time	3270.0	3314.4	3473.6	2853.6	2024.5	1873.4
Total	3961.0	4017.8	4200.4	3601.9	2809.4	2680.3

	08/09	09/10	10/11	11/12
Below 19	871.9	895.3	886.6	882.6
19+	1694.1	1505.9	1213.4	1518.0
Full-time	812.7	857.7	835.7	994.6
Part-time	1753.3	1543.5	1264.3	1406.0
Total	2566.0	2401.2	2100.0	2400.6

Sources: Foster Report (2005) and Skills Funding Agency (SFA/BIS). In the interests of compatibility, totals for 1996/7–2002/3 from the former source exclude numbers in the 'Other full-time' category that cannot be identified by age and therefore remain within the age breakdowns. These, therefore, sum to greater than the amounts shown in the totals columns for these years.

Younger learners – Participation

Full-time education for 16–18-year olds takes place overwhelmingly in schools, GFEs, and SFCs. At the end of 2013, 35.6 per cent of 16-year olds were in state schools, 11.7 per cent in SFCs, and 31.2 per cent in GFEs. Even if the independent sector (6.3 per cent of 16-year olds) is included, the majority of 16-year old students attend college, and the proportion grows for 17-year olds (28.4 per cent in schools, 27.9 per cent in GFEs and 10 per cent in SFCs). The vast majority of part-time education for young people goes on in GFEs (5.5 per cent out of 5.9 per cent).

Changes in total FE enrolments in the early 1990s were due mostly to adult participation, some of it a function of the rise and fall following the franchise scandal (see Chapter 2). There was no substantial rise in the overall proportion of 16-year olds in full-time education between 1994 and 2001 – the proportion fluctuated between 70 and 72 per cent. But between 2001 and 2009, full-time participation grew from 71 per cent to 83.8 per cent. A similar picture is seen in respect of 17- and 18-year olds. This is reflected in the figures in Table 3.1 – an increase of FE enrolments from 625,000 in 2000/1 to 882,000 in 2011/12. By 2013, the first year where the Raising the Participation Age legislation (Department for Education and Skills, 2007) took effect, 81.2 per cent of 16–18-year olds were participating in education and training, an increase of two percentage points from the previous year, and the highest since comparable records began in 1994. Full-time participation was also at its highest, at 70 per cent (Department for Education, 2014). Eighteen-year-old participation fluctuated around 40 per cent from 1994 to 2003, but rose to 50 per cent by 2011. This is a positive story, but it seems to yield no correlation between incorporation and changes in participation rates.

The period since incorporation was paralleled by an increasing concern about NEETs – those youngsters not in education, employment, or training – who constituted 14 per cent of the cohort in 2001. A number of measures brought the proportion of NEET 16-year olds to 6.8 per cent and 17-year olds to 12.9 per cent by 2009. The FE market segment – vocational programmes, often for those who had not made a success of their school career – was well placed to meet this need, though it can be argued that funding restrictions hampered the development of bite-sized, confidence-building programmes and the type of multi-agency provision necessary to attract the most alienated 16–18-year olds.

Adult learners and incorporation

So, for younger learners, there has been a modest but encouraging increase in participation. Ministers and pundits are given to telling their interviewers that the reason for the latest educational reform is that 'young people have only one chance to get an education'. (Googling 'youngsters have only one chance' yields quotations from sententious ministers from Nigeria to Australia.). This is not true, and for those working in further education, it is particularly galling. The majority of enrolments at colleges are adults, even if (as these are part-time students) the bulk of college workload remains with the younger age group. British life is enriched by people who took a second chance in education – from Colin Firth to Clive James, from John Prescott to Willy Russell, Mica Paris to Steven Fry. What impact did incorporation have on those who sought a second chance?

The early years of incorporation were accompanied by an enthusiasm for raising participation among older students (see Chapter 2). Lifelong learning was the watchword, a learning society the goal. The year 1997 saw the publication of *Learning for the Twenty-first Century*, named the Fryer Report after its chair (Fryer, 1997). The report called for 'a clear commitment to widening and deepening participation and achievement in learning ... enlarging substantially the existing constituency of lifelong learners and ensuring that many more people successfully get to the starting line, so that lifelong learning for them can begin' (Fryer, 1997: paragraph 1.10). Ironically, the report was issued at the start of a sustained period of contraction in adult learning. There was a brief upward swing between the end of the millennium and 2002/3, as a result of ministerial enthusiasm to count even three-hour courses. This effect was reversed in 2003 with the coming of the Skills Strategy (Department for Education and Skills, 2003) and the Train to Gain initiative, a scheme that grew out of the Leitch Report (HM Treasury, 2006). (It is striking that even a Conservative Government felt it was an expensive employer subsidy and moved to close it down in 2013.) In a short space of time, one million learners were lost. One reason for the squeeze on adult numbers under incorporation was an increasing emphasis on courses that were felt to help the economy, were qualification-led, and vocationally focused. Liberal adult education was saved in 1993 by some finessing of the new funding methodology, but generally the thrust of government policy was towards a Gradgrind usefulness. (The collection of the writings of Alan Tuckett, leading advocate for adult education, is significantly titled *Seriously Useless Learning* – Tuckett and Nash, 2014.) The Skills for Life adult literacy and numeracy strategy continued, but again it was justified on its workaday utility: improving adult literacy and numeracy to reduce unemployment and disengagement and providing courses of English for speakers of other languages (ESOL) to remove barriers for migrants and enable those from black and minority ethnic communities to enter the workforce.

The increasing emphasis on functionality was bad news for the traditional forms of adult education – what became known as 'non-voc'. It was sometimes possible to squeeze liberal education into a qualifications-driven funding regime (See Blackmore, 2009), but it was an obvious area to cut when budgets had to be shaped to hit targets, or pared to make economies. In 2002, Alan Tuckett of the National Institute of Adult and Continuing Education (NIACE) hammered out an agreement with Ivan Lewis, the junior minister in charge, to 'safeguard' spending on non-vocational adult education at a figure limited to £210 million (interview with the author, November 2014). This was effectively a cut of 3 per cent or so each year - leading an insider to comment that the Blair mantra of 'education, education, education' seemed to mean primary, secondary, and higher. The bald figures show a calamitous drop in adult enrolments in further education, from 3,480,000 in 2002/3 to 1,500,000 ten years later.

Part-time study had fallen by nearly a half, leading to reports of the 'death of the evening class'.

Towards the end of the period, the enthusiasm for loans-funded education came to further education, with grim effects on adult opportunities. BIS figures show a collapse in the number of people taking part in learning at Levels 3 and 4. In 2012/13 over 400,000 people aged 24 and over took part in learning at these levels. In comparison, in 2013/14 only 57,000 people paid for learning at this level with a loan. The Chief Executive of NIACE noted that 'huge numbers of people are no longer participating in learning that will help them to get on in life and in careers which will help the economy to grow' (NIACE, 2014). The 2015/16 settlement continued the grim sequence for adult learning with an overall reduction of 11 per cent (Evans, 2015), and a projection that within five years there would be no government subsidy at all for adult skills. This is an extraordinary policy for a country with an ageing population and a productivity deficit with its industrial competitors, and a sad commentary on the hopes of the early years of incorporation.

Student success

Volumes of enrolments are not a measure of how successful the system has been in increasing the stock of skills in the country. For that, we must look at the number of successful graduates – those who have reached the end of their course of studies and passed the assessments required to gain a qualification. Crude pass rates – the proportion of those that entered the final examination and passed – had been under scrutiny for some time, being reported to college governors and academic boards before incorporation. However, the broader 'success rate' measure – the proportion of those that started a course and gained success at the end – was slow to be recognized, though the issue of drop-out had been placed squarely on the agenda by the Audit Commission in 1993 (Audit Commission, 1993). At the turn of the century, there was an increased emphasis as part of what became known as the 'standards agenda'. Margaret Hodge, then a junior minister in the department, told the Learning and Skills Development Agency (LSDA) Conference in 2002 that 'one in five students drop out and you have only a 50:50 chance in post-16 education of successfully achieving what you set out to do'.

The reaction of the FE sector to this challenge was defensive. Principals and teachers drew attention to the disadvantaged nature of their client group; withdrawal was often attributed to insurmountable financial difficulties. Others pointed out that pass rates varied between different subject areas and different awards. For example, a college that achieved 80 per cent pass rates in A Levels or foundation courses was doing poorly; achieving the same success in craft NVQs or higher professional studies would be a strong performance (Mount, 2005). It was also claimed that attempts to reduce wastage rates would lead to the exclusion of students who deserved a chance.

Whatever the justification for these responses, however, it was clear that improvement was needed, and could be achieved. Complacency was challenged by Further Education Development Agency (FEDA) studies commissioned by two London colleges in 1994, the results of which were replicated subsequently by larger scale national surveys (Further Education Development Agency, 1998; Martinez and Munday, 1998; RCU Ltd, 1998; Davies, 1999b). All of these studies reached similar conclusions, which continue to hold good – that decisions to complete programmes of study are less strongly influenced by finance or other factors external to the college than they are by learners' experience at college. Completing and non-completing learners are strongly differentiated by their college experiences, notably in respect of their placement on appropriate courses, assistance with progression in employment and/or education, the timetabling of courses, the intrinsic interest of courses, and, especially, the perceived quality of the teaching, and their relationships with teachers. Poverty certainly affects participation, but once on course stayers-on are no less deprived than early leavers, and there are sharp differences in performance between equally challenged inner city colleges. It became clear that inspired teaching and well-organized support could shepherd the most challenged learner to course success.

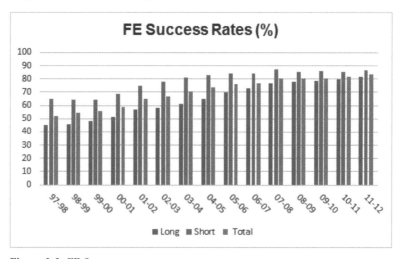

Figure 3.3: FE Success rates

In fact, an underlying improvement in the success rate was already under way at the time Hodge was making her influential speech (see Figure 3.3). By 2002, colleges in the bottom decile were performing as well as had those in the median percentile four years previously, and success increased markedly from 52 per cent in 1998/9 to 72 per cent in 2003/4 (Foster, 2005: 83). Some of this improvement was more apparent than real. Colleges worked on their ILRs to achieve the best image, ensuring the dropouts were massaged through to the right census date, and removing altogether failures who were not eligible for funding. But at least some of the rise in success rates was due to real improvements in pedagogic practice. By the end of the 1990s, the understanding of student retention and the remedial actions necessary to address the issue had assumed impressive proportions. (Arguably far more so than in higher education, where the attitude persisted that students should not be at university unless they were mature enough to cope with its demands. In school sixth forms, the issue continued to be largely ignored.) A new expertise in raising success rates, from better admissions counselling to early analysis and support of those at risk, was developed and shared.

Student satisfaction

A number of colleges had started satisfaction surveys before incorporation, usually focused on a particular college service – enrolment, libraries, cafeteria – with the aim of service improvement. Satisfaction surveys picked up steam when they became a part of the new public management systems of the 1980s and 1990s, with their desire that users of public services – now to be called clients and customers – should have a say in the quality of the service they were offered. Customer satisfaction surveys formed a major part of this approach. The 'voice of the learner' formed one of the main strands of Sir Andrew Foster's review of FE, undertaken in 2005, and he made a number of recommendations to strengthen mechanisms by which learners could be involved in the design and delivery of the education and training that they received (Foster, 2005). A number of developments followed, trying to ensure that learner satisfaction became an integral part of provider self-assessment and development planning. As part of the Common Inspection Framework, providers were asked to demonstrate that learners had been consulted on the key elements of their learning experience, and reveal what they said (see Chapter 8). Learner satisfaction was incorporated as one of the key performance indictors within the 'Framework for Excellence', the government's performance assessment tool for FE. A National Learner Panel for FE was established in November 2006, followed by a 14–19 Learner Panel. These developments were mirrored locally in efforts (in association with the National Union of Students) to improve the number and quantity of student governors and to develop other forms of student representation, such as course committees and focus groups. (A helpful review of this work can be found in Katsifli and Green, 2010.)

In parallel with these developments, the National Learner Satisfaction Survey (NLSS) was introduced by the Learning and Skills Council (LSC), the funding and planning body for all post-16 education and training except higher education from 2001 to 2010 (see Chapters 1 and 2), involving six large-scale studies of FE undertaken between 2001 and 2009. (The surveys continued in a modified form under the Conservative–Liberal Democrat Coalition Government from 2010, with the aim of providing greater disaggregation of information so as to enable colleges and students to assess their comparative performance more meaningfully.) In the last of these, 91 per cent of students expressed satisfaction with their learning experience, with just 6 per cent dissatisfied (Department for Business, Innovation and Skills, 2011). The findings from the NLSS confirmed those from earlier research in their indication that perceptions of the quality of teaching had the biggest influence on overall satisfaction levels. Teachers sometimes challenged these findings, concerned that they were being set up as the scapegoats for any supposed failings in college performance. As researchers were at pains to point out, however, the vital importance of teaching to the student experience was surely what the National Association of Teachers in Further and Higher Education (later the Universities and Colleges Union) would have wanted independent research to establish. A further key influence on satisfaction levels was the help and support provided. Other studies had also shown correlations between staff satisfaction, learner satisfaction, and learner retention and achievement (Owen and Davies, 2003). In comparison with other public and commercial undertakings, FE came out well from these surveys. In the 2002/3 survey, for example, 86 per cent were fairly, very, or extremely satisfied. This contrasted markedly with other institutions – schools 80 per cent, police 63 per cent, hospitals 78 per cent, rail 73 per cent, and dentists 52 per cent, as revealed in DfE background papers for the Foster Report. A separate study of student satisfaction with higher education saw FE colleges outscore most universities (British Council, 2014).

Summary

It is difficult to summarize the experience of millions of learners in a major sector of English education. However, a number of points can be made.

The first is that incorporation failed to deliver the expansion that was desired. College incorporation was motivated by a desire to see newly free and entrepreneurial colleges expand their learning market, as the polytechnics had done. The fact that this did not happen may reflect the fact that little freedom was in fact on offer. Increasingly austere management from national government determined the numbers to be recruited, the qualifications to be offered, and the definition of quality. It is difficult to see the coming of incorporation as a test bed for the benefits of increased autonomy when the perception of those who work in colleges is that it in fact delivered increased central control. Yet even then, colleges did not reap the rewards of being a national sector. They persisted in viewing themselves as competitors with neighbours, rather than partners in a national endeavour. As a result, there were few attempts at, for example, joint procurement or regional student recruitment campaigns. It was almost as if the sector had all the disadvantages of being a nationally controlled system – bureaucracy and lack of discretion, for example – with none of the advantages of scale economies and image.

The second point is that there is a need for a clear and consistent series of numbers to inform policy, showing recruitment data, success levels, ages, and vocational areas. The authors encountered substantial difficulty in assembling data, and it appears that some data were lost in the move to a standard 'gov.uk' platform. Even an insider finds difficulty chasing down the real figures – we ourselves have found different figures in different publications (e.g. Fryer, 1997, and Smithers and Robinson, 2000, on the early experience of incorporation).

A true analysis of the worth of incorporation would go beyond the crude figures enrolled, or even success rates. The criticism implicit in the Wolf report (Wolf, 2011), that many FE courses did not lead to worthwhile qualifications or employment, needs to be further tested and the conclusions reflected in policy changes that enhance rather than remove vocational pathways. At the time of writing, the Department of Business, Innovation and Skills (BIS) is piloting success measures that assess employment success, with a view to including them in funding systems (Department for Business, Innovation and Skills, 2014). It is more likely, however, that improved success in employment and life chances will be delivered by sharing good practice – as happened with retention – rather than clumsy attempts at financial incentives.

Nevertheless, we believe that there were benefits to students from some aspects of incorporation. This is particularly true of the drive to better success rates – the 'standards agenda' – in the early 2000s, which substantially increased the chances of a student finishing her/his course with a worthwhile qualification. The efforts and expertise to improve retention were groundbreaking. It is salutary to realize that in a large college this could mean several thousand better outcomes in a year. An additional advantage accrued to the student with learning difficulties and/ or disabilities, where the FEFC's additional learning support structures, and those of its inheritors, released real resource to support vulnerable learners. There were genuine improvements in communication with students and in student representation.

This is not to deny problems. There was an overall lack of strategic focus, which partly reflected the diversity of the student body but was also caused by the continual shifting of governmental priorities. Managers became adept at adjusting to new funding messages or inspection frameworks (see Chapter 8), but lost a distinctive view of their place in the local infrastructure, and neglected curriculum development. The failure to bring about sufficient progression to vocational courses above Level 2 is an example of lost opportunities amid the policy turmoil. Counterfactual history is popular at the moment. Applying this to the FE sector, one would ask 'what would have happened if colleges had remained with local authorities?' The question is unanswerable, but it seems implausible to believe that there would not have been progress on the student experience, and a better fit with other local provision.

References

Audit Commission (1993) *Unfinished Business: Full-time educational courses for 16–19 year olds*. London: HMSO.

Blackmore, S. (2009) 'The death of learning for fun'. *The Guardian*, 5 October. Online. www.theguardian.com/commentisfree/2009/oct/05/adult-education-evening-class (accessed 2 December 2014).

British Council (2014) 'UK student satisfaction hits 10-year high'. Online. www.educationuk.org/global/articles/student-satisfaction-at-10-year-high-says-national-survey/ (accessed 22 March 2015).

Burns, D. (2007) 'Conceptualising and interpreting organizational boundaries between further and higher education in 'dual sector' institutions: Where are they and what do they do?' Paper presented at the International Conference on Researching Transitions in Lifelong Learning at the University of Stirling, 22–24 June.

Callender, C. (1999) *The Hardship of Learning: Students' income and expenditure and their impact on participation in further education.* Coventry: LSC.

Chowdury, H., and Emerson, C. (2010) *An Efficient Maintenance Allowance?* London: Institute of Fiscal Studies.

Davies, P. (1999a) *Learning and Earning: The impact of paid employment on young people in full-time education.* Online. http://dera.ioe.ac.uk/2898/1/Learning%2520and%2520earning%2520-%2520the%2520impact%2520of%2520 paid%2520employment%2520on%2520young%2520people.pdf (accessed 22 March 2015).

— (1999b) *What Makes for a Satisfied Student?* London: FEDA.

Davies, P., Fletcher, M., Munoz, S., and Whittaker, M. (2008) *The True Cost of College: The price students pay for further education.* London: LSN /NUS.

Department for Business, Innovation and Skills (BIS) (2011) *National Learner Satisfaction Survey: Further education research study report.* (BIS Research Paper No. 2). Online. www.gov.uk/government/publications/national-learner-satisfaction-survey-further-education-research-study (accessed 2 December 2014).

— (2014) *Adult Further Education: Outcome based success measures. Experimental data 2010/11.* London: BIS.

Department for Education and Skills (DfES) (1995) 'School performance tables: National targets for education and training. Online. www.education.gov.uk/ schools/performance/archive/schools_95/sec7.shtml (accessed 16 Dec 2014).

— (2002) *14–19: Extending Opportunities, Raising Standards.* Norwich: The Stationery Office.

— (2003) *21st Century Skills: Realising our potential.* Online. www.nrdc.org.uk/ anr_details.asp?ID=2931 (accessed 2 December 2014).

— (2007) *Raising Expectations: Staying in education and training post-16.* Online. www.education.gov.uk/consultations/downloadableDocs/6965-DfES-Raising%20Expectations%20Green%20Paper.pdf (accessed 2 December 2014).

Department for Education (2014) *Participation in Education, Training and Employment by 16–18 Year Olds in England: End 2013.* SFR 18/2014. Online. www.gov.uk/government/uploads/system/uploads/attachment_data/file/322575/ Participation_SFR-Final.pdf (accessed 2 December 2014).

Eaton, G. (2013) 'Labour could reintroduce EMA, says Tristram Hunt'. *New Statesman*, 18 October. Online. www.newstatesman.com/politics/2013/10/ labour-could-reintroduce-ema-says-tristram-hunt (accessed 22 March 2015).

Evans, D. (2015) https://news.tes.co.uk/further-education/b/news/2015/02/26/ adult-skills-budget-cut-by-11-per-cent.aspx

Foster, A. (2005) *Realising the Potential: A review of the future role of further education colleges.* London: DfES.

Fryer, R. (1997) *Learning for the Twenty-first Century.* Online. www. lifelonglearning.co.uk/nagcell/index.htm (accessed 2 December 2014).

Further Education Development Agency (FEDA) (1998) *Non-completion of GNVQs.* (Research Report No 3). London: FEDA.

Further Education Funding Council (FEFC) (1992) *Letter Of Guidance to FEFC from the Secretary of State, July 1992* (Circular 92/08). Coventry: FEFC.

— (1996) *Inclusive Learning* (the Tomlinson Report). Coventry: FEFC.

— (1997) *Learning Works* (the Kennedy Report). Coventry: FEFC.

Gorard, S., Selwyn, N., and Rees, G. (2000) 'The "conveyor belt effect": A re-assessment of the impact of National Targets for Lifelong Learning'. Paper presented at BERA Conference, Cardiff University, September.

Hall, V. (1990) *Maintained Further Education in the United Kingdom*. Blagdon: The Further Education Staff College.

HM Treasury (2006) *Prosperity for All In the Global Economy: World class skills* (the Leitch Report) Online. www.delni.gov.uk/leitch_finalreport051206[1]-2.pdf (accessed 2 December 2014).

Hodgson, A., and Spours, K. (2001) 'Part-time work and full-time education in the UK: The emergence of a curriculum and policy issue'. *Journal of Education and Work*, 14 (3), 373–88.

Hubble, S. (2008) *Education Maintenance Allowances: Current issues*. London: House of Commons Library.

IFF Research Ltd (2003) *Study of Learners in Further Education*. London: DfES.

Katsifli, D., and Green, K. (2010) *Making the Most of the Student Voice in Further Education*. London: Blackboard and 157 Group.

Major, J. (1999) *John Major: The autobiography*. London: HarperCollins.

Martinez, P., and Munday, F. (1998) *9,000 Voices: Student persistence and drop-out in further education*. London: FEDA.

McNair, S., and Parry, G. (2004) *Learning Together: Age mixing in further education colleges*. LSRC.

Morris, A., Davies, P., and Bromley, R. (1999) *Sixth Form Centres in FE Colleges: A report for the DfEE*. London: FEDA.

Mount, P. (2005) *FE Review: Data evidence paper to inaugural meeting of external reference group*. London: DfES.

NEDO/MSC (1984) *Competence and Competition*. London: MSC.

NIACE (2014) 'A work in progress.' Online. www.niace.org.uk/blog/?p=2436 (accessed 22 March 2015).

Owen, J., and Davies, P. (2003) *Listening to Staff 2002*. Coventry: LSDA.

Pidd, H. (2014) 'Northern English councils demand more powers from Westminster'. *The Guardian*, 21 September. Online. www.theguardian.com/politics/2014/sep/21/northern-councils-greater-powers-devolution (accessed 22 March 2015).

RCU Ltd (1998) *National Retention Survey Report*. RCU Publications.

Skills Funding Agency (2014) 'FE Data Library: Further education and skills'. Online. www.gov.uk/government/statistical-data-sets/fe-data-library-further-education-and-skills (accessed 22 March 2015).

Smithers, A., and Robinson, P. (2000) *Further Education Re-formed*. London: Falmer Press.

Times Educational Supplement (2008) 'Deadline slips in audit havoc'. Created 16 February 1996, updated 11 May 2008. Online. www.tes.co.uk/teaching-resource/Deadline-slips-in-audit-havoc-107691/ (accessed 2 December 2014).

Times Higher Education (1996) 'Minister rubbishes media courses'. 25 November. Online. www.timeshighereducation.co.uk/features/minister-rubbishes-media-courses/91521.article (accessed 22 March 2015).

Tuckett, A., and Nash, I. (2014) *Seriously Useless Learning: The collected TES writings of Alan Tuckett*. London: NIACE/TES.

Wintour, P. (2012) 'Coalition's child poverty adviser: Bring back EMA'. *The Guardian*, 18 October. Online. www.theguardian.com/education/2012/oct/18/coalition-child-poverty-ema-1 (accessed 22 March 2015).

Wolf, A. (2011) *Review of Vocational Education: the Wolf Report* Online. www.gov.uk/government/publications/review-of-vocational-education-the-wolf-report (accessed 2 December 2014).

Chapter 4

What goes on in colleges? Curriculum and qualifications

Geoff Stanton, Andrew Morris, and Judith Norrington

Introduction

This chapter examines some alternative definitions of 'the FE curriculum', looks at a number of developments and initiatives as case studies, and draws some overall lessons about the process of curriculum change in FE. It addresses the situation in England, focusing on the last 21 years since the incorporation of English FE colleges, but also reviews some earlier developments that either set the scene or provide illuminating contrasts. Various influences on the curriculum are considered, of which the impact of FE incorporation is but one. The chapter is concerned primarily with the work of general FE Colleges (GFEs) rather than with independent vocational training providers, or Sixth Form Colleges (SFCs), for instance.

What is meant by 'the FE curriculum'?

Curriculum itself can mean different things. These include:

- the overall curriculum offer of the FE sector
- the curriculum offer made by individual colleges
- the content of courses and/or qualifications (as in 'the curriculum for A level history')
- the design and implementation of learning programmes for individuals.

We shall make reference to all of these, but will start here with the overall curriculum offer. Many commentators (e.g. Huddleston and Unwin, 2013) define this as consisting of:

- general education
- general vocational education
- job-specific training
- higher education
- adult education (cultural and recreational studies, usually non-examined).

Others (e.g. Frankel and Reeves, 1996) also add:

- compensatory education, including Adult Basic Skills
- preparation for higher education (Access courses for adults)
- courses for people with a variety of special needs, including those who had been attending special schools and who would now benefit from the wider environment of a college (See Further Education Funding Council, 1996).

In addition, each of these categories of provision may be offered on a full-time or part-time basis. Some, such as apprenticeships, are offered jointly with employers, such that learning takes place both on and off the job. Vocational courses may be classroom and/or workshop based, and some make use of 'realistic work environments', such as restaurants, hairdressing salons, farms, or travel agencies, run on a commercial basis by the college. So FE college courses taken as a whole cater for all ages from 14 upwards. (Provision for 14–16-year olds is often, but not always, offered jointly with a secondary school.) They cater for all levels of previous attainment, and may be academic or vocational, full-time or part-time.

The issue of diversity

This diversity has attracted criticism. In 2005 the government-commissioned Foster Review of the future role of FE colleges argued that: 'FE lacks a clearly recognized and shared core purpose' (Foster, 2005: vii), recommending that 'the Government should articulate a core role for FE colleges ... in supplying economically valuable skills.' However, the very next paragraph of the report had to compromise this clarity by adding, 'The Government should recognize that a primary focus on skills does not exclude other significant purposes in promoting social inclusion and facilitating progression' (Foster, 2005: 76).

As if to prove this point, FE was later given a major role in providing Adult Basic Skills (following the Moser Report, Department for Education and Employment, 1999), and recently it has been asked to ensure that 16+ school leavers attain at least Level 2 GCSEs in mathematicss and English before they are 18 (following the Wolf Report in 2011).

The issue of the diversity of FE provision, and whether this is a virtue or a problem, is ongoing. Our conclusion is that it is the very diversity of the FE curriculum offer that simplifies the life of school sixth forms and universities by enabling them to keep their more focused missions.

A consequence is that FE is more inclusive than either school sixth forms or universities (Kennedy, 1997). For instance, ethnic minority students make up 20 per cent of students in colleges, compared with 15 per cent of the general population, and 16 per cent of 16–18-year olds in colleges were claiming free school meals at age 15, compared with 9 per cent in maintained school and academy sixth forms (see Association of Colleges, 2014, and see Chapter 3 for more on the nature of students in GFEs.)

Compared with most schools, GFEs offer a wider range of learning experiences and assessment regimes, such as those related to the 'realistic work environments' mentioned above. Its vocational programmes are usually in the form of an integrated course, rather than one made up of disparate subjects as in the case of the secondary school curriculum. When delivered by an effective course team, this allows for a more coherent learning experience and better pastoral support, and, in our experience, helps learners who have not found their school curriculum congenial.

The variety of subject areas, learners, and learning environments present in FE is unique and this means that, potentially, FE staff are uniquely positioned to contribute to development and innovation. But ironically, the trend has been the other way, with policymakers suspicious of practices that do not fit the academic paradigm, in terms of course design, assessment methodology, and definitions of excellence, that their own experience has given them.

But it is important to admit that the FE curriculum has not always had these open characteristics. At one time provision was not comprehensive and followed the conventional wisdom that many school leavers would not benefit from more learning. Some of the things that contributed to this changing during the 1970s were:

- An increased demand from school leavers who wanted to spend at least another year after the end of compulsory schooling before entering, or feeling able to enter, the world of work. This led to the creation of 'pre-vocational' courses (Further Education Unit, 1979).
- Funding from the Department of Employment, in the form of the Manpower Services Commission (MSC), to put on schemes of 'unified vocational preparation' (UVP) for young employees whose jobs required no specific training (Jamieson Wray *et al.,* 1989).
- The recession in the 1980s, which came to dominate the training agenda. By 1983 there were almost three million people out of work, and introducing work-related opportunities was seen as one of the solutions. A variety of MSC-funded schemes required innovative approaches to pedagogy and course design (Cantor, 1989).

Design of the vocational curriculum

However, since the teacher-led innovations prompted by these demands, FE staff have had, we shall argue, decreasing influence over the content of the vocational curriculum, while receiving criticism about its relevance. Teachers have also had to adapt to a shift from the content of vocational qualifications being described in terms of topics (as most academic degrees, for instance, still are) to one in which learning outcomes or occupational competences are specified. This process began when the Business and Technician Education Council (BTEC) introduced its programmes in the 1970s. BTEC set up working groups of teachers and employers to specify the required learning outcomes. Interestingly, BTEC also checked on the capacity of providers, preventing most schools from involvement, while in suitable cases allowing experienced colleges to propose their own schemes for BTEC validation.

The outcomes-based approach was much extended by the National Council for Vocational Qualifications (NCVQ) when it was created as a regulatory body in 1986. Qualifications were to be described in terms of 'competences' or 'occupational standards', specified by 'Industry Lead Bodies'. There was no required learning programme. This approach had many virtues, particularly when applied to experienced workers who had learned on the job, but there was little involvement of experienced teachers in the process. We argue that when linked with the use of qualifications as performance indicators and triggers for funding (Stanton, 1996), as happened post-incorporation in 1992, the ability of FE staff to respond to the needs of individual learners and employers was hindered.

Government assumed at first that all post-16 qualifications that were not GCSEs or A levels would be fitted into the NVQ framework, including full-time courses (Eggar, 1991). This could have been the case if NCVQ had kept to its original brief of creating a framework 'to incorporate and embrace existing vocational qualifications' (Raggatt and Williams, 1999: 78), but for the most part NCVQ's requirements were such that brand new qualifications had to be designed. Also, the specified assessment regime often required access to the workplace. Therefore, NVQs came to be used for apprenticeships and for adult workers, rather than for full-time provision for younger learners.

Structure of this chapter

Rather than continue to address the FE curriculum as a whole, we shall now offer four case studies that we believe will provide specific examples of the

FE curriculum and its development, and from which we shall draw further conclusions in the final part of the chapter.

A key feature of college activity has always involved working closely with employers and especially providing support for work-based learning. This form of vocational education is illustrated in our first case study, with a particular emphasis on apprenticeships.

Our second case study concerns full-time vocational education for school leavers. Many people do not realize that nearly twice as many 16–18-year olds study full-time in colleges as in school sixth forms (840,000 in 2013). Many of them study A levels, as in schools, but vocational courses are the distinctive FE offer, so we focus on them. They are important even though apprenticeships get more attention. Despite a considerable recent increase in overall apprenticeship numbers, the under-19 figures have remained static for decades, and still only make up about 5 per cent of the cohort.

Some 2.2 million adults studied or trained in colleges in 2013, often part-time. But not all FE provision for adults is directly vocational, and our third and fourth case studies illustrate two forms of adult provision that are not. These are 'Access courses' that provide an alternative route to Higher Education (over 140,000 higher education students study in colleges, but we focus on provision that is special to FE), and 'adult basic skills' – literacy, numeracy, and ESOL (English for speakers of other languages).

In the space available none of the case studies can be comprehensive. Our intention is just to illustrate some patterns of curriculum change. The first two case studies may be confusing, because there has been considerable turbulence, with oscillations in national policy. The other case studies describe developments that have also evolved, but with fewer abrupt changes of direction. They also have more involvement of FE practitioners in their design. You may think that this is not a coincidence.

1. Work-based learning

The tradition of FE working with employers to meet their training needs has often involved providing the theoretical component of apprenticeships on a day-release basis, but has also included systematic workshop practice and enabling older people to retrain. For many occupations, FE involvement has helped to assure a sustained national standard of skills, knowledge, and performance that could be relied on. However, this has always proved to be a complex area of curriculum development and delivery, as employment requirements are not homogeneous.

NVQs

In 1986 a review of the whole vocational qualifications system (Manpower Services Commission/DES, 1986) recommended the creation of a new framework, in order to simplify what was seen as an over-complex system. It was initially envisaged that all existing vocational qualifications would, after being modified as necessary, be inserted into the new framework (Raggatt and Williams, 1999), and would then be dubbed National Vocational Qualifications (NVQs). The report also urged that a national council, NCVQ, should be established as a regulator to work with the existing bodies to set up that framework. But, as described earlier, because of the nature of the specifications, for the most part new qualifications had to be designed.

A system of competence-based qualifications at five levels was created, intended to be independent of any location, mode, or duration of training. The competences were specified by lead bodies for each industry. This approach provided the opportunity for experienced workers to accredit their prior learning. As a result, new roles as external assessors of workplace performance were created for staff from colleges and independent training providers. However, there were many problems about the way in which competences were defined and the assessment regime designed. This led to the Beaumont review in 1995 (Beaumont, 1996).

After 1997 NCVQ was subsumed into what became a succession of other regulatory bodies, each of which had a general rather than a specifically vocational brief. After 2008 NVQs were progressively replaced with Qualifications and Credit Framework (QCF) awards, certificates, and diplomas. The QCF rules were themselves abandoned in 2014 as being too rigid. Nevertheless, the valuable features of competence-based qualifications continue to be available for many occupations, though not always under the NVQ label.

Apprenticeships

NVQs were an important component of apprenticeships, the next area for reform. A serious decline in numbers led to a White Paper in 1994 (Department of Trade and Industry, 1994), which introduced the Modern Apprenticeship. The White Paper's ambitious objectives were to have 150,000 new apprentices in England at any one time and over 40,000 young people each year achieving qualifications at NVQ Level 3 or above via the one-year Foundation Modern Apprenticeship (FMA) and the two-year Advanced Modern Apprenticeship (AMA). Both were based principally upon the achievement of an NVQ – at Level 2 in the case of the FMA and at Level 3 for the AMA – together with, as a minimum, key skills in communication and application of number. AMAs included underpinning technical knowledge and skills delivered through a taught programme of off-the-job learning. Sector Skills Councils (SSCs), which had by now replaced Industry Lead Bodies, could also specify any additional qualifications.

By 2001 there were still issues with the approach and delivery of apprenticeships, leading to another review (Cassels, 2001). This set out an entitlement to apprenticeships for all 16–17-year olds who achieved a GCSE at grades A to C, but problems with finding enough employment-based provision led to the introduction of a so-called 'programme-led apprenticeship', which took the form of up to six months of full-time, off-the-job training mainly done in colleges. This was intended to lead on to employment, but frequently did not do so. In 2003, therefore, a Modern Apprenticeship Task Force was set up to encourage employers to become involved. In 2004, Young Apprenticeships for 14–16-year olds were introduced, in which students followed a programme of work-based learning for two days a week.

Programme-led apprenticeships were removed in 2009, following concern that in some areas they were of very short duration, and that some involved employees already trained and in post. New rules were introduced to ensure that apprenticeships lasted for at least a year.

A further review, published in November 2012, clarified the position that apprenticeships should relate to new staff in new roles, and argued for them all to be at Level 3. The author made it clear that he supported off-site learning, describing it as adding 'real value', and expressed his support for GFEs, describing the best as 'world leaders' and innovators in the delivery of apprenticeships (Richard, 2012). In 2013 there were 510,000 apprenticeship starts, but 78 per cent were for those over 19 and 57 per cent were at Level 2.

The Leitch Review

The Leitch Review was published in 2006, and exhorted the nation to be more ambitious in relation to the skills development of employees. It was suggested that 90 per cent of the adult population should be qualified to at least Level 2 by the year 2020 (an increase from 69 per cent in 2005), with four million adult Level 3 attainments expected over the same period. It was also suggested that an employer-led Commission for Employment and Skills should be established and that only those vocational qualifications signed off by an SSC should be funded. A 'Train to Gain' scheme of subsidized training was introduced, but in January 2010 the Public Accounts Committee reported that 'in the face of evidence of what was achievable targets were too ambitious' and that 'half of the employers involved said that they would have arranged similar training in any case, without public subsidy' (Public Accounts Committee, 2010). The scheme was withdrawn later that year.

Commentary

It is noticeable that despite the importance of the role played by colleges in supporting off-the-job training, they are not always present at the early policy discussions where their extensive experience could be helpful.

Many of the White Papers employ phrases such as 'putting employers in the driving seat'. What perhaps has not been practised so well in the recent past is the joint responsibility for creating and planning the curriculum. Employers have a right to expect that training programmes will be up to date with industry's needs and that colleges and training providers will be flexible and responsive. But they also have a responsibility to articulate their current and future skill requirements clearly. The succession of employer bodies over past decades suggests that there is something fundamentally difficult about their fulfilling their proper role in the UK system. Since the 1960s, Industry Training Boards have been followed by Industry Training Organizations, then Industry Lead Bodies, then Occupational Standards Councils, and now we have SSCs. Colleges have been a constant during the whole period and their contribution to work-based learning, together with that of independent training providers, should not be underestimated.

2. Full-time vocational education for school leavers

GNVQs

By the early 1990s there was a realization by policymakers that the NVQ framework was not after all suitable for full-time provision, particularly if the learners were not yet employed. This was because such learners needed a broad vocational preparation, and the evidence of their ability to progress, whereas NVQs were occupationally specific, and required access to the workplace for valid assessment of their occupational competence.

The need to develop a coherent range of more general vocational qualifications (GNVQs) was flagged up in the 1991 Education and Training White Paper (Raggatt and Williams, 1999). NCVQ was asked to coordinate the necessary work. Ministers requested that the first GNVQs should be accredited in time to be available in colleges and schools from September 1992. This was a strenuous schedule, to say the least, but it was suggested by ministers that, 'it should be possible to make rapid progress towards modifying some existing qualifications to bring them in line with the new criteria very quickly, and accrediting them' (Eggar, 1991). However, NCVQ set about designing a new qualification from scratch. Significant problems resulted, and in 1996 prompted an urgent review into GNVQ assessment (Capey, 1995).

The Dearing Review

In 1996 the Dearing Review of 16–19 Education confirmed the position of GNVQs as a middle path between GCSEs/A levels and NVQs, but also suggested that they should be modularized in a way that made it possible to 'mix and match' with modular A levels (Dearing, 1996). This brought them closer to being vocational subjects, to be taught alongside other subjects, rather than, as they started out, integrated vocational courses. In time, GNVQs at Levels 1 and 2 were replaced by vocational GCSEs, and at Level 3 by Advanced Vocational Certificates of Education (AVCEs) – vocational A levels.

Curriculum 2000

Despite the name, this was actually a qualification rather than a curriculum reform. It introduced AS levels, five of which could be taken by students at the end of one year of study post-16, before focusing on fewer full A levels a year later. This was intended both to promote a broader A level curriculum, which could include vocational as well as academic subjects, and to provide a stepping stone, in the form of AS, for those who found the direct move to A level difficult. Here is not the place to analyse this innovation in detail, but it is mentioned for two reasons. (For more detail on Curriculum 2000 see Hodgson and Spours, 2003.)

One reason is the attempt it made to integrate academic and vocational provision into the same qualifications framework. Such links had already been created organizationally. Ministries had been merged to form the Department for Education and Employment in 1995 (it became the Department for Education and Skills in 2001), and between 1996 and 1998 government put pressure on awarding bodies offering A Levels and GNVQs to merge in order to fund 'unitary awarding bodies' that could offer a 'single point of accountability' for all qualifications intended for 16–18-year olds.

The second reason is the nature of the problems it ran into. In 2002 an inquiry into what had gone wrong with the marking of the new qualifications blamed near-universal confusion about standards. The author, Mike Tomlinson, a former chief inspector, made it clear that the problems could have been avoided if the government had not rushed to introduce Curriculum 2000 without extensive testing of the new arrangements beforehand (Tomlinson, 2002). At the same time, Ofsted was reporting that the Vocational A Levels had not been well designed, being 'neither seriously vocational, nor consistently advanced' (Ofsted, 2004: 5).

The Tomlinson 14–19 working group

The following year Tomlinson was again called upon to chair a working group with the brief to 'consider how to develop a unified framework of qualifications that can stretch the performance of learners, motivate progression and recognise different levels of achievement' (Tomlinson, 2004: 75).

A contemporary BBC education correspondent said of the report: 'Rarely has a government-commissioned inquiry done its job so thoroughly. For two years, Sir Mike's working group sifted the evidence, took advice, cajoled and persuaded. By the end he had achieved the near impossible: a very broad consensus in favour of wholesale reform of the examination system' (Baker, 2005). Working group members were therefore very disappointed, even offended, to hear that the Prime Minister, Tony Blair, had rejected the proposals because of a concern that they might be seen to threaten the position of A levels. Instead, the government announced its intention to develop new 14–19 Diplomas, to be launched in 2008 to replace GNVQs.

14–19 Diplomas

Despite the previous existence of GNVQs and the ongoing presence of BTECs, the new 'employer designed' Diplomas were described as filling a gap (House of Commons Education and Skills Committee, 2007). The then Secretary of State said in evidence to a Select Committee enquiry: 'It is the bit that is missing and has been missing from our education system historically. We have had, on the one side, theoretical study and, on the other side, workplace training, job training, and there has been nothing that mixed the theoretical with the applied to any great degree.' This was particularly odd, given that GNVQs did do this, and when they were abolished the government itself stated that, before the new Diplomas came on stream, existing alternatives were BTEC diplomas and certificates, OCR Nationals, and City & Guilds progression awards. Indeed, the select committee asked about existing provision:

> The question remains as to whether more use could and should have been made of existing "tried and tested" qualifications such as BTECs at the outset. What appears to have happened is that a 'blank slate' approach has been adopted ... this seems wasteful to us and makes it likely that old lessons will have to be learned again.
>
> (House of Commons Education and Skills Committee, 2007: 26)

What lent even more power to the criticism of the Select Committee was the fact that, just as in the case of GNVQs, a highly ambitious development schedule was set out for the Diplomas, with no provision for piloting and little initial involvement of FE practitioners.

Another feature of these awards was a requirement that they be offered jointly by consortia of schools and colleges. This meant that they were expensive to provide, and attempted to address a variety of purposes. When in 2010 Michael Gove, the incoming Secretary of State, removed the funding for Diplomas and proposed the 'English Baccalaureate', a performance measure for 16-year olds that only included GCSEs in traditional academic subjects, it became clear that the integration of the academic and the vocational was no longer in favour.

The Wolf Review

In 2011 yet another report into 14–19 vocational education was commissioned, this time from Professor Alison Wolf. Wolf made a number of pertinent criticisms, for instance about the weak vocational content of much school-based provision at Levels 1 and 2, about the faulty basis for the claimed equivalences between academic and vocational qualifications, and about the consequences of funding individual qualifications rather than a whole learning programme (Wolf, 2011). What was made less clear was that all these were the consequences of 'reforms' introduced by previous governments of both main parties.

In general, Wolf commended the work of colleges, but she did criticize the fact that general education in the form of GCSE English and mathematics did not continue after the age of 16 for those who had not already achieved grade C. She argued that only GCSEs had currency with employers, and was dismissive of alternatives such as Key Skills. But this debate continues, since the term 'currency' confuses the value of qualifications for selection purposes, which diminishes, of course, the more people achieve them, with their relevance for the workplace, for which GCSEs were not designed.

Commentary

This case study provides evidence of much government-created turbulence. While government schemes have come and gone, qualifications such as BTEC have continued, in amended forms, throughout the past 21 years. More recently, the awarding body OCR has developed its Cambridge Technicals, and City & Guilds is developing its TechBac.

All three awarding bodies would have gone bankrupt had their own products needed the same degree of early revision as the government schemes. As it is, the failed government initiatives cost the state, the awarding bodies, and FE providers considerable sums of money. They also damaged the interests of learners who had experienced these 'product recalls'.

We suggest a number of related explanations for the failure of government-designed qualifications to be sustained and to succeed in the market place:

1. Over-complex assessment regimes and an unrealistic schedule.
2. The failure to learn lessons both from previous problems and from tried and tested qualifications that have mostly worked – the attraction of a 'clean sheet' to people new to this kind of development work.
3. An inclination to blame problems with 14–19 provision on inadequate vocational courses (and by implication colleges), rather than re-examining the appropriateness of the traditional academic diet, now that it is being asked to meet the needs of far more of the age group.
4. The use of linear rather than iterative development processes, without piloting, and with teachers being regarded as implementers of schemes rather than having a role in their design.

3. The Access movement

The origins of the Access to HE movement lie well before the period captured in this book and the story continues to unfold today.

Originally inspired in the late 1970s by a central government initiative to attract greater numbers of black and minority ethnic people into teaching and social work (Parry, 1996), the idea of an alternative route to higher education (HE) rapidly took off. Local authorities in Manchester and London started providing courses for mature students with few qualifications. Within a few years the range of courses was broadening and an increasing number of colleges were offering them. Courses were locally designed and progression routes were often negotiated with specific local HE institutions, which were asked to specify the qualities they required. The radical departure from mainstream vocational and academic provision was that course design and content were determined locally by practitioners. In the early days, Access courses with guaranteed progression to HE were a form of affirmative action at a time when widening participation was neither a general policy nor practice.

It became clear that the courses were succeeding in attracting students, retaining them, and progressing them into HE, where most of them flourished. Large numbers of adults, given a second chance to learn, were having their lives and prospects transformed. At the same time, universities were finding new markets for their courses, and many professions were finding new sources of recruits. The success at local level meant that some form of coordination and mutual recognition became necessary at regional and national level. Open College Networks formed, beginning in Manchester, which were loose federations of the active partners. They developed new ways of accrediting learning, based on the flexibility of units and the accumulation of credit. As Access became increasingly recognized as the 'third route into HE', Authorised Validating Agencies (AVAs) were formed in the late 1980s that provided a 'kitemark' to guarantee standards. National recognition for Access courses was jointly overseen by the organizations responsible for polytechnics and universities. More recently, the Quality Assurance Agency, which had taken over responsibility for regulating the AVAs, produced a national specification for Access courses, including the requirement for them to be credit-based.

The act of FE incorporation did not significantly alter the course of development for Access provision, but it did introduce a difference to the funding of it. Prior to 1993 there had been wide variation in the ways in which local authorities organized funding; some even provided grants to support the students. When funding units were introduced in 1993, the degree of variation was reduced.

However, the 'coming of age' process has not been without its controversies. Access's origin as a tailor-made response to a specific kind of demand reflects the best of the further and adult education traditions, as does its rapid development by teachers on the ground. The involvement of teachers as course designers, syllabus writers, setters of standards, and judges of quality had an empowering effect that no doubt spilled over to students on these courses. The infrastructure to support local provision was built by the very people who were in touch with the students and the institutions to which they belonged. Yet, as Access courses began to be recognized as mainstream provision, standardization and regulation of the procedures associated with them gradually became more centralized, so the very success of bottom-up, locally determined initiatives ultimately gave way to a more tightly prescribed national specification.

From the student point of view, however, the ever-increasing range of courses and numbers of Access graduates entering the professions bore witness to the enormous impact of the provision. From the point of view of society and the economy, significant pent-up demand for higher skill development had been revealed from a previously neglected segment of society. Unprecedented collaboration between the further, adult, and higher education communities had met it.

4. Literacy, numeracy, and ESOL for adults

The story of literacy and numeracy learning is as old as education itself. Social movements throughout the nineteenth and twentieth centuries extended the ability to read and write beyond the confines of the privileged few. More recent developments that immediately preceded the incorporation of colleges in 1993 were often driven by local education authorities (LEAs), especially in urban areas. The Inner London Education Authority's Language and Literacy Unit in London was an example. National initiatives included the creation of Industrial Language Training Units and a national advertising campaign on television. During the 1980s the Basic Skills Agency (BSA) ensured that basic skills (as they were then known) remained on the agenda. The extent of basic skills needs and the lifelong impact of poor literacy and numeracy were demonstrated by pioneering research, commissioned by the BSA, using data from the longitudinal birth cohort studies.

Incorporation in 1993 marked a breakthrough in support for literacy, numeracy, and English for speakers of other languages (ESOL) thanks to the mainstreaming of funding for provision through the newly formed FEFC. They were weighted favourably in the funding formula, in recognition of the necessarily small group sizes. The extent of provision varied between colleges and for some in the inner cities basic skills became a major part of the offer.

Greater public recognition of literacy and numeracy needs resulted from the poor showing of the UK in international surveys of adult basic skills and in the 1999 report, *A Fresh Start*, by Claus Moser (Department for Education and Employment, 1999). This suggested that one in five adults had 'low literacy skills' and half the population had 'numeracy skills below the level expected of an 11-year old'. The issue was taken up by the Labour Government and the *Skills for Life* strategy (Department for Education and Employment, 2001), launched by the Prime Minister in 2001, was its response. The strategy set out how the government intended to reach what it set as a Public Service Agreement (PSA) target to improve the basic skill levels of 2.25 million adults between 2001 and 2010.

The DFE *Skills for Life* strategy, headed by Susan Pember, a former FE college principal, led to the creation of national qualifications for learners and also for teachers. The early years saw several professionals being brought into government which helped ground the plans and activities. However, in the view of some, over reliance on targets had some distorting effects – a preference for selecting the learners most likely to succeed, leaving others behind (See Hodgson *et al.*, 2007). The strategy gave rise to the National

Research and Development Centre for Literacy and Numeracy, which researches key issues and provides evidence-based materials to support practice. It also led to the gradual professionalization of the workforce (Carpentieri, 2007), from a mixture of qualified and unqualified teachers and volunteers to professionals trained both as teachers and subject specialists.

The strategic response to adult basic skills has aroused some controversy since incorporation. In the early days, the importance of ESOL was under-recognized, missing the predictable impact of migration trends. There was also a tendency to believe that the problem had been caused simply by inadequacies in schooling and therefore the need for Level 1 and 2 provision in FE and adult education would gradually die out as school improvement policies worked their way through. The issue of qualifications to accredit this type of provision divided practitioners, some arguing that they bestow confidence in learners with a history of repeated failure; others arguing that the very process of testing undermines confidence (Waite and Wolf, 2007).

Nevertheless it is clear that countless thousands of learners, who previously would have been overlooked, have benefited enormously. Since 1993 provision has been steadily extended, teachers gradually professionalized, and standards improved through an increasingly student-centred approach. But as we look to the future, the 2013 OECD survey of adult learning offers a salutary reminder of how much still has to be done: the UK remains stubbornly below the OECD average in both numeracy and literacy acquisition (see OECD, 2013: 258 – literacy; OECD, 2013: 263 – numeracy). Also, progressive reduction since 2011 in the weighting for this area of work has meant real-term cuts in funding for providers.

Summary and conclusions

Inspection reports show that, in general, over the past decades colleges have improved the overall quality and reliability of their teaching, and the level of student achievement as measured by qualifications. In our view, GFEs have done an increasingly complex job increasingly well, often stimulated by developments in funding and inspection methodology, but often despite rather than because of shifts in national policy with regard to their overall curriculum offer. However, it could also be argued that colleges have not been sufficiently assertive in exerting their authority in curriculum matters, which they could legitimately claim because of the breadth and nature of their expertise.

The overall curriculum offer

GFEs have been required to play a central role in the delivery of a rolling programme of national initiatives. But as the first two of our case studies have illustrated, there have been pendulum swings in policy. A recent report from City & Guilds (2014) points out that since 1981 skills and employment policy has been subject to 28 major Acts of Parliament, 10 transfers of responsibility between government departments, and has been overseen by 61 Secretaries of State. NVQs, GNVQs, AVCEs, and 14–19 Diplomas were all strongly advocated by the then government, but subsequently ran into design problems and had government support withdrawn (See Stanton, 2008). Also, at the time of FE incorporation, academic and vocational programmes existed in separate silos, then came a period when various attempts were made to bring them within a single framework, and most recently they have been treated separately again. There have also been a series of reviews and policy changes with regard to apprenticeships and work-based learning.

The development of Access courses and adult basic skills provision provides an interesting contrast. There has of course been professional debate about the best way forward and many changes as a result, but the experience is one of evolution rather than revolution. (However, recent funding changes appear to have produced a significant drop in adult participation – see Chapters 2 and 3.)

Aims and target groups

Over time, GFEs have been asked, and indeed have sought, to respond to changing priorities with regard to specific target groups. Policy about the relative priority to be given to certain aims has also changed; whether, for instance, it is more important to help individuals maximize their potential, to provide skills for the economy, or to promote social cohesion and healthy communities.

There has also been policy confusion as to whether the curriculum offer of colleges should be determined by the colleges themselves, using their knowledge of the local community; by national, local, or sector-based planning systems; or by the market in a competitive environment. At the same time GFEs have been criticized for not having a clear focus for their activities.

The vocational curriculum

Development of the quality of vocational teaching and learning has been hindered by ongoing turbulence with regard to vocational qualifications.

The situation is not improved by equating vocational education reform with qualification reform, and the assumption that this type of reform should be the primary means of 'driving' change. Pressure on the curriculum is exacerbated by the use of qualifications as performance measures that influence both inspection grades and funding, and the assumption that more 'rigorous' academic-type written assessment will improve quality and status. The concept of vocational rigour, linked to the ability to perform in the workplace, is less well recognized. Compared to the vast sums spent on qualifications development, few resources have been spent on discovering how to enable people to acquire workplace competence.

There have been repeated claims of inadequate employer involvement in the determination of course content, for which responsibility has been given to a series of employer representative bodies (see the section on work-based learning in this chapter). The fact that the structure and boundaries of these employer bodies have been changed many times over several decades is evidence of continuing problems. We suggest that during this time there has not been the necessary level of involvement of teachers, awarding bodies, and trades unions to bring about effective qualification design.

We have described a tendency for some curriculum innovations initially to be practitioner-led and flexible, but then to become formulated too rigidly into national systems that unnecessarily restrict the ability to meet individual and local needs. It remains to be seen whether increased use of information technology and social media will allow more flexible provision to be re-introduced, as recent reports suggest (see Department for Business, Innovation and Skills, 2014).

Government has repeatedly favoured a 'clean-slate' approach to the design of new vocational provision, and has ignored, or been ignorant of, tried and tested programmes that would have provided a sounder and more economical foundation for necessary further development.

What is distinctive about the FE curriculum?
As we have seen, some of the FE curriculum overlaps with that of schools and universities. But aspects of it are distinctive. The 'signature' FE curriculum is:

- integrated rather than subject based
- vocational in several senses, namely:

  ➢ a preparation for work
  ➢ designed to up-skill or retrain those in work
  ➢ a vehicle for providing continuing general education via an integrating vocational theme

- modular to allow for flexibility but with modules that are designed to relate to one another
- multi-level to allow access from different levels of achievement
- concerned with learning processes as well as outcomes
- delivered by a course team able to manage the learner experience across the curriculum.

Policymakers have often been unable to recognize the value of these features, influenced as they are by the secondary-school paradigm. This assumes separate subjects, all at the same level, designed and taught without planned reference to one another; recognizes as progression only increasing academic levels in the same subject area (rather than, for instance, applying learning in a new context); and has a narrow view of what constitutes 'excellence'.

Looking forward

The Commission on Adult Vocational Teaching and Learning (CAVTL, 2013) was announced by the government in December 2011, and reported in April 2013; it may provide some pointers for the future. In many ways this commission was a break from the past because it:

- focused on teaching and learning rather than on qualifications
- addressed the needs of adults, and not just those at or just leaving school
- was chaired by someone from the FE sector, but had membership from industry, learners, and charities and independent training providers
- recruited its membership by open application, rather than using a government nominated individual or working group
- held meetings hosted in a variety of education and training locations countrywide.

Possibly as a result, it reframed the traditional debate in new and helpful ways. Among other things it argued for:

- a shared responsibility for curriculum design and implementation between employers and colleges, rather than a customer–client relationship
- vocational qualifications with a common core, plus options to meet local needs and to use local facilities and expertise
- principals and other FE staff engaging directly with local companies, reducing the role of intermediaries
- recognition of the 'dual professional' role of vocational teachers: their need both to develop their pedagogy and keep up with innovations in their industry.

Finally, CAVTL advocated the creation of a national centre to act as a focus for the development of teaching and learning in what it called the 'VET system'.

A final comment

The CAVTL experience provides the note on which we would like to finish this chapter. We hope for a future emphasis on collaborative efforts by the FE sector and its leaders, jointly with industry partners, policymakers, and researchers, leading both to continual improvement of teaching and learning in FE, and to ongoing adaptation to new requirements and target groups. This will require:

- at a *policy* level, an increased level of trust, a willingness to learn from the past, and avoidance of an obsession with just one factor as a lever for change, such as funding, assessment, or the employer voice
- from *researchers*, a willingness to work from practice to theory, and to engage with the problems of practitioners and the application of findings, as well as pursuing their own research agendas
- from *teachers*, a willingness to make use of theoretical insights and of effective practice elsewhere, in order to innovate, and to develop their own reflective practice as FE professionals
- from *managers,* providing the space and time for teachers and programme leaders to focus on teaching, learning, assessment, and the curriculum and to take the kind of calculated risks that are required in an increasingly unregulated FE system.

The time is ripe for a move forward but, given the history of volatility in government policy, and the increasingly short-term existence of the agencies it sets up, this will require clear, authoritative, and consistent leadership from the world of FE itself.

References

Association of Colleges (2014) *College Key Facts*. Online. www.aoc.co.uk/sites/default/files/AOC%20KEY%20FACTS%202014.pdf (accessed November 2014).

Baker, M. (2005) 'Why Tomlinson was turned down'. *BBC* News, 26 February. Online. http://news.bbc.co.uk/1/hi/education/4299151.stm (accessed 22 March 2015).

Beaumont, G. (1996) *Review of 100 NVQs and SVQs*. London: DfEE.

Cantor, L.M. (1989) *Vocational Education and Training in the Developed World: A comparative study*. London: Taylor & Francis.

Capey, J. (1995) *GNVQ Assessment Review*. London: NCVQ.

Carpentieri, J.D. (2007) 'Double-check these figures'. *Reflect*, 8,16–17.

Cassels, J. (2001) *Report of the Modern Apprenticeship Advisory Group.* London: DfES.

Commission for Adult Vocational Teaching and Learning (CAVTL) (2013) *It's about Work: Report of the Commission on Adult Vocational Teaching and Learning.* Online. www.aoc.co.uk/sites/default/files/Its%20About%20Work.pdf (accessed 22 December 2014).

City & Guilds (2014) *Sense & Instability: Three decades of skills and employment policy.* Online. www.cityandguilds.com/news/October-2014/skills-policy-review#.VJLw1dKsWSo (accessed 22 December 2014).

Dearing, R. (1996) *Review of Qualifications for 16–19 Year Olds.* London: School Curriculum and Assessment Authority.

Department for Business, Innovation and Skills (BIS) (2014) *The Government Response to the Report of the Further Education Learning Technology Action Group (FELTAG).* London: BIS.

Department for Education and Employment (DfEE) (1999) *A Fresh Start: Improving literacy and numeracy.* (The report of the working group chaired by Sir Claus Moser.) Online. www.lifelonglearning.co.uk/mosergroup/index.htm (accessed 30 November 2014).

— (2001) *Skills for Life: The national strategy for improving adult literacy and numeracy skills.* Online. http://rwp.excellencegateway.org.uk/Archive/Policy,%20strategy%20and%20archive%20resources/ (accessed 22 December 2014).

Department of Education and Science/Department for Employment/Welsh Office. (1991) *Education and Training for the 21st Century.* London: DES/DoE/WO.

Department of Trade and Industry (DTI) (1994) *Competitiveness: Helping business to win.* London: HMSO.

Eggar, T. (1991) Department of Education and Science, press release, 21 March.

Foster, A. (2005) *Realising the Potential: A review of the future role of further education colleges.* London: DfES. Online. www.theresearchcentre.co.uk/files/docs/publications/he0039.pdf (accessed 22 March 2015).

Frankel, A., and Reeves, F. (1996) *The Further Education Curriculum in England: An Introduction.* Bilston: Bilston College Publications, 14–15.

Further Education Funding Council (FEFC) (1996) *Inclusive Learning: Findings of the Learning Difficulties and/or Disabilities Committee* (Chaired by Professor John Tomlinson). Coventry: FEFC.

Further Education Unit (FEU) (1979) *A Basis for Choice: A report of a study group on post-16 pre-employment courses.* London: FEU.

Hodgson, A., and Spours, K. (2003) *Beyond A Levels: Curriculum 2000 and the reform of 14–19 qualifications.* London: Kogan Page.

Hodgson, A., Edwards, S., and Gregson, M. (2007) 'Riding the waves of policy? The case of basic skills in adult and community learning in England'. *Journal of Vocational Education & Training*, 59 (2), 213–29.

House of Commons Education and Skills Committee (2007) *14–19 Diplomas: Fifth report of session 2006–07.* Online. www.publications.parliament.uk/pa/cm200607/cmselect/cmeduski/249/249.pdf (accessed 22 March 2015).

Huddleston, P., and Unwin, L. (2013) *Teaching and Learning in Further Education: Diversity and change.* 4th ed. London: Routledge.

Jamieson Wray, M., Moor, C., and Hill, S. (1989) *Unified Vocational Preparation: An evaluation of the pilot programme.* Windsor: NFER.

Kennedy, H. (1997) *Learning Works: Widening participation in further education.* Coventry: FEFC.

Manpower Services Commission (MSC)/DES (1986) *Review of Vocational Qualifications in England and Wales.* London: HMSO.

OECD (2013) *OECD Skills Outlook 2013: First results from the survey of adult skills.* Online. http://dx.doi.org/10.1787/9789264204256-en (accessed 22 December 2014).

Ofsted (2004) *Vocational A levels: The first two years.* London: Ofsted.

Parry, G. (1996) 'Access education 1973–1994: From second chance to third wave'. *Journal of Access Studies,* 11 (1), 10–33.

Public Accounts Committee (2010) *Train to Gain: Developing the skills of the workforce.* Online. www.publications.parliament.uk/pa/cm200910/cmselect/cmpubacc/248/248.pdf (accessed 22 March 2015).

Raggatt, P., and Williams, S. (1999) *Government, Markets and Vocational Qualifications: An anatomy of a policy.* London: Falmer. Press.

Richard, D. (2012) *The Richard Review of Apprenticeships.* Online. www.gov.uk/government/publications/the-richard-review-of-apprenticeships (accessed 22 March 2015).

Stanton, G. (1996) *Output-Related Funding and the Quality of Education and Training.* London: Institute of Education. Publications

— (2008) *Learning Matters: Making the 14–19 reforms work for learners: by emphasizing learning programmes as well as qualifications; by learning from previous initiatives.* Reading: CFBT.

Tomlinson, M. (2002) *Inquiry into A level Standards.* London: DfES.

— (2004) *Working Group on 14–19 Reform: Final Report.* London: DfES.

Waite, E., and Wolf. A. (2007) 'Reaching the learners that other provision does not reach'. *Reflect,* 9, 10. Online. www.nrdc.org.uk/uploads/documents/doc_3840.pdf (accessed 22 December 2014).

Wolf, A. (2011) *Review of Vocational Education: The Wolf report.* Online. www.gov.uk/government/publications/review-of-vocational-education-the-wolf-report (accessed 30 November 2014).

Chapter 5

The further education workforce

Mick Fletcher, Norman Lucas,
Norman Crowther, and Dan Taubman

Introduction

A key change introduced by the incorporation of colleges in 1993 was that institutions themselves rather than local government became responsible for employing college staff (see Chapter 1). This chapter traces the subsequent changes to the size, structure, and circumstances of the further education (FE) workforce and assesses how far they can be seen as a direct or indirect consequence of this different status. The major focus is on FE teachers as both the largest group and that about which most is recorded. Wherever possible, however, it explores the implications for all staff groups.

The chapter starts with one issue clearly determined by incorporation: the changing locus of collective bargaining on pay and conditions of service as colleges became employers. It provides a narrative account of, and commentary on, the changing nature of industrial relations, noting the strongly held and divergent views concerning what took place and its implications. It also summarizes the outcomes of this process, not only in terms of pay and conditions but also on the 'climate' in further education: how it felt to work in the sector during this period.

The following section describes how the staffing profile has changed over the past 21 years, looking at the changing proportion of part-time staff and the balance between teaching and support. An analysis of staff numbers leads naturally into a consideration of equality; how the gender balance and the proportion of black and ethnic minority staff changed since 1993 and whether any inferences can be drawn about the specific impact of incorporation.

Alongside continuing debates about pay, conditions, and staffing levels has been a dialogue about professionalism and professional standards, linked with, though not limited to, discussions about the qualifications required by FE staff.

The concluding section draws the various strands together and assesses how far changes affecting the workforce have been driven by what one might call 'the logic of incorporation'. Its general conclusion is that incorporation was a precondition for the development of a quasi-market which facilitated the policy goal of reducing unit costs; driving changes to teachers' conditions of service was a conscious part of that agenda. Incorporation also enabled, though did not require, the development of a more centralized system of government control of FE (see Chapter 8), which provided an important context for action relating to the workforce.

Reaching agreement on whether incorporation has been beneficial to the workforce will always be difficult. What a manager sees as increased flexibility an employee may perceive as decreased security: an improvement in efficiency can also be an increased workload. For this reason such judgements are left to the reader.

Industrial relations 1993–2014

The period before incorporation is often seen by older staff and the FE unions as a golden age, although with hindsight it is clear that a relatively stable period of industrial relations, conducted between local authority employers and the FE unions, was coming to an end. (The FE Unions are NATFHE – from 2006 UCU – UNISON, ATL, the ACM – until 2010 when it merged with ATL to become the Management Section of ATL – AMiE, the GMB, and T&G, which became AMICUS and then UNITE.) National negotiations determined pay scales and conditions of service, codified in the 'Silver Book'. They were good: a 30-hour week, 14 weeks holiday (6 to be taken in the summer), and a teaching week of no more than 21 hours. Lecturers' pay followed that of school teachers though it had already fallen behind in the 1970s, possibly as a result of the FE unions deciding to negotiate separately. Shortages of teachers in certain subjects were filled by hourly paid staff but also by full-time staff undertaking large amounts of systematic overtime. (Non-teaching staff were represented by UNISON, the T&G, and GMB Unions. They too had national pay scales and conditions of service, codified in what was known as the 'Burgundy Book'.)

> The main teaching union, the National Association of Teachers in Further and Higher Education (NATFHE) was strongly represented among college leaders as well as teachers. College principals often took the lead in developing union policy on educational issues. NATFHE even published the main text on college management. Such involvement of senior staff was facilitated by the fact that negotiations around key services, such

as payroll, human resource management, personnel, and legal services, were undertaken by local government staff.

This changed with incorporation, though there were clear signs of change before 1993. FE colleges' traditional clients, such as day release students, began a long-term decline in the 1970s and colleges faced mounting pressures to become more efficient, reduce costs, and modernize working practices. In the late 1980s local authorities began to challenge the Silver Book. Hereford and Worcester for example introduced their 'Gold Book' with conditions less favourable to staff, and in 1988 a division of academic staff into teaching and management grades was agreed, with the latter receiving a substantial cut in leave entitlement.

Initial conflicts 1993–7

The first years of incorporation were marked by conflict. One of the authors of this chapter wrote in 2000 that 'the story of staff relations is a narrative of almost unrelieved misery' (Taubman, 2000: 82), noting that for two years in the early 1990s FE had proportionally more days lost to strike action than any other sector in the British economy (Taubman, 2000: 83). FE industrial relations were conducted in the context of new laws on trades unions that hampered their ability to take action; college employers were not slow to use this legislation.

Conflict between NATFHE and the College Employers' Forum (CEF) began in 1993 with a dispute over conditions of service. There was an assumption at the time among leaders in the sector that lecturers' conditions of service needed to be 'modernized' to give greater flexibility and adapt to a new business model (Burton, 1995). The government encouraged reform by holding back some college funding until lecturers' conditions of service had been changed, though some argue that CEF requested the holdback itself (Ward, 1995). Thus in 1993, CEF proposed increases in teaching hours and the working year. A walkout by NATFHE members was stopped by the employers taking legal action. Throughout 1994 there was a series of local and bitter disputes as colleges pressed staff to sign new contracts with diminished conditions of service.

Divisions in the workforce were emphasized by incorporation. Many managers, squeezed between senior management and teachers, left NATFHE for the newly formed ACM. Low-level conflict continued throughout 1994 with colleges giving CEF contracts to new and promoted staff and offering financial inducements to others. NATFHE trumpeted local deals with better offers. The result was that fewer staff were on Silver Book conditions, while some 1,500 full-time posts and over 8,000 part-time posts were lost (Taubman, 2000: 85).

Over 200 local disputes were recorded in 1995. Stalemate at national level continued into 1996. Redundancies continued to grow, with 3,500 full-time posts lost. Colleges increasingly abandoned national pay scales, instituting narrow pay bands. Gaps in teacher numbers were filled by part-time hourly paid staff, many of whom were not qualified teachers. Some colleges used non-teaching staff in quasi-teaching roles such as 'instructors' and 'demonstrators'. A House of Lords decision on part-time workers' rights in 1994, giving some protection to part-time staff, was quickly undermined by college use of third-party agencies to provide temporary workers (Burchell, 1998).

The contracts dispute was disastrous for NATFHE; in the late 1990s membership fell to an all-time low (Burchell, 1998). The workforce was divided and NATFHE had small but serious rivals – ACM for managers, and ATL for teachers who rejected the NATFHE positions. (And NATFHE had no representation in sixth form colleges.) National pay bargaining was in tatters, staff pay restricted to narrow bands within national scales and national pay rates largely abandoned. Very few lecturers remained on the Silver Book and they could easily be ignored by management. Indeed by standing out against locally agreed pay and conditions, they saved colleges money.

Return to negotiation 1997–2004

1997/8 saw changes that were to bring the contracts dispute to an end and usher in a period of negotiated change. In May 1998 a Labour Government was elected and the policy context for FE shifted. Key moments in this change of policy were the publication of the Tomlinson Report (Tomlinson, 1996) on inclusion, and the Kennedy Report (Kennedy, 1997) on widening participation. David Blunkett, the first Secretary of State for Education actually to have attended and benefited from FE, signalled a clearer articulation of the place of adult and further education in skills and regeneration (Department for Education and Employment, 1998). The FEFC had changed Chief Executive in September 1996 (the new Chief Executive was David Melville) and took a more supportive and softer tone.

> There was still stalemate in industrial relations. Most college staff (55 per cent) were on locally negotiated contracts, but the percentage of part-time teachers on non-permanent contracts exceeded 30 per cent – the standard pre-incorporation. In 1997 there were another 5,000 redundancies. The arrival of a Labour

Government, however, opened up the opportunity for more political approaches by the unions around increased funding for the sector where they could make strategic alliances with the Association of Colleges (AoC), the new employers' organization for FE colleges. (The CEF was superseded by the AoC when the two bodies merged in 1998.)

The AoC, had a new CEO in the shape of David Gibson, a college principal. From around 2000, college principals rather than college governors took the lead in negotiations. NATFHE too had a new and strong General Secretary, Paul Mackney, a NATFHE official and ex-FE lecturer, who had stood on a platform of resolving the contracts dispute. He had the courage to tell his members that they had lost, but that there were still many issues and concerns for FE teachers that had not been lost.

Feelers for peace were made over the summer of 1998. A new and thinner minimum national framework of conditions of service was hammered out (Taubman, 2000: 85) within which colleges could develop their own institutional conditions. The yearly maximum number of teaching hours rose from 750 to an average of 850. The working week increased from 35 to 37.5 hours and leave was cut back, the exact details varying with the college and the strength of NATFHE locally. By 2000, teaching hours had on average increased to 825–50 per annum, though not the 1,000 hours that had been the employers' initial proposal. There was a series of local disputes in colleges as some tried to push the boundaries, usually as a result of worsening financial situations.

The dispute clearly affected the morale of the workforce. In 1996 an independent survey for NATFHE (Kinsman, 1996) found 35 per cent of its respondents actively seeking work outside the profession with 60 per cent considering leaving FE and 80 per cent seriously considering early retirement. An inspectorate report in 1995 also points to poor morale in some colleges (*TES*, 1995).

On the other hand, the evidence from staff perception surveys is mixed. In 2002 Owen and Davies found 'the large majority of those surveyed answered that "overall I enjoy my job" and a clear majority would recommend their college as a good place to work' (Owen and Davies, 2002: 2). A later study (2008) however found that many employees in FE 'enjoy their jobs but are less positive about their institutions' with only 31 per cent of teachers describing their college as 'a good place to work' (Villeneuve-Smith *et al.*, 2008: 1). The timing of these surveys may suggest that the dispute itself was not the major or enduring cause of staff dissatisfaction.

A new White Paper, *Success for All* (Department for Education and Skills, 2002), published in June 2002, was to have a profound and direct impact on industrial relations in colleges. Even before it was published, government announced an extra £500 million for FE pay (National Association of Teachers in Further and Higher Education, 2002). Each college had its own allocation for 2001/2 and indicative allocations for 2002/3 and 2003/4 from a sum of £54 million known as the Teachers Pay Initiative (TPI). The FE unions and AoC created a National Framework giving guidelines to individual colleges on using these extra resources (National Association of Teachers in Further and Higher Education, 2002). This allowed colleges flexibility to fund their priorities and existing pay structures, to be accomplished through local negotiations with the unions.

Most felt that the overall impact of the TPI on the morale of staff was 'modestly positive' (Association of Colleges, 2002: 3) though, as AoC commented, 'most feel they are still disadvantaged in comparison with teachers in schools and that if the allocations so far received are not consolidated in future settlements, then their position would be further eroded' (Association of Colleges, 2002). Moreover, the TPI for the FE workforce only applied to teachers. Support staff were left out of the arrangements.

A new equilibrium 2004–14

The final element of TPI concerned modernizing pay. There were to be improved pay structures supported by new job evaluation schemes in colleges. Agreement was reached on guidelines for the development and use of new career families and pathways. There was also agreement in May 2004 on guidelines for performance management in colleges, which meant a new system of targets with changes to individual staff roles and responsibilities. In 2005, NATFHE balloted for strike action in 71 colleges that had not fully implemented the harmonization framework agreement, and non-implementation was the major concern in industrial relations right up to 2007/8.

The new settlement was intended to provide for stability in industrial relations and to enable colleges to plan their staffing while modernizing pay and structures. Government, having intervened to drive change in the first period and to help normalize relations in the second, now withdrew and left industrial relations to the two employer bodies, the AoC and the Sixth Form Colleges' Assocation, and the trades unions.

The normalization of industrial relations may have been threatened by the financial crisis that hit in 2008 and the subsequent adoption of 'austerity policies', which include proposals for substantial cuts in FE budgets. A reduction in the size of the public sector and a freeze on public sector pay are key elements of the policies adopted by the Conservative–Liberal Democrat Coalition Government. However, since these policies are not strongly contested by the official opposition party there seems little chance of their changing in the short to medium term. The impact on pay was made clear with the announcement of an end to automatic pay progression for teachers (from September 2014), civil servants (by 2015–16), prison officers, police officers (whose pay was frozen), and most health workers.

Currently, however, FE industrial relations remain unusual. Unlike many privatized services, staff still access public sector pensions; unlike school teachers FE lecturers negotiate with independent employers and employer bodies not government.

The changing workforce

Teaching staff

Since the transfer of employment responsibilities from local authorities to colleges was followed by unprecedented industrial conflict in the sector, it is important to analyse how the size and shape of the workforce actually changed. There is much anecdotal evidence, most particularly relating to the increased employment of part-time and temporary teachers, but much less by way of hard data. There is also commentary on the wider use of non-teaching staff in a variety of roles, but even less firm evidence.

There are no benchmark data on staff numbers at the time of incorporation, but Hall (1994) reports that in 1990/1 the total number of lecturers in colleges and polytechnics in the UK was 88,000. This implies around 70,000 in England, a modest increase from the 55,000 reported some twenty years previously. The numbers in FE colleges alone would be considerably lower; the 50 polytechnics and colleges of HE had around 280,000 full-time students at the time of incorporation (Hall, 1994) implying 15,000 to 20,000 lecturers. The best estimate of FE lecturer numbers in 1993 therefore is around 70,000 posts, though this excludes some 15,000 staff in sixth form colleges and understates part-timers paid as creditors, not through the payroll.

The most recent figures for FE employees come from the Staff Individualised Record (SIR), a return made on a voluntary basis by colleges and therefore incomplete. In 2012/13, however, the most recent year for which analysis is available, the authors state that the average FE College has 642 employment contracts (a small number of employees may have more than one contract), of which 307 relate to teachers (The Education and Training Foundation, 2014: 4). Since they also state that the sample is fully representative of the sector and that there are 359 colleges, we can extrapolate to a total of 230,000 staff contracts of which just under half, 110,000, relate to teachers.

The earliest SIR record available, for 2003/4, implies 260,000 staff contracts, of which 140,000 relate to teachers, which is consistent with the 2012/13 report (Lifelong Learning UK, 2005). At first sight these figures seem difficult to reconcile with the narrative of cuts and redundancies that emerges from the industrial relations story (see for example Taubman, 2000). They suggest that a decade after incorporation the number of teachers in colleges had grown by over 50 per cent and that it is still well above the initial figure. One explanation is that the first decade after incorporation saw a rapid increase in student numbers. The redundancies that were certainly a feature of the 1990s reflected restructuring rather than contraction and while the demands on lecturers grew, the number of students grew still faster. The result was a sector that was both larger and more efficient. Also the apparent trends are confused by the changing balance between full- and part-time staff. If, other things being equal, a proportion of full-time lecturers were replaced by part-time employees, numbers would seem to rise at the same time as staff faced redundancy. The proportions of staff on part-time contracts rose but not perhaps as dramatically as some suggest.

Part-time teachers

Hall states that prior to incorporation around 20 per cent of teaching in FE was undertaken by part-time staff but 'as colleges moved to financial independence there has been a growing tendency to use more part-time staff...' (Hall, 1994: 147). Since part-time staff in general work fewer hours, however, 20 per cent of teaching hours implies more than 20 per cent of staff numbers. If the average part-timer worked a third of the hours of a full-time lecturer, for example, they would constitute a little over 40 per cent of staff.

Evidence presented to the Education and Employment Select Committee suggested that in 1995/6 39 per cent of staff worked part time (Select Committee on Education and Employment, 1998: paragraph 174). Witnesses to the committee agreed that there had been an increase in the use of part-time staff, but were not able to quantify its growth. Some of the commentary to the committee conflates part-time employment with temporary employment; while both seem to have risen after incorporation, they are not the same thing and an increase in temporary status does not change staff numbers.

A report by the FEFC Inspectorate in 1999 gives useful information on the proportion of teaching undertaken by part-time teachers and the proportion of part-time staff. According to this analysis, 30 per cent of teaching in 1997/8 was undertaken by part-time staff who accounted for 62 per cent of all teaching posts (82,000 out of a total of 131,000). Assuming that the average full-time teacher workload was 21 hours per week, the average part-timer taught for around 5.4 hours.

The SIR return for 2003/4 suggests that the same proportion – 62 per cent of FE teachers – were on part-time contracts at that date and the same figure is reported almost ten years later in the 2012/13 analysis. It suggests that in the first few years after incorporation there was indeed a rapid increase in the proportion of teachers on part-time contracts, but by 1997 it had reached a new equilibrium position and thereafter did not change.

There are three observations arising from this analysis. One is that those giving evidence to the Select Committee about the growth in part-time teaching were prescient both in identifying concerns about its potential impact on quality and also in identifying that it had probably reached a natural limit. Future debate in the sector concerned the treatment of part-time staff rather than their overall numbers.

Secondly, if the average hours taught by individual part-time staff was around five to six per week pre-incorporation, the subsequent growth in teaching staff numbers was almost all accounted for by part-time posts. Full-time teacher numbers, in sixth form colleges as well as general further education colleges seem to have fallen somewhat initially but since then have remained constant at a little over 40,000 employees.

The final observation is that the period during which this change happened coincides almost exactly with the period of most acute industrial conflict. It is perhaps not surprising.

Support staff

The high-profile disputes associated with changes to the teaching workforce tend to overshadow some equally important changes in relation to other categories of staff. Anecdotal evidence suggests that both the numbers and proportions of support staff grew after incorporation and new staff roles were created, some blurring the boundary between teaching and support. Arguably the changes to non-teaching roles might be expected to be more profound since both national negotiations and college articles of government had limited the influence that local authority HR departments were able to exercise over teaching staff, but had not limited their powers in relation to other categories of employee. Many college principals (e.g. Ashton, 1995) had found local authority HR departments to be unhelpful or even obstructive when seeking to introduce change (see also Kingston, 2008).

The majority of staff in FE currently are not teachers. The breakdown for the SIR analyses for 2012/13 and 2003/4 are shown in Table 5.1.

Table 5.1 Proportions of FE staff (FTEs)

Occupational group	Proportion of FTE staff	
	2003/4 (%)	2012/13 (%)
Administrative and professional staff	8	8
Technical staff	6	7
Word processing, clerical, and secretarial staff	11	11
Service staff	15	15
Teaching staff	54	44
Assessors and verifiers		2
Senior managers	6	1
Other managers		9
Unknown		3

The major change over nearly a decade is a reduction in the proportion of teachers from just over to just under 50 per cent of the total. This change is probably overstated by the separate recording of assessors and verifiers in the later period and a more detailed analysis of managerial roles. The main message in respect of other staff groups seems to be one of consistency rather than change.

The identification of similar evidence from earlier periods is difficult. A report in the *TES* in 2010 suggested that the proportion of teaching staff fell from 60 per cent of the workforce in 1997 to 52 per cent in 2006, a trend that is consistent with the SIR data. A source of data from earlier periods on the teaching workforce (Hall, 1994), however, makes no mention of other categories of staff.

Despite the lack of numbers there is evidence on the changing and widening role of support staff. Colin Flint, for example, in evidence to the Foster Review of FE states:

There are many roles within the term 'support staff', and the distinction between teaching staff and non-teaching will continue to narrow. Most if not all colleges now employ staff on support conditions of service (longer working week and year) and pay (lower) in quasi-teaching roles. Teaching technicians, instructors, assessors, learning support workers and others under different titles are an indispensable part of the FE workforce.

(Flint, 2005)

A different interpretation of the same phenomena is offered by a Unison spokesperson quoted by the *TES*:

'Increasingly, demonstrators and technicians are being asked to "instruct" students as pressures on lecturing staff have grown,' the union says. NVQs and portfolio methods of assessment have also drawn support staff into the borderline between teaching and learning supervision. One respondent admitted: 'I now find I do work which I don't feel adequately qualified for and most support staff have taken on extra responsibilities.'

(Crequer, 1998)

A study carried out for the Learning and Skills Research Centre in 2005 identified growth in the number of Learning Support Workers (LSWs) as one of the most significant changes in FE staffing in the previous twenty years, with most growth occurring following incorporation (Robson *et al.*, 2006). A key factor in encouraging growth to a point where LSWs accounted for 4 per cent of the FE workforce was the Additional Support Mechanism used by the FEFC to fund resources for learners with learning difficulties and/or disabilities. Interestingly they comment that this substantial change occurred without central direction and without any of the conflict that accompanied other staffing changes.

Incorporation had a direct impact on college staffing structures by requiring colleges to take on new roles in relation to HR, finance, and estates in particular. The view that some aspects of a teacher's role might be better undertaken by instructor grades or demonstrators is also evident from the earliest days of the new sector and seems linked with proposals to reform teachers' conditions of service (Burton, 1995). The former difference can be seen in changing proportions of managerial staff in the SIR but the latter is less evident in the data than debates around the issue might lead one to suspect.

The growth agenda pursued by government in the early 1990s and the more competitive environment in education also led to an expansion of posts in marketing; and the demands of the new systems introduced for funding and performance management led to the creation of new roles in information management. The increase in functional specialists in these roles, as well as HR, finance, and estates explains why 'other managers' now account for 9 per cent of FE staffing – one for every five teachers.

Equality issues

Gender

The period since incorporation has seen a marked increase in the proportion of women in the FE workforce and now almost two-thirds of employees are women – 60 per cent of teachers and managers and just under 50 per cent of senior managers. This represents a dramatic reversal of the position in 1993 when, according to Hall, 62 per cent of FHE teachers were men (Hall, 1994; note that there is some inconsistency in Hall's figures – he states the proportion of men in the 1990s as both 62 per cent and 70 per cent).

To some extent the change seems part of a longer-term trend. Hall notes that in 1970/1 the workforce was 81 per cent male. It is probable that this reflects the changing balance of FE students, with a decline in technical subjects relative to courses in business, foundation studies, care, and hospitality. Three-quarters of teachers on courses in English, foundation studies, and care are female, while engineering and construction show the opposite picture. (Unless otherwise stated, the figures in this section are taken from the SIR analyses for 2012/13 and 2003/4.)

It also seems that the change in the profile of the sector was concentrated in the early years after incorporation since the change from 2003/4 to 2012/13 is negligible. An initial rapid change followed by a return to a more stable position is compatible with other evidence about the impact of incorporation.

Incorporation required new roles to be created in colleges (principally finance and HR) and encouraged or allowed the development of others (marketing, learning support). The SIR figures support anecdotal evidence that most of these posts were filled by women – three-quarters of administrative and professional staff are female. Earlier sections have also charted the growth of part-time teaching staff and once again the SIR confirms that this is associated with increased female employment; women comprise 70 per cent of part-time teachers but 54 per cent of full-timers.

These changes have been consequences of incorporation but not intended consequences. In contrast, one of the most dramatic changes – the increase in the number of female chief executives – does appear to have been an objective of policy, though not of those who framed the legislation changing the status of FE.

The change over 21 years has been substantial. In 1993 only 13 college principals were women; around 3 per cent of the total. By 1996 the figure was 15 per cent and at the end of 1997, 20 per cent (Stott and Lawson, 1997). More recent figures published by the Women's Leadership Network show increases to 36 per cent in 2010 and 42 per cent in 2014 (Women's Leadership Network, 2014). Although still less than the proportion of women in the sector workforce, it is a not inconsiderable achievement.

In part the change might be attributed to determined action by individuals and sector organizations. Bodies such as the Further Education Development Agency (FEDA) and the Centre for Excellence in Leadership (CEL) attached increasing importance to equal opportunities, running events and training programmes intended to support women into leadership roles. Their efforts were supported by membership bodies such as the Women's Leadership Network.

Incorporation may have helped the process by raising the consciousness of FE as a distinct sector and in later years providing sector-wide data about staff characteristics. A larger indirect impact will have been the changing mix of staff in the sector as a whole increasing the pool of potential candidates for senior leadership positions. While this may help explain the recent growth in the numbers of female leaders, however, it does not explain why, at a time of turbulence and conflict in the early 1990s, their numbers should increase fivefold.

Ethnicity

The FE workforce is overwhelmingly white, more so than the population at large and more so, in particular, than the FE student body, which attracts a disproportionate share of black and ethnic minority students. In 2003/4 almost 88 per cent of staff were reported as White British. In 2012/13 the proportion had reduced to just over 84 per cent of all staff (though it was still 90 per cent of managers). In contrast in 2012/13 over 19 per cent of adult learners were from black or other minority ethnic groups as were 14.6 per cent of England's population in the 2011 census (ONS, 2012).

Figures on the numbers of black and minority ethnic staff from the early years of incorporation are difficult to find. Increased attention has been paid to the issue since the establishment of the Commission for Black Staff and the Network for Black Professionals following the Stephen Lawrence enquiry in 1999. Concern about under-representation at that time led to a series of interventions by agencies such as CEL focused in particular on increasing the numbers of black and minority ethnic staff in leadership positions.

An evaluation of the Black Leadership Initiative (BLI) from its inception in 2002 (Walker and Fletcher, 2013) describes a wide range of development activities addressed primarily at increasing the number of potential candidates for senior leadership positions and in particular the post of principal. It succeeded according to its headline measure; the number of black principals rose from three to thirteen over the period, or from under 1 per cent to around 3 per cent of the sector. There was less progress at lower grades; the percentage of managers from black and minority ethnic groups rose by one percentage point over the period (though this is more impressive when presented as a 15 per cent increase). In any event, for 7 per cent of managers to come from black and minority ethnic groups when they account for 8.5 per cent of total staff does not appear to constitute serious under-representation in terms of promoted posts even if there remains a problem at the level of overall staffing.

As with gender issues, progress (or lack of it) in relation to black and minority ethnic representation does not appear to be directly linked with incorporation. It may be argued, however, that there is a powerful indirect link as a result of the establishment of a national identity as a sector. National organizations, both statutory and voluntary, have begun to address equity issues at a sector level in a way that was unknown if not impossible when colleges came under the control of disparate local authorities.

Teacher education and professionalism

In technical colleges FE lecturers avoided pedagogic issues, seeing themselves as trainers not teachers and their previous industrial, craft, or trade expertise as an adequate basis for teaching (Venables,1967; Bristow, 1970; Carlton *et al.*, 1971; Gleeson and Mardle, 1980; Lucas, 2004a). As colleges changed from technical to FE colleges from the 1970s, new and more diverse traditions emerged, resulting in no clear professional identity among teachers and, some have argued, an impoverished professional culture (Robson, 1998; Lucas, 2004b). In the last decade the increasing regulation of FE teaching has brought an expectation for the FE teacher to be a proficient professional as well as a subject or vocational specialist giving rise to the term 'dual professionalism', (Robson, 2006) which though criticized by some, emphasizes combining occupational and pedagogic expertise as a key strength of the sector.

Despite a steady increase in qualified FE teachers between 1944 and 1993, (Young *et al.*, 1995) FE initial teacher education (ITE) was largely unregulated and at incorporation was mostly in-service, ad hoc, and uneven with no statutory requirement for qualifications. Furthermore, colleges' spending on staff development fell after incorporation to under 1 per cent of budgets (Young *et al.*, 1995), although it increased following regulations in 2001 and 2007. The last two decades have seen much more intervention aimed at raising the standards of FE teaching (Lucas, 2007) but little evidence links it to incorporation. The identification of competences needed by FE teachers started in the early 1990s (Chown and Last, 1993), alongside similar developments in schools, higher education (HE), and the public sector more generally. The reason why workforce development, teacher training and qualifications, mentoring, and continuing professional development (CPD) have been persistent but unresolved concerns in the sector may be that incorporation directed attention elsewhere.

Table 5.2 summarizes the main regulatory changes. They involve the development and imposition of occupational standards; then, following a critical inspection report in 2003, making CPD, qualifications, and membership of a professional body (IfL) mandatory before withdrawing these requirements less than a decade later following the Lingfield Review.

Table 5.2 There and back again: state regulated professionalism of FE teachers

- 1996: FE Staff Development Forum established to develop NVQ-type occupational standards for FE.
- 1997–9: DfES consultation on introduction of standards and qualifications for FE teachers.
- 1999: Formation of FE National Training Organisation (FENTO) and publication of the national occupational standards for teachers.
- 2001: Statutory instrument. New teachers required to gain a teaching qualification based upon FENTO standards. Ofsted given responsibility for inspection of FE ITE.
- 2002: Subject specifications for teachers of adult literacy, numeracy, and ESOL. Institute for Learning (IfL) established as a voluntary professional body for FE workforce.
- 2003: Publication of the critical HMI national survey on the FE ITE and DfES consultation on future reforms.
- 2004: Publication by DfES of *Equipping our Teachers for the Future: Reforming initial teacher training for the learning and skills sector.*

- 2005: DfES pilots – subject mentoring, observation of teaching practice. Lifelong Learning UK (LLUK) and Standards Verification UK (SVUK) replace FENTO.
- 2006: Publication of LLUK standards for teachers in the learning and skills sector. Publication of draft criteria for the award of Centre for Excellence in Teacher Training (CETT) status. Publication by DfES of *Professionalisation of the Learning and Skills Sector* announcing plans for a compulsory CPD requirement for FE teachers.
- 2007: Publication of LLUK mandatory units of assessment for initial teacher training (ITT) (England). Regulations introduced by Department for Innovation, Universities and Skills (DIUS) introducing Qualified Teacher Learning and skills (QTLS) status and a compulsory CPD requirement. IfL designated as a mandatory body.
- 2008: Implementation of reforms – ITT providers go through SVUK endorsement and commence teaching and assessing ITT qualifications based upon the new LLUK standards and assessment units.
- 2011: LLUK and SVUK abolished. Functions passed to the Leaning and Skills Improvement Service (LSIS) and IfL.
- 2012: Lingfield report on *Professionalism in Further Education*. Revocation of 2007 regulations. QTLS and CPD no longer compulsory in the FE sector.
- 2013: Abolition of LSIS and the establishment of the FE Guild, which became the Education and Training Foundation (ETF).
- 2014: IfL closes and its functions are passed to the ETF. The ETF aims to set up a 'professional arm' for former IfL members.

Source: Based upon Lucas, 2013.

There seems little doubt that the reforms outlined above represent a genuine attempt by government to improve the professional practice of FE teachers and it is important to analyse why it failed. Some argue that the 'standards-led approach' to professionalism was problematic (Lucas, 2007), since it did not lead to thinking about alternative ways of teaching but rather the validation of existing divided practices between different subjects and different teaching and learning traditions. It emphasized 'ticking boxes' and 'mapping' standards against practice to show 'coverage'. Behind strategic compliance many aspects of ITE carried on in the same way as before (Lucas,

2004a). For FE teachers the application of standards had little meaning for their specialism (Bathmaker, 2000; Hill, 2000) and in any case they were open to wide interpretation (Nasta, 2007).

Lucas and Nasta argue that the impoverished professional culture in FE and the absence of broader discussions about teaching and learning meant that the tensions between subject knowledge and pedagogy were not reconciled. Another factor was the relative weakness of intermediary bodies – employer organizations, trades unions, and professional organizations that could have mediated the standards as in schools or HE (Lucas and Nasta, 2010).

Others (Lucas *et al.*, 2012) suggest that statutory regulation has not produced what policymakers intended. Research on FE teachers undergoing in-service teacher training in FE colleges (Lucas and Unwin, 2009) illustrates how the demands and pressures that shape the workplace in colleges restrict the capacity of trainee teachers to develop their professional expertise. Recent policy initiatives to regulate and support trainee FE teachers have taken place in a culture with a weak tradition of supporting professional development (Ofsted, 2010; Ofsted, 2011; Skills Commission, 2010; LLUK, 2010).

The introduction of compulsory teacher training and CPD was (and still is) broadly supported by teachers in further education colleges. Yet Orr (2009) suggests that while college managers have constructed systems to report that numerical targets have been achieved, little has changed in terms of quality. Compliance with external standards and regulations may have diverted attention from addressing more fundamental weaknesses, by developing stronger mentoring and workplace support and achieving a better synergy between the taught and practice elements of ITE courses.

The Lingfield review (2012) was established primarily to resolve a conflict with UCU over compulsory membership of IfL. It produced wider recommendations leading to the revocation of the 2007 framework, arguing that despite good intensions FE professionalism had been weakened by the sheer amount of external intervention. One of the main recommendations of the report was that power to determine professional standards and the qualifications needed by staff should be devolved to colleges themselves because both the sector and FE professionalism had matured beyond the need for central government regulation.

While one may dispute some of these recommendations, much of the criticism of two decades of standards-led reform rings true. This leaves the question of whether FE professionalism has been enhanced in the period since incorporation. A recent small-scale research project among FE teachers

(Smithers, 2013) found that they saw themselves as professionals, describing the concept in terms of values, beliefs, ethics, specialist knowledge, and qualifications. Respondents said that the IfL had failed to raise the status of the profession and that the CPD requirement had been a meaningless logging of hours. However, all respondents had a sense of being an FE professional, albeit challenged in ways that undermined their autonomy as teachers, and unlike previous generations of FE teachers saw formal teaching qualifications as important. This suggests that after 21 years of incorporation the identity of FE teachers as professionals has advanced.

Conclusions

The 21 years since the incorporation of colleges have seen significant changes to the size and structure of the FE workforce and the experience of those working in the sector. Of course, that is not to say that incorporation caused them all directly or even indirectly. This section seeks to identify where the removal of colleges from local government and their establishment as independent legal entities had a significant impact on staffing and staff relations in the sector.

Incorporation was rapidly followed by a period of intense industrial conflict, particularly with the main teaching union, NATFHE, over conditions of service and pay. It is tempting to conclude that the change of employment status 'caused' the conflict, though the reality is more nuanced. There are, for example, signs that the conflict was waiting to happen; certainly it seems part of a more general attack on trade union power pursued by government during the 1980s. It was also the view of many college principals that they needed greater flexibility in staffing to respond to changing patterns of demand.

The conflict was initially encouraged by government holding back a proportion of funding until contracts were changed, giving weight to the view that a principal aim of incorporation was to develop a business-driven culture in FE as opposed to a collegial or public service ethos. This is reflected in the rhetoric of the times. Colleges as independent entities were much more exposed to financial pressures than they had been as branches of a local authority, which gave management the incentive to negotiate vigorously to control costs. The creation of institutions that needed to focus strongly on their financial viability was probably more important in changing the climate of FE than the initial conflict. Many later concluded that such conflict had not been necessary (Flint, 2005). A direct consequence of institutional control over staffing was some reshaping of the workforce; partly driven by financial considerations but partly reflecting aspirations frustrated by local authority rigidities. New posts blurred the boundary between teaching and learning support though perhaps not as dramatically as supporters or opponents claim. More obviously evidenced is the growth in functional management posts reflecting new responsibilities but also an increasingly detailed external performance management regime (see Chapter 8). The proportion of teaching undertaken by part-time staff increased rapidly, but equally rapidly reached a new equilibrium.

Incorporation seems to have given the sector a clearer identity, which has facilitated action by voluntary organizations and official agencies on equality. Progress in closing the gender gap in senior management roles has been substantial, aided perhaps by a major shift in the balance of the sector to a mainly female workforce. Despite equally sustained attention, progress in relation to black and minority ethnic leadership has been slower, perhaps reflecting the under-representation of black and minority ethnic staff at all organizational levels.

Finally there seems to be a set of important issues where the impact of incorporation is difficult to pin down. Despite considerable attention from national government and its agencies, and the enhanced capacity to influence the sector provided by incorporation, progress in relation to the quality and qualifications of the workforce is difficult to detect. The professional identity of FE teachers is weaker than in schools or HE and not noticeably stronger than two decades ago. Some will argue that the logic of incorporation creates a managerial culture necessarily in conflict with notions of professionalism, though it is important to note that it was strong trade union opposition that gave government a rationale for withdrawing support from IfL. Others will argue that the impact of incorporation was to direct leaders' attention elsewhere; to financial solvency and compliance with inspection and audit for example. This is true but does not seem to be the whole story.

Finally there is the question of the impact of incorporation on the experience of staff in the sector. The evidence is mixed. The morale of teachers in particular seems to have been low in the immediate aftermath of incorporation, a reflection no doubt of industrial relations conflict. The subsequent evidence from perception surveys is that staff, and teachers in particular, enjoyed and were strongly committed to their work and their students but were much less positive about their organizations. The factors that appear to drive these reactions relate to managerial style and the demands of external performance management systems, both contingent on but not necessary outcomes of incorporation.

References

Association of Colleges (AoC) (2002) *Teaching Pay Initiative in FE Colleges: Implementation research project*. London: AoC.

Ashton, J. (1995) 'The management of change in further education: Some perspectives of college principals'. PhD thesis, Loughborough University.

Bathmaker, A-M. (2000) 'Standardising teaching: The introduction of standards for teaching and supporting learning in further education in England and Wales'. *Journal of In-service Education*, 26 (1), 9–23.

Bathmaker, A., and Avis, J. (2006) *Becoming a Lecturer in Further Education in England: The construction of professional identity and the role of communities of practice*. Online. http://eprints.uwe.ac.uk/117/2/JET_2005_becoming_a_lecturer_pre_pub_version.pdf (accessed 5 January 2015).

Bristow, A. (1970) *Inside the Colleges of Further Education*. London: Department of Education and Science.

Burchell, F. (1998) *Five Years of Change: A survey of pay, terms and conditions of service in FE*. London: NATFHE.

Burton, S. (1995) *Factors Affecting Quality in the New FE: Principals' views*. (Coombe Lodge Report, Volume 24 No 5). Blagdon: Coombe Lodge.

Carlton, D., Gent, W., and Scammels, B. (1971) *The Administration of Technical Colleges*. Manchester: Manchester University Press.

Chown, A., and Last. J. (1993) 'Can the NCVQ model be used for teacher training?' *Journal of Further and Higher Education*, 17 (2),15–25.

Crequer, N. (1998) 'Union fears for safety'. *TES*, 20 March. Online. www.tes.co.uk/article.aspx?storycode=303931 (accessed 23 March 2015).

Department for Education and Employment (DfEE) (1998) *The Learning Age: A renaissance for a new Britain*. London: DfEE.

Department for Education and Skills (DfES) (2002) *Success for All: Reforming further education and training*. London: DfES.

The Education and Training Foundation (2014) *Further Education Workforce Data for England: Analysis of the 2012–2013 staff individualized record data*. Online. www.et-foundation.co.uk/wp-content/uploads/2014/09/SIR-Report.pdf (accessed 23 March 2015).

Flint, C. (2005) *Staff in FE*. (Think piece commissioned for the Foster Review of Further Education.) Online. http://webarchive.nationalarchives.gov.uk/20060214030141/http://dfes.gov.uk/furthereducation/fereview/evidence.shtml (accessed 23 March 2015).

Gleeson, D., and Mardle, G. (1980) *Further Education or Training?* London: Routledge and Kegan Paul.

Hall, V. (1994) *FE in the UK*. London: Collins/The Staff College.

Hill, R. (2000) 'A study of the views of full-time further education lecturers regarding their college corporations and agencies of the further education sector'. *Journal of Further and Higher Education*, 24 (1), 67–75.

Kennedy, H. (1997) *Learning Works: Widening participation in further education*. Coventry: FEFC.

Kingston, P. (2008) 'Remembering 1993 and all that'. *The Guardian*, 1 April. Online. www.theguardian.com/education/2008/apr/01/highereducation.furthereducation (accessed 23 March 2015).

Kinsman, G. (1996) *Occupational Stress and Health Among Lecturers Working in Further and Higher Education*. London: NATFHE.

Lingfield, R. (2012) *Professionalism in Further Education: Final report of the independent review panel established by the Minister of State for Further Education, Skills and Lifelong Learning*. Online. www.bis.gov.uk/assets/biscore/further-education-skills/docs/p/12-1198-professionalism-in-further-education-final (accessed 3 March 2015).

Lifelong Learning UK (LLUK) (2005) *Further Education Workforce Data for England: An analysis of the staff individualised record (SIR) for 2003/2004*. Online. http://dera.ioe.ac.uk/2979/7/analysis_of_sir_data_20051124_04.pdf (accessed 23 March 2015).

— (2010) *Recent Trends in the Initial Training of Teachers of Literacy, Numeracy and ESOL for the Further Education Sector in England*. London: LLUK.

Lucas, N. (2004a) 'The "FENTO fandango": National standards, compulsory teaching qualifications and the growing regulation of FE college teachers'. *Journal of Further and Higher Education*, 28 (1), 35–51.

— (2004b) *Teaching in Further Education: New perspectives for a changing context*. (Bedford Way Paper.) London: Institute of Education Publications.

— (2007) 'Rethinking initial teacher education for further education teachers: From a standards-led to a knowledge-based approach'. *Teaching Education*, 18 (2), 93–106.

— (2013) 'One step forward, two steps back? The professionalisation of further education teachers in England'. *Research in Post-Compulsory Education*, 18 (4), 389–401.

Lucas, N., and Nasta, T. (2010) 'State regulation and the professionalisation of further education teachers: A comparison with schools and HE'. *Journal of Vocational Education and Training*, 62 (4), 441–54.

Lucas, N., Nasta, T., and Rogers. L. (2012) 'From fragmentation to chaos? The regulation of initial teacher training in further education'. *British Educational Research Journal*, 38 (4), 677–95.

Lucas, N., and Unwin. L. (2009) 'Developing teacher expertise at work: In-service trainee teachers in colleges of further education in England'. *Journal of Further and Higher Education*, 33 (4), 423–33.

Nasta, T. (2007) 'Translating national standards into practice for the initial training of further education (FE) teachers in England'. *Research in Post-Compulsory Education*, 12 (1), 1–17.

National Association of Teachers in Further and Higher Education (NATFHE) (2002) *Advice to Members on the Teachers' Pay Initiative*. London: NATFHE.

Office for National Statistics (ONS) (2012) '2011 census: Key facts for England and Wales'. London: ONS.

Office for Standards in Education (Ofsted) (2010) *Progress in Implementing Reforms in the Accreditation and Continuing Professional Development of Teachers in Further Education*. London: Ofsted.

— (2011) *The Annual Report of Her Majesty's Chief Inspector of Education, Children's Services and Skills 2010/11*. London: Ofsted.

Orr, K. (2009) 'Performativity and professional development: The gap between policy and practice in the English further education sector'. *Research in Post-Compulsory Education*, 14 (4), 479–89.

Owen, J., and Davies, P. (2002) *Listening to Staff 2002*. Online. www. itslifejimbutnotasweknowit.org.uk/files/LSDA%20Listening%20to%20 staff%202002.pdf (accessed 23 March 2015).

Robson, J. (1998) 'A profession in crisis: Status, culture and identity in the further education college'. *Journal of Vocational Education and Training*, 50 (4), 585–607.

— (2006) *Teacher Professionalism in Further and Higher Education*. London: Routledge.

Robson, J., Bailey, B., and Mendick, H. (2006) 'Learning support in further education colleges in England: Its development and implications for teachers'. Paper presented at the EARLI SIG Conference, Herleen, the Netherlands, 11–13 October.

Select Committee on Education and Employment (1998) *Sixth Report*. Online. www.publications.parliament.uk/pa/cm199798/cmselect/cmeduemp/264/26413. htm (accessed 23 March 2015).

Skills Commission (2010) Teacher training in vocational education. Online. www. policyconnect.org.uk/sc/news/skills-commission-inquiry-teacher-training-vocational-education (accessed 5 January 2015).

Smithers, M. (2013) 'The quest for professionalism in the further education sector'. Institutional focused study as part of a Doctor in Education programme, Institute of Education, University of London.

Stott, C., and Lawson, L. (1997) *Women at the Top in Further Education*. London: FEDA.

Taubman, D. (2000) 'Staff relations'. In Smithers, A., and Robinson, P. (eds) *Further Education Reformed*. London: Falmer Press, 82–8.

TES (1995) 'Leaked report attacks college complacency'. 22 September. Online. www.tes.co.uk/teaching-resource/Leaked-report-attacks-college-complacency-16103/ (accessed 23 March 2015).

Tomlinson, J. (1996) *Inclusive Learning: Principles and recommendations*. Coventry: FEFC.

Venables, E. (1967) *The Young Worker at College: A study of a local tech*. London: Faber and Faber.

Villeneuve-Smith, F., Munoz, S., and McKenzie, E. (2008) *FE Colleges: The frontline under pressure? A staff satisfaction survey of further education colleges in England*. Online. www.itslifejimbutnotasweknowit.org.uk/files/Frontline_ Staff.pdf (accessed 23 March 2015).

Walker, E., and Fletcher, M. (2013) *The Black Leadership Initiative: The first ten years*. Coventry: LSIS.

Ward, L. (1995) 'Relief after £50 million penalty is axed'. *TES*, 8 December. Online. www.tes.co.uk/article.aspx?storycode=14573 (accessed 23 March 2015).

Womens Leadership Network (2014) *Principals & Chief Executives of Colleges in the FE Sector: Gender statistics report 2009–February 2014*. Online. http://79.170.44.115/wlnfe.org/wp-content/uploads/2015/01/WLN-PursuingParityFeb2014withcharts-genderstats2009-Feb2014.pdf (accessed 23 March 2015).

Young, M., Lucas, N., Sharp, G., and Cunningham, B. (1995) *Teacher Education for the Further Education Sector: Training the lecturer of the future.* London: Institute of Education Post-16 Education Centre/Association for Colleges.

Chapter 6

Space and place: Colleges rebuilding

Paul Grainger, Chris Wilderspin, Joanna van Heyningen, and Tony Pitcher

Introduction

This chapter covers new approaches to the design of colleges following their increased freedom to make important strategic decisions after further education (FE) incorporation. These new ideas embraced both the buildings themselves and the internal environments, including the reception, social areas, and learning areas within them. The chapter is specifically about colleges and their buildings, not the buildings of the wider FE sector. The freedoms following incorporation led to a period of innovative thinking about design and purpose, as colleges expanded and reacted to the changing nature of students (see Chapter 3) and the curriculum (see Chapter 4). The conscious move towards marketing, with managers actively seeking to recruit increasing numbers of students based on a positive image of the college, led to efforts to renew and refresh the college environment, making it attractive to students. Coupled with this, colleges having control of their budgets led managers to seek buildings that were more cost efficient to run and many also looked to adopt the green ideas current at that time. The impact of technological advances led to new views on how learning could adapt to the enhanced use of information technology, and how this could be encouraged through the internal layout of the building. There was a desire to create better spaces for learning at a time when the challenges of greatly increased numbers of students and enhanced scrutiny of outcomes (see Chapter 8) caused college managers to look for new strategies to improve results. Principals looked abroad, particularly to the United States, for new ideas. College leaders turned to new technologies for potential solutions. There were changes to the workforce too (see Chapter 5) as nationally binding contractual arrangements were scrapped and managers looked to provide more flexible responses to the requirements of the expanding client group.

New ideas

After incorporation there was a phase of renewed energy and innovation in college construction. Initially, during the period of the Further Education Funding Council (FEFC), there were relatively tight constraints imposed with regard to design, with strict formulae on space utilization and guidelines to be met before college corporations were permitted to proceed with any capital spend (e.g. Further Education Funding Council, 1997). These formulae related to space per student multiplied by anticipated student numbers. Initially this hampered innovation and led to cramped designs. The formulaic approach was abandoned after 2001 under the Learning and Skills Council (LSC), leading to an extensive and imaginative building programme, which came to be described as 'Building Colleges for the Future' (Grainger, 2004). The term was borrowed from the contemporary 'Building Schools for the Future' programme, an aspirational £5 billion Labour flagship policy for the rebuilding of schools proposed in 2003 by Education Ministers, Charles Clarke and David Milliband (DfES, 2003). This initiative envisaged exciting and innovative designs in the building of learning environments (Greany, 2005). The LSC supported a similar approach to innovation in college design, establishing a design competition and advisory partnership with the Royal Institute of British Architects (Grainger, 2005).

By this time colleges were more able to dispose of unwanted assets in order to reinvest in new buildings or extensive renovation of old ones. Sometimes these assets were unfit or redundant sites, but, more controversially, some colleges sold off playing fields and other amenities. Incorporation had involved the transfer of assets from the local authority to the incorporated college. This involved a certain amount of bartering, and not all those assets transferred were conveniently located or fit for purpose. College boards of corporation could also transfer money between capital and revenue budgets. As a result, designers became far more sensitive to the lifecycle costs of buildings. The easing of the bureaucratic distinction between revenue and capital enabled boards to invest in buildings that, although initially more expensive, were cheaper to run in the long term, and that were greener in their approach, getting away from the quick-fix thinking associated with short-term capital funding. Savings were made by severely restricting the amount of unnecessary corridor and circulation space, which had the effect of lowering long-term costs such as heating, cleaning, and staffing. New approaches to teaching and learning meant that classrooms were no longer necessarily an unimaginative series of boxes off a central corridor, constructed for proscenium arch style front of class teaching. New curriculum innovations meant lessons involved less formal pedagogic instruction. New and expanding qualifications (see Chapter 4) such as General National Vocational Qualifications (GNVQs) and Business and Technology Education Council awards (BTECs), and new approaches to teaching, involved more interactions between students and between students and a wider range of staff. Students could move around more freely. There were spaces that helped promote group work and discussion, and other spaces for seminars and, particularly in the case of adults, more spaces for tutorials. As colleges became more sophisticated in their financial planning, consciousness of staff–student ratios increased, with a consequent interest in more flexible spaces. For example, sixth form colleges built in Lancashire in the 1970s were built to an anticipated staff–student ratio of 1:12. Such numbers were financially unviable after incorporation, and these classrooms became a financial liability.

Wider benefits of new college designs

Older style buildings had disguised bullying. This had been, perhaps, less recognized until managers became more interested in the retention of students, in part because of funding considerations (see chapter 8). Colleges began to ask departing students why they were leaving, with a system of exit interviews. Harassment was often cited. For example, it was the main reason given for non-participation by the 30 per cent of students who chose not to stay on after 16 who were surveyed in a Widnes and Runcorn College internal management report in 2003. Harassment takes place in covert, unsupervised areas; openness encouraged more, and more subtle, behaviour management, with an emphasis on visibility and clear lines of sight. Open spaces, more glass, and CCTV designed out the old, hidden areas which concealed furtive behaviour. Security measures were also designed into these new buildings. As a result, security could become more relaxed. For example, fewer entrances, but with monitoring, enabled greater freedom of circulation within buildings, and the provision of equipment that did not need to be bolted down. The main building of Wigan College in 1995 had 19 entrances, for example. It was impossible to separate students from any members of the wider community who chose to come into the building, or to prevent access by drug abusers and homeless people looking for warmth and privacy. In inner London colleges small, portable cassette recorders were screwed to large, wooden panels to make them harder to remove.

By the year 2000 most colleges had moved to a single, attractive entrance, staffed by an alert receptionist, and perhaps a professional security team, creating an area that was monitored and secure. After passing through, students could feel they were in a safe environment. Reception areas frequently featured an atrium to introduce more light and a sense of space. These areas then led into pleasant restaurants and student social spaces, then on to study spaces, open classrooms, and 'real-life' working environments. These were not just the old, 'oily rag' workshops, but catered for dance, theatre, media, and computing. During this period, many colleges also changed their emphasis towards their A Level, BTEC, and GNVQ courses and some older style workshop learning was franchised out to other providers (see Chapter 4). In the last two or three years, however as colleges seek to recover their identity as providers of employment and skills training, there has been a renewed emphasis on workplace preparation, and in some of their buildings colleges are returning to the idea of high-standard, industry-compatible, facilities.

The period of increasing independence, innovation, and investment instigated by the LSC came to a sudden halt when, in 2009, the council was shown to be over-committed financially. As a result it was forced to renege on a number of financial commitments that had been pledged to colleges to support rebuilding programmes. This caused many colleges severe financial hardship as investment in feasibility studies and designs had already commenced. Very large sums of money were entirely wasted. The resulting national scandal led to the resignation of the LSC chief executive, Mark Haysom, and the council itself was wound up in 2010.

Since then, within the funding regime of the succeeding Skills Funding Agency, the trend towards independence of corporations has continued, and colleges have continued to become freer from central control (see Chapter 7). Slowly, cautiously, a modest rebuilding programme has recommenced. Over this recent period colleges have also, in the main, become larger, often through merger, with multiple-site operations. They have begun to diversify by investing in newly emerging institutions, such as those initiated or promoted by the Conservative–Liberal Democrat Coalition Government since 2010 – university technical colleges (UTCs), academy chains, and studio schools. These have created new challenges for the design of colleges across a wider estate. The Hull College Group, for example, which is developing a leading role in the regeneration of the Humber region, is developing a capacity in 'strategic leadership' (see Chapter 9). Formed from the old Hull,

Goole, and Harrogate colleges, it has acquired an independent training provider based in Glasgow, and a raft of academies and studio schools. It has over 28,000 students, and is further developing a range of new markets, including significant 14–16 (i.e. school-age) provision. The chief executive, Gary Warke, sits on the Local Enterprise Partnership (LEP), and is in regular dialogue with the major companies of the area, including Siemens, and the four local authorities within the regeneration region.

College managers continue to be aware of the need to escape from the oppressive, carceral designs of the post-war years. In an interview in June 2014, Tony Pitcher, a former principal and current chair of governors, commented:

> I often used the word 'custodial'. Prisons, modern budget hotels, and traditional educational establishments all use the same basic (custodial) architecture – corridors and closed cells with minimal shared support services, locations where the community might interact informally, socially, or in unpredictable, creative ways.

In an interview in July 2014, Gary Warke said that new college buildings: 'need to have some fun in them, the "wow" factor, but in the end it's classrooms and science labs. The building is not what makes the difference. However customer expectations are changing – fees, loans, discerning clients, readier to complain. This leads to more emphasis on "front of house" activities'.

College managers drew many of the ideas for these new-look college buildings from the US community colleges. The Further Education Staff College (based at Coombe Lodge, with its archives now held by the UCL IOE) promoted visits by principals to the US. They returned with ideas of big libraries, congregating spaces, peer tutoring, a wide range of ancillary staff, and the appointment of college managers who were not educators. There was a wide debate about the nature of the learner within a rapidly changing society (e.g. Kennedy, 1994; Gates, 1995; McRae, 1996; Negroponte, 1996; Barber, 1997), and the organizational requirements necessary to support this (e.g. Moss Kanter, 1990; Jacques, 1997). College building mirrored an educational landscape – a series of different environments reflecting a range of different activities. For example, interviewed in August 2014, Tony Pitcher recalled:

I found that pedagogy in US Community Colleges was very conservative – both staff and students – but that 'the administration' (a sharp distinction from 'the faculty'), unable to have much influence on the classroom, used central resources to enlarge the function of libraries and the shared 'educational landscape' of the college to ameliorate the inflexibility of the student classroom experience. I saw several examples of impressive innovations in college architecture, particularly centralized facilities like libraries and large, well-furnished, informal social areas with direct access to support staff; these were very influential for me.

Design implications and outcomes

New versus old: Students as clients

One of the assumptions of the LSC in the Colleges for the Future programme was that the majority of colleges would be rebuilt wholesale. While it is true that many colleges were managing to deliver learning in outdated and inappropriate buildings, the assumption for demolition was potentially a wasteful idea.

Many colleges had a need for simple, traditional classrooms to deliver a good proportion of their curriculum, and for these, refurbishment of their current buildings would have been a sensible option. Some colleges recognized this and supplemented their traditional spaces with extensions that contained more flexible spaces that answered the other areas of their brief, such as leaning centres, cyber-cafes, break-out spaces, and so on.

A good example of this is City and Islington College in Finsbury Park, at their Lifelong Learning Centre, with a curriculum tending towards the older student and returning learners. The core of the scheme is a Victorian school, which has been adapted to new uses. The new-build accommodation wraps around this to create a strong dynamic between new and old and a real sense of spatial diversity, all enhanced by several specially commissioned artworks. A new space is created that combines the contemporary with the traditional – see Figure 6.1. The building also houses a public branch library within the new element and facing the street, the intention being that library users will become inspired to enrol for a course at the college.

Figure 6.1: Atrium at City and Islington College's Lifelong Learning Centre – new meets old (image ©James Brittain Photography, courtesy of Wilkinson Eyre Architects)

The notion that technology can liberate space can be equally true in older buildings as in new. Older buildings benefit from the effects of new technology, which sometimes gives spaces potential new uses that would not have been possible without the technology. For example by allowing access to the internet via Wi-Fi, spaces can be used for research that previously would not have been possible outside the traditional library, or for small-group or peer-to-peer learning.

Rethinking the place

Thankfully, not all college plans involved the wholesale demolition and rebuild of sites. The idea of re-imagining an existing campus challenged the notion that total rebuild was the only option that was economically sensible, and gave the opportunity to keep the best of what existed while redeveloping less satisfactory areas. In many cases this led to a more imaginative outcome.

Many colleges had grown up ad hoc with no overall plan, resulting in buildings that had become unsatisfactory because of their age and configuration. They also often had an unsatisfactory site layout that gave little sense of place or identity, and that was confusing to navigate around.

Before embarking on the design of new elements, colleges that had decided to retain some elements of their estate sensibly took a metaphorical step back and took stock of their current physical assets. The removal of unsatisfactory buildings to be replaced either by new buildings or open space, in effect a form of architectural surgery, allowed tired estates to be given a new lease of life relatively economically. Removal of unused buildings often let campuses breathe and become more easily navigable again, an important ingredient in making places welcoming and usable, and something that could then be strengthened by the introduction of new buildings that would reinforce that order. (This is often referred to as legibility.)

Figure 6.2: Enfield College – unattractive, out-of-date buildings with no identity (photo courtesy of van Heyningen and Haward Architects)

Enfield College in North London had grown up from an existing 1960s system-built school. It also contained some inefficient low-rise workshops that were inflexible and that the College found difficult to timetable – see Figure 6.2. The new buildings on the site had been erected to satisfy an immediate need rather than a long-term vision.

The college initially had a brief for a new entrance and general teaching building to replace the workshop block, but the architects took time to reconsider the assumed location and layout of the new building, looking also at the long-term redevelopment options for the rest of the campus. They imagined an adapted campus plan that would simplify circulation by means of a series of linked external spaces – see Figure 6.3. With the addition of a new entrance forecourt facing the main road, which would give a single point of entry and a clear, easily monitored security line, the environment and the student experience were improved before the buildings themselves had been designed – see Figure 6.4.

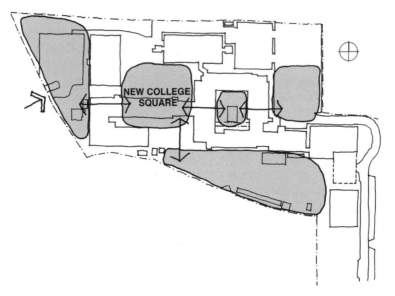

Figure 6.3: Diagram of proposed new spaces at Enfield College

Figure 6.4: Entrance forecourt at Enfield College (photo courtesy of van Heyningen and Haward Architects)

A similar approach was taken by the architects at Sussex Downs College, which started life as a business park on the outskirts of Eastbourne. The windswept campus had no focus, no sense of arrival or place – see Figure 6.5. New buildings were carefully placed to create a series of courtyard gardens that related to the buildings that opened onto them, allowing a sense of identity to develop – see Figure 6.6. For example, the performing arts centre opened out to a stepped terrace that could be used for socializing by students or for informal performances, and a second courtyard opened from the central student refectory and learning centre to provide external learning spaces that would allow social learning styles, such as peer-to-peer interaction, outside the classroom.

Figure 6.5: Sussex Downs College – unsatisfactory buildings surrounded by unattractive parking (photo courtesy of van Heyningen and Haward Architects)

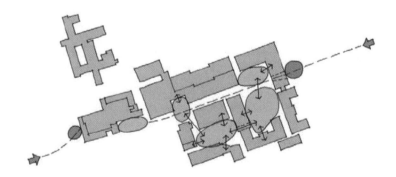

Figure 6.6: Sussex Downs College diagrammatic site plan of proposed new external spaces

Rethinking their campus also allowed individual departments to assert their identity more clearly, and allowed those with a closer potential relationship to relate to each other in a more positive way. For example, the existing art department faced the new performing arts centre across a new court;

thus invoking a dynamic relationship that could lead to a more creative working relationship between the departments. In turn the performing arts centre faced the expanded construction and engineering facility, which also became more open and transparent in its relationship with the outside world. This subtle shift offered the possibility of collaboration between the two curriculum areas, with the construction department making stage sets for performances in the arts centre becoming a possibility – see Figure 6.7.

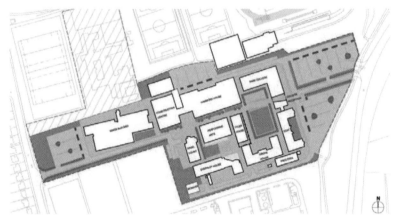

Figure 6.7: Sussex Down College - final proposed site plan

In this way the architects sought to make the campus feel more like a place to which students and staff wanted to belong, and in which they could take pride.

Making attractive buildings (on limited budgets)

As we have noted, the opportunity to invest led managers to focus on making their colleges more attractive to students, by means of improvements to the physical environment. However although large sums of money were available, budgets were still relatively constrained. Managers and designers faced the challenge of doing more with less, which in turn provoked creative responses to budget and design questions.

Many colleges focused on the 'shop window' as a means of encouraging students through their front door. An attractive reception with low-key but effective security and easy access to information and reception staff was one of the recurring features of new colleges, for example at City and Islington College – see Figure 6.8. In order to maximize efficient use of the budget, these spaces were often combined with other common uses, such as dining halls, internet cafes, or learning centres.

A reasonable proportion of colleges spent disproportionate amounts of money on their front-of-house spaces, chasing the 'wow-factor' that would distinguish them from other colleges. Complex sweeping entrance canopy features, or expensive materials used around the entrance certainly made colleges distinctive, but added little to the learning experience. Some of these were more successful than others, depending on how the internal spaces were used and the effect this had on creating stimulating usable learning spaces – see Figure 6.9.

Figure 6.8: City and Islington College – College Hall, main street on left (image ©James Brittain Photography)

Figure 6.9: South East Essex College entrance hall with break-out 'pods' (image by Gareth Gardner, courtesy of KSS Architects)

Figure 6.10: City and Islington College – typical classroom (photo courtesy of Nick Kane and van Heyningen and Haward Architects)

Other colleges spread their budget more evenly throughout the college making good quality spaces of a standard which would benefit all users. Key principles of the provision of good levels of natural light, natural ventilation, and robust yet well detailed attractive materials laid the foundations for pleasant learning environments that would also stand the test of time (see Figure 6.10), crucial when maintenance budgets were also restricted. Keeping things simple not only helped with the budgets, but also continued the notion of a legible place into the design of individual buildings, allowing users to find their way around more easily and as a result be more relaxed about spending time there – see Figure 6.11. This has had a notable effect on retention rates and behaviour in some colleges. Senior staff at Enfield College reported a far calmer atmosphere in their new building, which has large windows between corridors and classroom, when compared to the rest of the college – this they put down to the benefits of good passive supervision – see Figure 6.12. City and Islington College reported far higher student retention rates associated with their new buildings when compared to before the rebuild.

Figure 6.11: Staircase at City and Islington College with street views (photo courtesy of Nick Kane and van Heyningen and Haward Architects)

Figure 6.12: Enfield College – generous views into classrooms raised image and improved behaviour through better passive supervision (photo courtesy of Nick Kane and van Heyningen and Haward Architects)

Technological changes

Learning within the classroom

Technological advancement has taken many different forms, but the greatest for the education world has been the use of the internet for research and digital-based assignments.

Learning has shifted from the traditional 'chalk and talk' lesson, coupled with background research carried out in a dedicated library environment, to more immersive teaching styles, making use of interactive media, such as whiteboards connected to the web, and research carried out digitally on computers and wireless devices, such as laptops and tablets.

Although the presumption of these changes was for total rebuilding of some colleges, it should be noted that the changes in teaching patterns and pedagogy mentioned would be equally applicable to the re-use of existing buildings, where colleges still required more traditional teaching spaces (for example, for sixth form style lessons).

Learning outside the classroom

The main effect of advances in technology has been to shift learning out of the classroom into a wider variety of spaces. Learning has also become much more of a social pursuit to be combined with other activities such as drinking coffee or watching films or media online. The phrase 'continuous learning environment' is one that has been used to describe this shift in approach. An associated benefit has been that students are better able to make use of the downtime between more structured learning, and have been encouraged to remain on college premises in these periods.

In turn, the emphasis on the design of spaces has focused more heavily on the spaces outside the classroom, such as cafes, libraries, and even circulation spaces, to make them more suitable for new styles of learning. Students no longer desire to learn in silence, leading to 'differentiated space' that ranges from places for silent study through to peer-to-peer exchanges in public places.

Even the design of libraries (more often called Learning Centres or Resource Centres), has had to adapt to reflect these shifts. Different types of space became available, such as spaces with Wi-Fi access (blanket Wi-Fi was still not the norm in the mid-2000s), and a blurring of catering and learning spaces – some colleges even integrated their cafes within their libraries.

The key outcome has been the development of a range of spaces for learning, giving students the resources to take control of their own territory and empower them to work in their own way. It could be argued that students have become more relaxed yet purposeful in their approach to study.

Learning outside the college

Advances in technology have also brought about changes in how students communicate, both with each other and with their tutors. Firstly, in a similar manner to the internal college environment, students can now access information outside of the college at any time of the day, and anywhere access to the internet became possible. This further diversified the learning environment, making it yet more continuous and stretching it further from the traditional classroom. A bedroom or local café or a municipal library or the park could all be considered places where learning could take place, and students could exchange knowledge.

In the same way, access to tutors and coursework also became more and more possible through digital means. Colleges set up digital platforms, which allowed assignments to be downloaded and submitted online, without the need to venture into the college itself. In this way the role of the traditional teacher can be seen to have changed, with a wider variety of professionals supporting learning, such as teaching assistants and learning support staff.

Security

Advances in smart technology, particularly in the world of security, also transformed how colleges were managed on the front line. Many colleges previously had no defined security line, with visitors, students, staff, and strangers alike being able to enter the college site without restriction. The introduction of smart-card access, and later electronic registration, allowed colleges to control and monitor who was on their premises in a more immediate yet discreet way. Open sites could now have clearly defined secure lines, usually with public facilities, such as reception, enrolment, and any public facilities such as libraries (as we have seen at City and Islington College in Finsbury Park), on the non-secure side of the line.

Financial considerations

The greatest opportunity was to be more efficient about the use of space. Colleges that were housed in converted Victorian schools and office buildings were often making poor use of the space they had. There was a huge disparity in the condition and quality of space that they occupied. On the other hand, some colleges struggled to find space for the functions that local education authorities had previously carried out, such as finance and HR departments. But the overall trend was that colleges were simply too big and inefficient. The result was new assessment methods devised by the FEFC, which aimed at that time to put space standards on a more equal footing.

Enlightened colleges saw an opportunity in having too much space, in that they could dispose of surplus assets to help fund the new building works they desired. For example, Sussex Downs College saw an opportunity to sell off for development a number of redundant buildings on the edge of their campus, which also happened to be close to a residential area. City and Islington College took the opportunity to reduce their large portfolio of inefficient sites down to just four, which in one stroke made their estate very much more manageable. This grand move took a number of years to accomplish, with some deft phasing and decanting of departments, but ultimately the college is reaping the benefits of a tighter estate.

But this disposal strategy also allowed colleges to pick which of the buildings inherited from the local authority they wished to retain. This was crucial in terms of estate rationalization, giving managers the opportunity, if they decided to take it, of keeping the best buildings and disposing of those that were a financial liability. Generally older Victorian buildings, although thought to be less flexible, are very well built and have a longer life expectancy than many newer more cheaply built estates, and the lack of flexibility can be addressed by imaginative design and the use of technology. If carefully re-used and updated, older buildings can have their life expectancy extended well into a very positive future.

In order to make the best use of limited budget, a number of colleges (with their designers) took a highly creative approach to the use of 'balance space' (that space allowed for circulation and other non-teaching space). For instance, there was an increased allocation of space for circulation, including space that allowed for dining, in order to make room for other individual spaces that could be used in a number of different ways for flexible learning outside the classroom. Some colleges cleverly designed circulation to create 'break-out' spaces – often simply a widening of the corridor in order to create small seating areas for one-to-one teaching or small groups.

Although budgets did not allow for a great deal of experimentation with renewable technology as a means of reducing running costs, in rethinking their estate, colleges were more likely to invest in passive 'green' solutions, such as good levels of insulation, natural ventilation as opposed to air conditioning (even in some city centre locations), and the use of robust materials. Making sure new buildings were well orientated (where possible) to take advantage of daylight and natural breezes, and then designing the windows such that those natural resources could be used to best effect, are the key to low-cost, low-energy buildings.

Conclusions and a look to the future

Since incorporation, four major drivers for a rethink on college design, both new build and renovation, can be identified:

1. In 1993, on incorporation, students became perceived and described as clients. Money followed the students. Colleges could recruit from a wider catchment area, unrestricted by old local authority boundaries. Up until this time, since students were funded by the LEA, most authorities insisted that students attended one of their local colleges rather than let the students go expensively 'out county'. This restricted competition and led to some unnecessarily long journeys for students close to LEA boundaries having to go to distant in-county towns. This new language of 'customers' introduced retail analogies. Most colleges established a marketing department for the first time, and took

to advertising themselves. Many sought high street locations, as with South East Essex College, which constructed a new building as part of a shopping complex on Southend High Street. Colleges were under pressure to increase numbers and the quasi-market established by the FEFC promoted competition. College managers felt the need to improve the physical appearance and general ambience of their buildings in order to attract and retain students, introducing stylish, welcoming reception areas, bright, airy social spaces, and improved learning environments. This came with a new approach to staffing (see Chapter 5). Much more attention was given to student movement through these new spaces, both in terms of minimizing unnecessary movement, and in creating the appropriate atmosphere for study, or for work-related activity. Science departments had traditionally required laboratory space. However, the majority of an A level physics course, for example, is seminar work, requiring different accommodation. Before incorporation this simply had not been thought through.

2. Technology was developing rapidly and becoming more central to a student's learning experience, and expanding the reach and potential of lecturers. Rather than thinking in terms of a simple timetable, with contact time and free time, managers developed the notion of a learner's journey – through an open and attractive reception area, into the social and advisory areas of the college and a wider variety of learning areas, allowing a mix of formal teaching and supervised study. Some spaces were designed to promote access to the equipment on which the new technologies sat. In the early years after incorporation this mainly meant computers. At this time student–computer ratios were improving from around 1:6 to 1:2. In a slightly later phase, screens began replacing blackboards, and interactive screens and access to the internet increased teachers' capacity for illustration and opened up new possibilities for the management of learning. Computerized resources were introduced into the teaching of new, high-tech occupations, and also radically changed the teaching of traditional ones. Teaching staff began to use laptops for the preparation of materials for these new environments. Other study areas were designed to enable students to get away from the clutter of keyboards and screens. At this time the word 'library' was tending to be replaced by 'learning centre' or something similar. This was not just a trendy term, but reflected a wider range of activities taking place in these areas. South Thames College in Wandsworth created such a space in 1994 with the intention of giving

students areas in which to study, singly or collaboratively, with light-touch supervision from the wider range of professionals that were emerging at this time. In some instances this went to over-enthusiastic extremes. By 1997 Stoke-on-Trent College had ditched almost all the books from the library and replaced them with computers. Other colleges managed to achieve a balance between old and new forms of information retrieval.

3. New approaches to learning and student support were developing within these innovative spaces. In most colleges there was an increasing role for study supervisors, learning assistants, support workers, advisers, and centre coordinators, who could operate in the wider learning spaces without disruption to formal teaching hours and without the heavy hand of 'support' in class, or extraction from class activity for 'special needs'. The increasing popularity of BTEC and, later, GNVQ courses, made possible by more flexible means of study, replaced an emphasis on the essay and homework. New forms of assessment introduced the concept of assignments, which were often collaborative, and had to be generated on site. The broader student population entering colleges could also mean that 'homework' was unpopular, not welcomed in some households, and conflicted with the needs of part-time employment that, in the late 1990s and early 2000s, was very common among college students (Hodgson and Spours, 2001). Colleges were becoming much more general learning areas. As class contact hours were reduced (see Chapter 8) there was greater emphasis on student learning beyond the timetable. This involved technology-based tracking systems. Within the building there was a new synergy, a sense of space, and a wider range of professional interactions that accompanied the widespread deployment of technology. The role of the teacher became disaggregated. Some colleges created two sets of study spaces: areas for intense, silent study, and others for more relaxed conversational study. For the latter South East Essex College used a restaurant analogy – a reasonable hubbub of noise was acceptable, but rowdiness was not. The new learning support roles, such as centre coordinators, tutors, and support staff, worked alongside subject specialists. The need for access to both equipment and a wider range of staff led to the opening up of large, multifunctional learning centres.

4. The delegation of financial responsibility and the reduction of bureaucratic constraints such as the easing of the distinction between capital and revenue budgets led to a new approach to determining the

cost of a building. College corporations were freed up both to dispose of assets and to invest. Unused land and inefficient, dilapidated buildings could be disposed of to fund new, more efficient buildings with built-in security, clear lines of sight, and passive monitoring of access and behaviour. College boards of corporation became much more hands-on (see Chapter 7), employing specialist consultants to undertake feasibility studies and to present fiscal and design options. As a result, running costs were driven down and time-wasting circulation was minimized. It was understood that an efficient building could cut long-term running costs. Income, too, could be enhanced. Managers focused on the productive use of space, with a new emphasis on management formulae, such as room utilization, which could help identify wasteful, underused accommodation. More colleges prepared to sub-let their facilities, or to share them with neighbouring institutions, or the community. There was a focus on how the building, or its location, might increase student numbers. Coupled with this was a heightened awareness of ecological issues, with colleges experimenting with socially responsible eco-friendly designs.

Common to all the six stages of development since incorporation identified in Chapter 1, there has been a drawing together, an increasing closeness, of the college and its community. This may constitute the local, geographical community; the more abstract specialist 'market' that a college seeks to attract, perhaps in terms of a national occupational expertise (as with the development of niche acoustics courses at Colchester Institute); or an ethos that might attract online learners (as with the focus on entrepreneurialism in the Gazelle group of colleges). This has influenced the nature of college design and also the physical location, with more attention being paid to accessibility, visibility, to transport 'corridors', and 'hubs'. There is an enhanced sense of place, together with innovation in locations for the delivery of learning to sub-sets of learners (for example on employers' premises – Prospects College, Southend, has a classroom that overlooks 'airside' activity at Southend airport.). Moreover, there has been an impact on the design of learning environments resulting from the much larger and inclusive range of students that has emerged since incorporation (e.g. students aged 14–16, reluctant learners), the changing nature of adult provision, and the introduction of higher education (see Chapter 3).

The identity of a college has thus developed far beyond the notion of a single building. The emerging college occupies a number of spaces, and through online learning can reach wider communities of learners. Gary Warke sees the next big change in design coming from keyboardless computing. He anticipates a continuing shift towards blended learning (a combination of face-to-face and online learning), but not the realization of the theories around the management of student learning which were in vogue in the 2000s. In fact, there has been a move away from the open-space ideal. The move to the high street has been followed through, but the basics of pedagogy have not changed. There is, however, more direct community engagement, with community use of college facilities. Gary Warke views the collapse of the LSC as a watershed: college corporations have become much more cautious, and aware of the financial risks. The direction of travel for large colleges if they are to survive is to diversify and to become national players. He feels that the innovations developed by colleges are driving the change in school models, such as studio schools and UTCs.

Victorian buildings, with their ecclesiastical flourishes and sturdy construction, had in their time expressed the sense of the value of education that was felt by their funders. Over succeeding years, pressure on capital budgets and lack of imagination had often pared LEA college buildings down to functional, but poorly planned spaces. Incorporation introduced a change. Over the last 21 years college buildings have become more than accommodation. They represent the increasingly individual nature of colleges, and a new relationship with their communities.

References

Barber, M. (1997) *The Learning Game: Arguments for an education revolution.* London: Gollancz.

Department for Education and Skills (DfES) (2003) *Building Schools for the Future: Consultation on a new approach to capital investment.* London: DfES.

Further Education Funding Council (FEFC) (1997) *Circular: 97/37: Guidance on floor-space management.* Coventry: FEFC.

Gates, B. (1995) *The Road Ahead.* New York: Viking Penguin.

Grainger, P. (2004) *Colleges of the Future.* Coventry: LSC.

— (2005) *World Class Colleges.* Coventry: LSC.

Greany, T. (2005) *From the Inside Looking Out: A new perspective on learning environments.* London: Design Council.

Hodgson, A., and Spours, K. (2001) 'Part-time work and full-time education in the UK: The emergence of a curriculum and policy issue'. *Journal of Education and Work*, 14 (3), 373–88.

Jacques, E. (1997) *Requisite Organization: Total system for effective managerial organization and managerial leadership for the 21st century.* London: Gower.

Kennedy, P. (1994) *Preparing for the 21st Century.* London: Fontana.

McRae, H. (1996) *The World in 2020: Power, culture and prosperity.* London: HarperCollins.

Moss Kanter, R. (1990) *When Giants Learn to Dance: The definitive guide to corporate success*. London: Simon & Schuster.

Negroponte, N. (1996) *Being Digital*. New York: Alfred A. Knopf.

Chapter 7

Governance and governors
John Graystone, Kevin Orr, and Rob Wye

Introduction

FE governance was little researched in the UK before the late 1980s. Indeed a senior civil servant described the study of governing bodies as 'esoteric' (Thompson, 1983). Now FE college governance has been heavily researched and reviewed.

In 2015, there are around 8,000 governors in FE colleges (GFEs) and sixth form colleges (SFCs) in England. The Association of Colleges (AoC) Governors' Council, launched in February 2009, influences national education and skills policies and shares good practice. In late 2014, the Minister for Skills and Equalities wrote directly to chairs pointing out the importance of effective governance (Boles, 2014). From being on the periphery, governors have moved centre stage.

The governance of FE colleges before incorporation (1993)

Before the Education Reform Act (ERA) 1988, the education system in the United Kingdom can be described as a 'national system locally administered' (e.g. Parkes and Locke, 1978; Kogan, 1971). Central government established policies and laid down standards while the local education authorities (LEAs) had the powers and duties to provide education. In Northern Ireland this role was fulfilled by school and library boards.

Reforms set out in the Education (No. 2) Act, 1968 and taken forward in Department for Education and Science, 1970 required LEAs to establish governing bodies for their FE colleges with a balanced representation of employment interests and LEAs. Governing bodies gave colleges a degree of independence from local authority control and provided some public accountability. Governors were essentially representatives of a wide range of bodies and it was unclear whose interests came first – those of the body they represented or those of the college.

The average size of governing bodies before 1989 was very high. The largest governing body had 40 members and only 1.9 per cent had fewer than 20 governors, with an average of around 27. LEA nominations made up 36.6 per cent of members followed by employers with 22.3 per cent. A governing body typically had four staff and two student governors (Graystone, 1999).

As one principal reported, an FE governing body sometimes resembled the FE sub-committee of an LEA's education committee – dominated by political parties. The 1970s and 1980s saw a gradual move towards increased autonomy for institutions and a gradual reduction in LEA powers. (For example, Training for Jobs (1984) gave the Manpower Services Commission (MSC) increased responsibilities from 1986 to purchase a quarter of work-related non-advanced FE provided by local authorities.)

Under the radical changes set out in the Education Reform Act (ERA) 1988, LEAs retained control over their colleges for funding, strategic planning, and employment of staff (Department of Education and Science, 1989). Other powers were delegated to newly reconstituted business-led governing bodies that were expected to ensure their colleges became more responsive to the needs of industry and their managers more efficient and effective (Department of Education and Science /Welsh Office, 1987).

Employers now made up 50 per cent of governors, with LEAs reduced to no more than 20 per cent. The average size of a governing body fell to between 18 and 19. In 2013 the average size was fairly similar – 19.2 (Association of Colleges, 2013).

These important reforms barely had a chance to work, although there was time for tension to emerge between LEAs and governing bodies over who had responsibility for the future direction of colleges. Incorporation ended the direct involvement of LEAs in the running of FE colleges.

Governance of FE colleges following incorporation

Following incorporation, the governance of GFEs was regularly reformed as they moved from the early 'salad days' to 'austerity and deregulation', as outlined in Chapter 1. (The legal term for FE governing bodies is 'FE corporations'. In this chapter the term 'governing body' which is the common public term is mainly used. FE corporation' is used when specific reference is made to legislation or to distinguish FE corporations from other governing bodies.) The newly incorporated colleges, with the shackles of LEA interference removed, were encouraged to be competitive (The author chaired a conference where one principal stated – to wide applause – that he saw success as 'turning the college up the road into a car park'.) and follow the success of the incorporated polytechnics by ensuring an overall increase in student numbers and greater efficiency (Department of Education and Science/Welsh Office, 1991). Many business-led governing bodies welcomed this challenge, and, initially at least, saw their role as focusing on financial rather than academic performance – the latter being seen as the responsibility of the principal.

There were early concerns about FE governance. Two reviews supported by the Further Education Funding Council (FEFC) (Shattock, 1994; Caines, 1994) drew attention to a breakdown in the relationship between the governing body and senior management in two colleges (Derby College, Wilmorton and St Philip's Roman Catholic College) and a lack of rigour in the procedures for conducting the business of the colleges. The Education Secretary used her powers under Section 57 of the FHE Act 1992 to dismiss a number of governors and appoint others in their place. The National Audit Office (NAO) reports (National Audit Office, 1999a; National Audit Office, 1999b) on two other colleges drew attention to the lack of financial monitoring by the governors and weaknesses in the financial data provided to governors. It recommended that senior post-holders should have a duty to provide accurate information to the governing body and emphasized the importance of the clerk's independence.

Recognizing that governors needed to have authoritative central guidance on their roles and responsibilities, the FEFC published guidance and notes for governors and for clerks (FEFC, 1994; FEFC, 1996a; FEFC, 1996b; FEFC, 1996c). These were among the first of several publications by various organizations aimed at improving governance.

In spite of some concerns about governance, four years after the introduction of incorporation, Gillian Shephard, the outgoing Education and Employment Secretary, noted the success of the reforms::'further education colleges are well run. The many hard working, highly committed voluntary governors and their staff deserve praise for doing an excellent job.'

The incoming Labour Government was less positive. The Labour Party's manifesto for the 1992 general election had pledged to reverse incorporation. The incoming government chose instead to introduce reforms. Competition was now deemed 'unhelpful', with GFEs encouraged to develop partnerships with other bodies (e.g. Department for Education and Employment/Welsh Office, 1998). The approach adopted was more interventionist than that of the outgoing Conservative Government, encouraged by some poor practice. (For example at Bilston College, Gwent Tertiary College, Halton College, and Stoke-on-Trent College.) While according to inspection reports most colleges were well run and well governed, a number had financial difficulties, poor inspection reports, or were involved in questionable business activities. Such cases were 'relatively few and far between' – the Education and Employment Committee (1998) drew attention to the fact that 61 per cent of inspections carried out by the FEFC inspectorate were awarded grades 1 or 2 for governance and management – but their influence on policy within government was very significant.

In line with the new government's overall educational approach, a 'stakeholder' model of governance (Blair, 1996) was introduced; a 'stakeholder' being defined as: 'any group or individual who can affect or is affected by the achievement of the organization's objectives' (Sternberg, 1997: 3). Membership was widened to include staff, students, and members of the local community as well as business people. The Education and Employment Committee, reflecting the new emphasis on improving transparency, recommended that every college should maintain a register of interests and appoint an independent clerk. A number of themes – the membership of governing bodies; the relationship between funding bodies and colleges; accountability and openness – became key features of the debate over effective governance.

Governing bodies were urged by government to take a closer interest in the academic and vocational work of their colleges by establishing quality committees to enable governors to be more involved in monitoring college performance (Blackstone, 1999) and to boost quality, which, the minister, Margaret Hodge, said, was 'uneven'. The emphasis had shifted from increasing student numbers and improving efficiency towards raising standards.

A number of significant reports on further education followed. For example, Foster's key report on FE (Foster, 2005), which emphasized the economic contribution of colleges, was positive about FE college governance. Baroness Sharp's 2011 report highlighted the tensions that sometimes arose in a governing body that sought to engage with its local community while fulfilling its statutory responsibilities in relation to quality and financial performance and responding to the 'top-down' prescription and regulation by Ofsted and the Skills Funding Agency. Both reports had significant implications for governing bodies, which had to balance the mixed demands of individual learners, communities, and the local and national economy.

From 2010 the Conservative–Liberal Democrat Coalition Government ushered in a period of austerity and deregulation, with increased emphasis on choice. Governing bodies found their colleges more than ever before competing for 16–18-year-old learners with new sixth forms opened in free schools, university technical colleges, and the new expanded academies. There was also competition for employed adults with employers and other training providers.

The Office for National Statistics (ONS) announcement that FE colleges in the UK would be reclassified as 'central government public sector entities' underlined the view that colleges were not independent. The Education Act 2011, however, gave colleges greater autonomy including the freedom to change their governance arrangements, subject to an amended Schedule 4 of the FHE Act 1992. But with these changes came increased risks. One major bank stated that as a result of this increased autonomy from central government, it would look more closely at each college to ensure strong management and effective governance before making a decision on whether or not to loan money (Kenny and Murray, 2012). Governing bodies thus had greater autonomy than they had ever had. But the rose of increased responsibilities coincided with the thorn of increased competition and considerably reduced funding.

Reforms to instrument and articles of government

The instrument (determining membership and conduct) and articles (determining responsibilities) of government of GFEs remained virtually unchanged between 1970 and 1989. However, in the 21 years of incorporation, the instrument and articles were revised six times – around once every three or four years (in 1992 at incorporation, and then in 1999, 2001, 2006, 2008, and 2012).

Despite these changes, the core responsibilities of governors for strategy, finance, and performance remained broadly the same. Their principal powers were set out in legislation (FHE Act, 1992). An FE corporation 'may provide further and higher education, [and] supply goods and services in the provision of education'. Other powers included acquiring and disposing of assets, borrowing and investing sums of money, and entering contracts. New powers were added in 2000 (Learning and Skills Act, 2000).

But membership went through several changes. From 1993 to 1997, at least 50 per cent of governors (maximum 14) were independent – appointed from business including a nomination from the local Training and Enterprise Council. Co-opted, staff, student, LEA, and community governors became optional but the principal was usually a member if he or she wished. In the early stages of incorporation, just over 10 per cent of governing bodies had no elected staff or elected student governors (Graystone, 1999).

The DfEE (Department for Education and Employment/Welsh Office, 1998) took forward the Labour Government's 'stakeholder' model by proposing three categories – internal college interests (i.e. staff and students); business interests; and external college interests (i.e. local authorities, local community groups, and parents). Proposals were included for making decision-making more open to the public. These changes were incorporated in the revised instrument of government in 1999 and further minor changes were introduced in 2001. Following a major review of FE governance (Department for Education and Skills, 2004), a number of significant changes intended to make governance more transparent came into effect in 2006.

But there were more developments. From 1 January 2008, greater flexibility was introduced in appointing governors, reflecting one of the NAO 2005 recommendations (National Audit Office, 2005). Business, local authority, community, and co-opted categories disappeared, leaving only staff and student governors as separate categories. As a further move towards openness, the minutes of every meeting of the governing body had to be published on the college's website. To underline the crucial role of governors in the academic performance of the college, the governing body was required to review periodically the college's educational character and mission and approve the quality strategy.

The 2011 legislation brought in major reforms. Under Schedule 12, 'a further education corporation in England may modify or replace their instrument of government or articles of government' (Education Act, 2011). FE college governing bodies were required to ensure the appointment of a chief executive and the clerk and the instrument 'must provide for staff and students'. The articles had to set out the respective responsibilities of the corporation, chief executive, and the clerk. Governing bodies were free to explore new models of governance but were not allowed to make changes that would result in the corporation 'ceasing to be a charity'.

These reforms marked a major turning point in the governance of colleges. The instrument and articles of government, which before 1989 had been drawn up by LEAs and tightly prescribed by central government in the first 15 years of incorporation, were now determined by governing bodies that had the power to choose the form of governance that suited them.

Most colleges in England have yet to make substantial legal changes under these new powers although a number have sponsored academies or university technical colleges or established joint venture companies (Pember, 2013). Around 10 per cent have set up a group structure (Association of Colleges, 2013).

Who serves on governing bodies?

Before and just after incorporation, the appointment of governors was not transparent. There was anecdotal evidence that many governors were appointed because they knew the chair, the principal, or an existing governor. There was little scrutiny of potential recruits and, until the 1999 revised articles of government, colleges were not required to have search committees to identify and recommend governors. The way that appointments were carried out in many colleges made it unlikely that membership would reflect the wide diversity of the local population or provide sufficient challenge to senior management.

Now, after over 21 years of incorporation, most governors are appointed on the basis of their skills and expertise. Governing bodies have had less control over the appointment of staff and student governors who are elected from their respective constituencies.

Now governors are typically recruited after skills audits to identify gaps; advertising via various forms of media using job descriptions and person specifications; and search committees approaching individuals followed by formal interviews. There was a move away from governors nominated by external organizations. Experience and expertise were typically sought in areas such as finance, law, estates, strategy, and senior management, as well as vocational education and post-16 curriculum. Business and employer governors are the largest category of governor (38 per cent). 'Other governors' make up 31 per cent and staff and student governors 11 per cent respectively (Association of Colleges, 2013).

Some colleges continue to struggle to recruit suitably qualified governors, especially from minority groups or those with financial skills or of working age (Schofield *et al*, 2009; Humphreys, 2011). Also, small and medium sized enterprises have found it difficult to release staff for governance duties whereas some larger companies encourage their managers to take on community responsibilities. A consistent challenge has been to ensure diversity in membership. Governing bodies have been dominated by white, able-bodied, and middle-aged or retired males.

Table 7.1 shows the results of various surveys carried out on membership. The average proportion of female governors is around one-third, the highest average being 38 per cent recorded in 2012 and 2013. Only 13.1 per cent of chairs were female in 1999 – the figure before incorporation being 9.5 per cent. By 2013 it was around one-quarter. Figures for governors from black and minority ethnic groups are considerably lower than what would be expected from the population. In 1999, 71.1 per cent of governing bodies had no black and minority ethnic governors at all. The proportion with black and minority ethnic governors rose to 9 per cent in urban areas with relatively high black and minority ethnic populations (Graystone, 1999) and to 8 per cent and 9.6 per cent in two 2013 studies. Whereas the male–female ratio does not vary much throughout England and Wales, the proportion of black and minority ethnic groups varies considerably between parts of the country. This might partly explain different patterns of membership but not the overall low averages. (The 2011 census data showed that the ethnic minority population was 14 per cent in England and 4 per cent in Wales but was 55 per cent in London.)

Table 7.1 Figures from various reports on membership of GFE and SFC college governing bodies by gender, ethnicity, and age

	Female governors	Black and minority ethnic governors	Governors aged over 50	Retired governors	Female chairs	Ethnic minority chairs
Graystone 1999	21.7%(17.8% before 1993 and 20.5% just after 1993)	3%(1.2% Afro-Caribbean 1.7% Asian)	51.1%	14%	3.1%	
Davies 2002	30%	5%	71%		12%	2%
Cornwall College 2003	c. 30%		75%	30%		
Foster 2005						2.3%
FE Women's Leadership Network 2012	38%		74.1%		20%	
ColegauCymru (Wales) 2012	27%	4%	56% 45–64 20% 65+		27% (2014)	0%
ACER 2013	33%	9.6%	66.3% (45+)		24%	
AoC 2014	38%	9%	59% (45+) 14% 65+			
Chwarae Teg (Wales) 2014	32%	8%	45% (55+)		27%	

Governors' ages do not reflect the working population. A recent study (FE Women's Leadership Network, 2012) showed 74.1 per cent aged over 50, revealing fewer younger governors being appointed in 2012 than in 1999. A 2012 survey in Wales found that 6 per cent were registered disabled and in another England survey 2 per cent 'self-assessed' themselves as having disabilities (Association of Colleges, 2013). In Wales around one-fifth of people are disabled, the equivalent figure being 18 per cent in England (Census, 2011).

Therefore it appears that a 'governors' ceiling' has kept women's membership of FE college governing bodies stuck at around a third. In addition, black and minority ethnic groups and people with disabilities are under-represented. It may be speculated that other minority groups, such as gay men, lesbians, and transsexuals, are also under-represented although research is needed to test whether this is the case. Successive governments have chosen not to legislate on this matter, leaving it up to individual governing bodies to choose appropriate governors. Quotas have never been on the agenda.

Colleges are not alone in facing this diversity challenge. In the 1990s, a study showed that the proportion of female governors was highest in primary schools (42.9 per cent) and progressively fell in secondary schools (31.8 per cent), FE colleges (21.7 per cent), and higher education institutions (16.0 per cent) (Graystone, 1999). In the private sector, women made up only 12.5 per cent of board members in FTSE 100 companies (Department for Business, Innovation and Skills, 2013b), which were set a target of 25 per cent by 2015.

Governors are unpaid volunteers. Several reports have recommended that governing bodies be given the power to remunerate chairs and governors (for example, Schofield *et al.*, 2009 and Humphreys, 2011). Under charity legislation, there has been some relaxation in rules covering payment of trustees. In a Department for Business, Innovation and Skills (BIS) review of FE governance (2013a, Annex B) in 2013, the Charity Commission set out exceptional circumstances when a governor might be paid. It appears, however, that time rather than money is a major factor in recruiting high calibre governors.

To whom are FE college governing bodies accountable?

Some North American states hold elections for community college governors (trustees as they are called), who can be voted out of office. The general pattern in most countries, however, is that FE governors are appointed, usually by the governing body. (In Northern Ireland governors are appointed by the relevant minister; in Scotland chairs are appointed by the minister.)

Concern over lack of accountability was of particular significance to those who opposed incorporation, particularly the lecturer unions. Some governors also felt uncomfortable taking major decisions affecting their colleges with little accountability. The FEFC (1994) did not help by defining accountability in terms of the powers of intervention of the Education Secretary and the legal definition of 'unreasonable behaviour' by governors.

The accountability of public bodies became of increasing political interest in the 1990s. The two seminal reports of the Committee on Standards in Public Life chaired by Lord Nolan (Committee on Standards in Public Life, 1995 and 1996), aimed at MPs and members of government quangos, and then public-appointed bodies, recommended seven key principles of public life (selflessness, honesty, integrity, objectivity, accountability, openness, and leadership), which have remained in force to the present day, as a proxy for accountability. Nolan argued that appointments to boards should be based on merit. He supported the continuation of unpaid voluntary service by governors, and stated that the extension of terms of office (normally four years) beyond two terms should be the exception rather than the rule. The underlying themes of the Nolan reports were the importance of openness wherever possible, and that governing bodies should be given more scope to run their own affairs.

Greer and Hogget's study of the accountability of local non-elected bodies pointed out that FE governing bodies had considerable autonomy to determine their own destiny but that their environment was shaped by central government and by the FEFC. Governments interpreted accountability as increasing regulation, setting targets, and introducing greater openness and transparency in the way business was conducted.

The FEFC, which had strongly commended a code of conduct containing twelve statements underpinning the behaviour of board members (FEFC, 1994), drew up its own code covering corporate responsibility and the individual conduct of Council members (FEFC, 1995). Clearly the code of conduct was an idea whose time had come. By June 1995, three-quarters of GFE and SFC governing bodies had drawn up a code of conduct or were in the process of doing so (Graystone, 1995).

Some governing bodies sought openness by holding annual general meetings (AGMs), occasionally combined with an open day or special event. Colleges also published annual reports, which were often publicity brochures outlining their key achievements. There was little opportunity for scrutiny by the local community.

In Wales, the Humphreys Report (2011) on governance recommended smaller boards and the setting up of membership bodies. Local bodies appointed from local stakeholders could comment on the college's strategic plan and the board's overall performance and, crucially, appoint governors. Several governing bodies in Wales welcomed the approach and set up membership bodies.

The theme of accountability is underlined in the AoC Foundation Code of Governance, which states that governing bodies should ensure decision-making processes are transparent and rigorous and encourage open discussion and debate (Association of Colleges, 2011). Sharp went further in recommending that governing bodies be given the statutory duty to account annually to their local communities on their performance in meeting local needs – an AGM with teeth.

Accountability for FE governors has generally been 'giving an account for actions taken' rather than 'being held to account for those actions' (Stewart, quoted in Skelcher and Davis, 1995: 10) by their local communities. The Learning and Skills Improvement Service (LSIS, 2012), echoing the point made by Sharp, drew attention to colleges focusing too much on 'vertical accountability' – to government and funders – rather than 'horizontal accountability' – to local stakeholders.

Relationships between governors, the principal, and the clerk

The working relationship between the chair, the principal, and the clerk – called by some 'the holy trinity of governance' – is a key determinant of the success of a governing body. The AoC code recommends that the respective functions of governance and management, and the roles and responsibilities of the chair, the principal, and the clerk as well as of individual governors should be clearly defined (Association of Colleges, 2011).

The principal's relationship with the governing body is multifaceted. The principal is the governing body's adviser, accounting officer, and chief executive while also being an employee of the governing body and a governor. The board has the responsibility to appoint the principal and determine his/her pay and conditions. The chair is appointed by the governing body and has a key responsibility for providing strategic leadership and ensuring it works effectively. (Many publications set out the responsibilities of the chair, for example, FEFC, 1994a; Humphreys, 2011; Griggs, 2012.)

According to the Department for Business, Innovation and Skills (2013a), a consistent characteristic of successful colleges is strong leadership and management, pointing out that Ofsted (2013) has highlighted 'the importance of the relationship between governors and college managers in ensuring a culture of accountability and success'. But the interpretation of the legal responsibilities of the governing body and the principal inevitably varies between colleges and between individuals. There is a 'grey area' between governance and management – when does governance end and management begin? In a number of high profile cases, the college principal was removed by the governing body. This could be a result of the college's poor financial performance; an inadequate inspection report; or sometimes a falling out between chair and principal. Where colleges have been judged to be underperforming, governors could be too close to management or, at the other extreme, stand back and offer only a rubber stamp, providing little challenge. The distinction between governance and management has often been unclear.

The relationship with the clerk is also crucial. The FEFC Guide for Clerks (FEFC, 1996c) was published in response to reports on college failure where the clerk was judged not to be independent of the college management nor given sufficient authority. This guide, the training materials for clerks (Learning and Skills Development Agency, 2001), and the clerks' qualification reinforced the importance of the role of clerk or 'governance officer' (Humphreys, 2011). The appointment of clerk was clearly a matter for the governing body, who worked on their own behalf and not on behalf of the principal or other senior managers. An effective clerk should have the authority to advise the governing body as well as to ensure the smooth organization of meetings including the distribution of papers. The clerk also played a crucial role in raising standards by facilitating monitoring arrangements and helping the board with its own self-assessment (James, 2001).

Many governing bodies appointed external clerks who were not employed in any other capacity by the college. Some colleges appointed full-time clerks with legal qualifications, taking on a role like that of a company secretary. 79 per cent were part-time, 35 per cent worked for more than one college, and 24 per cent had another role in the college (AoC clerks' conference quoted in FE commissioner's annual report – Department for Business, Innovation and Skills, 2014).

However, in spite of all these developments, the Learning and Skills Improvement Service (LSIS, 2012) drew attention to a lack of recognition of the crucial role of the clerk, and in 2014 the FE Commissioner identified the significant role of the clerk in the lessons learnt from his interventions in 11 poorly performing colleges (Department for Business, Innovation and Skills, 2014).

Improving and measuring performance

Before the late 1980s, what happened in FE college governance remained a secret garden for outsiders. But following incorporation, there was increased focus on what governors did, who they were, and how their performance could be monitored and improved.

There is now a vast literature on what makes an effective board and the range of publications and reports analysing FE governance and giving advice on improving performance is substantial. LSIS produced 22 comprehensive governance newsletters and a series of publications covering the performance of governing bodies. The AoC produces regular guidance covering areas such as appraising the chair and asking powerful questions.

Governing bodies are subject to external inspection and audit. The importance of governing bodies carrying out self-assessment and thus improving their performance is emphasized in the English Colleges Foundation Code of Governance (Association of Colleges, 2011). From 2001, the Learning and Skills Development Agency (LSDA) provided health checks on governing bodies. The report on the initiative recommended a key role for governors in assessing college performance with particular emphasis on ensuring they received accurate data on the quality of the learners' experience (Barclay, 2003), a view echoed by the National Audit Office (2005).

The training of governors contributes towards effective governance. It has never been a requirement that governors must be trained, unlike, for example, magistrates. Before 1993, LEAs had funded governor training through grants for education support and training (GEST). At incorporation, central government funding for governor training ceased and colleges were expected to invest in their own training. Many colleges did so, although such training was sporadic. In some cases governors actively resisted training on the grounds that they were bringing their own business expertise to transform colleges. In 2015, the Education Training Foundation (ETF) has taken forward LSIS functions on support and training and the AoC and ETF organize regular governor training and national governors' conferences.

The AoC and DES Standards Unit consultations with governors identified a number of concerns over their ability to perform effectively (AoC and DES Standards Unit, 2003). These included the view that the time governors could give to their role was limited and procedures were unnecessarily complex and bureaucratic. Governors also pointed out that board meetings often focused on detail and not enough on strategy, although it is perhaps surprising that they did not seek to remedy this themselves. Interestingly the long-established tension over who determines the strategic direction of colleges resurfaced, with governors reporting that they did not have enough control over their colleges' direction as external agendas were set by funding bodies and the government. The NAO pointed to the concern of many governors that they held substantial financial responsibilities when people 'not part of the college may have substantial influence on the strategy' (National Audit Office, 2005: 9).

Six key elements of 'good governance' were identified by the Good Governance Standard for Public Services (Commission for Good Governance in Public Services, 2005). This list curiously excluded the word 'challenge'. Hill (2001) argued that governors should be 'active', challenging senior staff and focusing on quality and learning. Most commentators emphasize the need for governors to work effectively as a team – the legal responsibilities of corporations reside in collective rather than individual actions.

Ofsted drew attention to the importance of governors who 'were well informed, received the right information, and could challenge managers vigorously on the college's performance' (Ofsted, 2012: paragraph 4). Its later report on further education and skills reiterated that a key task 'remains for college governors to hold their college to account for the quality of provision and for its true impact' (Ofsted, 2013: paragraph 30).

The lack of challenge was highlighted by Pember, who pointed out that governors at failed colleges commented that 'they knew something was wrong but did not feel able to speak up and were therefore unable to hold the senior leadership team to account' (Pember, 2013: paragraph 2.6).

The debate about what is effective governance and how it is measured continues and different models have been put forward (e.g. Greer and Hogget, 1997; Schofied *et al.*, 2009). It could be argued that none of these models is 'better' than any other if applied effectively, fairly, and well. But some may be more appropriate than others. Boards need to be clear as to the model they are adopting and regularly review their approach to ensure they are consistently adding value to their college.

In 2014, the AoC Governors' Council supported by the ETF appointed national leaders of college governance to contribute to the implementation of the Creating Excellence in Governance Programme. The leaders, often highly effective chairs, support chairs of governing bodies in other colleges to help raise standards.

Under this initiative and with their increased freedoms following the 2011 legislation, responsibility for ensuring governors' high performance increasingly rests with the FE sector itself, subject to external inspection by Ofsted and with the proviso that the government can intervene through its FE Commissioner if things do go wrong. David Collins was appointed the first FE commissioner in November 2013 following the White Paper (Department of Business, Innovation and Skills, 2013c). His role is to assess the capacity and capability of the governance and leadership of colleges.

Summary and conclusions

What FE college governing bodies did and how they performed were largely unknown before incorporation. Numerous reviews, reports, guidance, and training materials have been published with the aim of seeking to understand how governing bodies work and improve their performance. Their instruments and articles of government have been regularly revised.

Governing bodies moved from a business-led model to one where a range of stakeholders were involved. Now governing bodies have considerable choice over whom they appoint. More than it has ever been, the emphasis is on ensuring governors have the appropriate skills and expertise to conduct their colleges, which are increasingly complex organizations, often with large budgets, facing a variety of tough curriculum challenges, increased competition from other educational institutions, and tight financial constraints. The skills required early on in incorporation at a period of growth and expansion differ from those needed now at a time of austerity and deregulation.

Effective governors add value to the work of college senior managers by bringing an external perspective and providing challenge while also giving advice and support. But this drive for appropriate expertise is balanced by the need for governing body membership to reflect its local communities. Humphreys says a test of this ownership is when local citizens refer to 'our college' rather than 'the college' (Humphreys, 2011: paragraph 54).

Governors' frequent wish to have 'enabling' rather than 'restrictive" (Schofield *et al.*, 2009: paragraph 4.8) powers has been granted. The detailed intervention by government that, in the view of Lingfield, has 'prevented the quality of governing bodies being tested' and impeded good governance, has been lifted (Lingfield, 2012: 15). It is tempting to say that central reforms of governance structures by government are at an end. But much depends on how governing bodies perform, the policies of the incoming government beyond 2015 and whether ministers can resist the temptation to bring in further changes.

Different patterns of governance have emerged in the UK countries. The Griggs Review (Griggs, 2012) in Scotland recommended a clearer national steer for governing bodies and the establishment of regional colleges and public appointed remunerated chairs. Northern Ireland and Scotland have concurred with the ONS decision to classify colleges as government bodies, which limits the powers of governing bodies. Wales has taken forward the 'not for profit institutions serving households' model. This divergence in governance arrangements will be a fruitful source of future research.

Few governors are left who served before 1993. Governors surveyed in the 1990s welcomed the increased responsibilities of incorporation and this is reinforced by the generally positive response from governors to the recent increased freedoms.

It is worth reminding ourselves that since 1993 the use of technology has changed dramatically the way governing bodies operate. Mobile phones to communicate with governors; PowerPoint to improve presentations; email to send agendas and papers; iPad and laptops to reduce the amount of paperwork; video-conferencing facilities to improve attendance; websites for governors to obtain up-to-date information – few of these were widely available or even invented in 1993. Governors now have access to much more information than they did in 1993.

Consistent themes emerge throughout the last 21 years. The creative tension between government, funding councils, and governing bodies over who determines strategy; the increased focus on the accountability of governing bodies and how this can best be demonstrated; the evolving distinction between governance and management and particularly the crucial partnership between chair, principal, and clerk; the developments in measuring governing body board performance; and the continuing need to address the continuing poor performance of a few governing bodies.

In the light of increased autonomy, the legal structures of governance are likely to develop over the next 21 years. Some governing bodies have expressed interest in a John Lewis style of governance, in which staff are 'partners', playing a more active role in determining strategy and receiving rewards for success. Others have developed federal models, set up wholly owned companies or joint ventures to run schools or generate income. There may be an increase in the number of 'professional' paid governors and the appointment of executive directors, on the lines of National Health Service Trusts and private companies.

It must be a good thing that we know a lot more about governing bodies. The next 21 years will see further unforeseen changes as technology develops and the labour market evolves. Whatever happens, governing bodies will continue to exist. If they did not, the authors believe that colleges would lose that challenging but supportive external perspective and their direction – rather like racehorses without their riders.

References

Association of Colleges (AoC) (2011) *The English Colleges' Foundation Code of Governance*. London: AoC.

— (2013) *AoC Governors Council Request for Information*, October 2013: Summary Report on Data: London: AoC.

— (2014) *Composition of English Further Education Corporations*. London: AoC.

AoC and DES Standards Unit (2003) *Dialogue with Governors: Interim report*, November. London: AoC.

Barclay, N. (2003) *Governance Healthcheck for FE college boards*. Research Report 2001/02. London: LSDA.

Blackstone, T. (Baroness Blackstone) (1999) Letter to chairs of FE corporations, DfEE 9 February.

Blair, T. (1996) Speech to businessmen in Singapore. Reported on BBC News, 8 January.

Boles, N. (2014) Letter to all Chairs of FE College Corporations, College Principals. 10 November. Online. www.gov.uk/government/uploads/system/uploads/attachment_data/file/373733/bis-14-1201-update-on-further-education-reform-nick-boles-letter-to-fe-and-sixth-form-college-chairs-10-november-2014.pdf (accessed 31 March 2015).

Caines, J. (1994) *St Philip's Roman Catholic Sixth Form College: Report of an enquiry into the governance and management of the college*. Coventry: FEFC.

Commission for Good Governance in Public Services (2005) *The Good Governance Standard for Public Services*. Online. www.coe.int/t/dghl/standardsetting/media/doc/Good_Gov_StandardPS_en.pdf (accessed 16 December 2014).

Committee on Standards in Public Life (1995) *Standards in public life*. First report. vol. 1, Cmnd 2850-1. London: HMSO (chaired by Lord Nolan).

— (1996) *Standards in public life: Local public spending bodies*. Second report. vol.1, Cmnd 3270-1 London: HMSO (chaired by Lord Nolan).

Department for Business, Innovation and Skills (BIS) (2013a) *A Review of Further Education and Sixth Form Governance*. London: BIS.

BIS, Department for Culture, Media and Sport and Government Equalities Office (2013b) *Women on Boards*, Lord Davies Report, London: BIS.

BIS (2013c) *Rigour and Responsiveness*. London: BIS.

— (2014) *Further Education Commissioner Annual Report 2013/14*. London: BIS.

— (2015a) *An Assessment of the Impact of Governance Reform on Further Education Colleges: A Review of Expectations*. London: BIS

— (2015b) *Further Education Commissioner's Report on Greenwich Community College*. London: BIS (March)

Department for Education and Employment/Welsh Office (1998) *Accountability in Further Education: A consultation paper*. London: HMSO.

Department of Education and Science (DES) (1970) *Government and Conduct of Establishments of Further Education*. Circular 7/70, April.

Department for Education and Skills (2004) *FE Sector Governance – a Framework for the Future*. Discussion Document. London: DfES.

DES and Welsh Office (WO) (1987) *Managing Colleges Efficiently: Report of a study of efficiency in non-advanced further education: for the government and local authority associations*. London: HMSO.

DES (1989) *Local Management of Schools and Further and Higher Education Colleges: Order under Section 222 of the Education Reform Act 1988*. DES Circular 13/89, 9 June 1989.

DES/WO (1991) *Education and Training for the 21st Century Vol 1*. London: DES.

Education Act (2011) London: HMSO.

Education and Employment Committee (1998) *Further Education Vol 1, 19 May*. London: HMSO.

FE Women's Leadership Network (2012) *Report on Surveys of Further Education Governors and Clerks to Governing Bodies*. London: WLN.

Foster, A. (2005) *Realising the Potential: A review of the future role of further education colleges*. London: DfES.

Further and Higher Education Act 1992, London: HMSO.

Further Education Funding Council (FEFC) (1994) *A Guide for College Governors*. Coventry: FEFC.

— (1995) *Annual Report. 1994–95*. Coventry: FEFC.

— (1996a) *Governance and management of further education colleges*. May. Coventry: FEFC.

— (1996b) *College Governance: A guide for clerks*. Coventry: FEFC.

— (1996c) *Notes for Governing Bodies* (separate notes covering areas such as Financial Monitoring, Governance, Strategic Planning, Quality Assurance) Coventry: FEFC.

Graystone, J. (1995) 'Time to sound the alarm on integrity'. *Times Educational Supplement, College Management*, 21 July, 2.

— (1999) 'Developments in the governance of further education colleges, primarily between 1970 and 1997' PhD diss., University of Bath.

Greer, A., and Hogget, P (1997) *Patterns of Accountability within Local Non-elected Bodies: Steering between government and the market*. York: Joseph Rowntree Foundation.

Griggs, R. (2012) *Report of the Review of Further Education Governance in Scotland*, Edinburgh: Scottish Government.

Hill, R. (2001) 'Don't join the club'. In Horsfall, C. (ed.) *Governance Issues: Raising student achievement*. London: LSDA, 33–7.

Hodge, M. (2002) 'Keynote address'. Conference on Raising Standards, Learning and Skills Development Agency, 7 March.

Humphreys, R. (2011) *An Independent Review of the Governance Arrangements of Further Education Institutions in Wales, Cardiff, Welsh Government* WAG10-11171.

James, I. (2001) 'Governors and the standards challenge'. In Horsfall, C. (ed.) *Governance Today: Rising to the challenge of raising quality and achievement.* London: LSDA, 27–32.

Kenny, C., and Murray, M. (2012) *Impacts of the Education Act 2011.* Presentation at the Corporate Education conference 9 February.

Kogan, M. (1971) *The Politics of Education: Edward Boyle and Anthony Crosland in conversations with Maurice Kogan.* Harmondsworth: Penguin.

Learning and Skills Development Agency (2001) *Clerks' Training Materials.* London: LSDA (commissioned by LSC).

Learning and Skills Improvement Service (LSIS) (2012) *Challenges for FE college Governance and Priorities for Development.* London: LSIS.

Lingfield, R. (2012) *Professionalism in Further Education: Final Report of the Independent Review Panel.* London: BIS.

National Audit Office (NAO) (1999a) *Financial Management and Governance at Gwent Tertiary College. Report by Comptroller and Auditor General.* HC 253 Session 1998–99. London: NAO.

— (1999b) *Investigation of Alleged Irregularities at Halton College. Report by Comptroller and Auditor General. HC 357 Session 1998–99.* London: NAO.

— (2005) *Securing Strategic Leadership for the Learning and Skills Sector in England. Report by the Comptroller and Auditor General HC 29 Session 2005– 06.* London: NAO.

Office for Standards in Education (Ofsted) (2012) *How Colleges Improve.* September 2008 Ref no 120166. London: Ofsted.

— (2013) *Annual Report on Further Education and Skills 2012/13.* London: Ofsted.

Parkes, D. and Locke, M. (eds.) (1978) *A Handbook for College Governors.* Coombe Lodge Report, vol. 11, no. 10.

Pember, S. (2013) *Creating Excellence in College Governance.* London: AoC Governors' Council.

Schofield, A., Matthews, J., and Shaw, S, (2009) *A Review of Governance and Strategic Leadership in English Further Education.* London: Learning and Skills Improvement Service and Association of Colleges.

Sharp, M. (Baroness Sharp of Guildford) (2011) A Dynamic Nucleus: Colleges at the Heart of Local Communities. Report of Independent Commission on Colleges in their Communities. Leicester, NIACE.

Shattock, M. (1994) *Derby College: Wilmorton. Report of an enquiry into the governance and management of the college.* Coventry: FEFC.

Skelcher, C., and Davis, H. (1995) *Opening the Boardroom Door: Membership of local appointed bodies.* LGC Communications York: Joseph Rowntree Foundation.

Sternberg, E. (1997) 'The defects of stakeholder theory'. *Corporate Governance*, 5 (1), 3–10.

Thompson, N. (1983) *College Government Up To Date* (Coombe Lodge Report Vol 16, No 12). Bristol: Coombe Lodge.

Training for Jobs (1984) Cmnd 9135. London: HMSO.

Chapter 8

Levers of power: Funding, inspection, and performance management

Mick Fletcher, Julian Gravatt, and David Sherlock

Introduction

This chapter describes the evolution of policy levers used by government and its agencies to shape the national system of further education (FE) created in England in 1993, when just under 500 colleges gained self-governing status. The focus is particularly on colleges (general further education (GFE), tertiary, sixth form (SFC), and specialist), with reference also to other training organizations in private and charitable ownership.

The creation of statutory FE corporations in 1993 crystallized characteristics that still define colleges today. (The Further and Higher Education Act 1992 created FE corporations but the transfer of staff, legal powers, and budgets did not take place until 1 April 1993.)The legislation established:

- a common structure, including governing bodies, which allowed successive governments to apply common rules and policies to colleges
- a clear legal separation from schools and higher education, which has restricted mergers across these boundaries
- a hybrid status which is outside the public sector in national accounts, allowing some financial flexibility
- charitable status, which safeguarded college assets for education
- continuing membership of public sector pension schemes as a disincentive to privatization.

Colleges were not 'set free' in 1993, any more than independent training providers had been and continued to be 'free'. Incorporation involved a transfer of power over property, staffing, and courses from local government to college governing bodies and college leaders, giving them wide scope to make decisions. But the legislation also put new powers of oversight and intervention in the hands of central government. The new Further

Education Funding Council (FEFC) was led by a team that had supervised polytechnics. They had developed an increasingly detailed and sophisticated approach to funding, inspection, and regulation, which was introduced to colleges in 1993. This approach was adapted for the whole system between 1997 and 2001.

The Learning and Skills Act 2000 merged various agencies to create a Learning and Skills Council with wide funding and planning powers and also reorganized inspection arrangements so that they were shared by Ofsted and the Adult Learning Inspectorate. The inclusion of colleges in a wider learning and skills sector in 2001 did not change the legal framework for FE colleges or for the newly included private training organizations.. However it did change the language. The introduction of terms like 'learner' to replace pupil/student/trainee/client/inmate or 'provider' to replace school/college/trainer was a deliberate attempt to create a new common identity for the FE system. This common identity was also fostered by moving gradually towards common arrangements for contracting, inspection, and funding.

Government has used three main policy levers to regulate FE since incorporation: formula-based funding; regular inspection; and statistical performance data. The introduction of a single funding formula for the sector involved incentives and restrictions intended to encourage or restrain particular institutional responses. A second strand, perhaps even more powerful, has been a system of inspection used regularly to measure and grade college quality against an explicit set of criteria, and to publish the outcomes. The third element has been the evolution of performance indicators intended to provide colleges and policymakers with summary assessments of institutional practice. There have been distinct phases in the evolving nature of each of these levers and in the ways they have been used.

There have been four such phases in the evolution of FE funding:

- an early post-incorporation period focused on growth and increased efficiency, alongside the assimilation of all colleges into a common system
- a 'late FEFC' phase, marked by a reaction against some of the more dramatic instances of gaming the system by some colleges
- a third period of increased emphasis on planning and targets, introduced by the Learning and Skills Council (LSC) after 2001
- in the most recent period, greater freedom from targets, balanced by more elaborate eligibility rules.

The evolution of inspection over the period similarly falls into four phases, though on a different cycle:

- the FEFC established a new independent and college-focused inspectorate in 1993
- the Training Standards Council (TSC) developed inspection of work-based learning and employability programmes from 1997
- the Adult Learning Inspectorate (ALI) shared inspection of colleges with the schools inspectorate, Ofsted, from 2001 to 2007, focusing on work-based and adult programmes
- in a final phase, Ofsted became the inspectorate for all learning, from early years through compulsory schooling to all FE; while the FEFC inspectorate, the TSC, and the ALI were structured so as to be at arm's length from government, Ofsted is a non-ministerial government department.

The performance management regime has evolved in a rather different manner but has been impelled by similar forces. An early focus on indicators to inform policymakers has given way, at least at a rhetorical level, to a more recent emphasis on information that can inform users – learners and employers.: 'The Government cannot tackle the skills challenge on its own. Employers and citizens must take greater responsibility for ensuring their own skills needs are met, and to do this they will need from Government good quality information, the opportunity to influence the system to provide the training they need, and access to finance' (Department for Business, Innovation and Skills, 2010: 6). After years in which student success rates have been arguably the most important measures of effectiveness, the Department for Education has focused more recently on examination results, while the Department for Business Innovation and Skills (BIS) values outcomes rather than outputs – destination data and the impact of FE on employment and earnings, rather than student retention and achievement of qualifications alone.

To help understand the drivers behind the many changes and their impact on the sector, this chapter considers each of these policy levers in turn. For each one, a brief chronology sets out the sequence of changes in policy. A final section then seeks to bring the separate strands of control together and to draw some overarching conclusions.

Funding

The last two decades have been a turbulent period. In 1990, colleges were funded and managed by local authorities as they had been for much of the twentieth century. In 1993, responsibility for their oversight transferred to the FEFC, and in 2001 to the LSC. From April 2010, it was planned to return responsibility for funding provision for young people to local authorities, working with the newly created Young People's Learning Agency (YPLA). Provision for adults passed to another new body, the Skills Funding Agency (SFA). For a few months only, funding was paid via local councils, but following the general election of May 2010, control was re-centralized in the YPLA. Within a further two years, this organization had expanded its remit and changed its status to create a new Education Funding Agency (EFA), responsible for funding all public education up to the student's 19th birthday.

These institutional changes both mark and mask changes in the technical arrangements used to fund further education. There have been repeated changes to funding methods and constant tinkering with rules, formulae, and approved qualification lists. Evolution has not been linear, with some features first declining in importance and then being reasserted. It is with these changes, rather than the funding bodies themselves, that this section is concerned.

In 1990, colleges were primarily funded by local education authorities (LEAs). They received income from several sources – from overseas students for example, and from full-cost fees charged to employers – but the dominant source of funding, then as now, was the taxpayer. (Interestingly, colleges were less dependent on taxpayer income in the 1980s than they are now because employer spending has fallen and government has sought to direct funding towards employer needs.) LEAs had traditionally determined their own approach to calculating the funding for each college, resulting in significant variations in both the level of provision and its unit cost among different areas of the country. However, by 1990 a degree of standardization in the way they calculated funding had been introduced. The Education Reform Act (1988) required LEAs to use a formula based on weighted full-time equivalent (FTE) student numbers to distribute funds among their colleges. The government did not specify the total sum to be allocated, nor the values of the weighting to be included in the formula, but it did prescribe the general form. (The government currently prescribes the arrangements for funding schools in much the same way.) A major driver of this new imposition of central control was the availability of spreadsheets, without which the calculations necessary would have been impracticable.

FEFC funding

In 1993, FEFC offered a fresh start: an opportunity to experiment with a new funding approach. This was introduced in 1994, following a period of consultation with the sector during which several different models were considered (FEFC, 1992) and strong support was shown by college leaders for one option (FEFC, 1993a). The formula chosen was, in essence, a more complex version of the model operated by LEAs in preceding years, but now reflecting both the greater technical capability of information technology (IT) and a desire to use funding to enforce policies (McClure, 2000). The new funding system was based on units rather than FTEs. It was based on a standard definition of guided learning hours (GLH), and units were earned by colleges for student enrolment (entry), attendance (programme), and achievement, with adjustments made to take account of the relative cost of different subjects.

Staff in the new national body had no special interest in preserving the original distribution of resources. In an environment of spending restraint in the mid-1990s, they introduced a relatively rapid process of convergence of unit costs across England. The unit costs of colleges inherited by FEFC varied by as much as three-fold. Adjustments led rapidly to real reductions in many colleges, though these were mitigated by some subsequent innovations. The Kennedy Report on widening participation, published in the first weeks of the new Labour Government in 1997 (FEFC, 1997), prompted FEFC to introduce 'widening participation' units (which later became disadvantage funding). This, as well as changes in area costs and the opportunity to secure growth-related funding, saved some colleges from closure. The financial pressures in the second half of the 1990s were nevertheless severe, causing many colleges to merge.

The FEFC initially paid less attention to questions of eligibility for public funding, though it was required by law to restrict funds to courses listed in Schedule 2 of the 1992 Further and Higher Education Act. At this stage of its development, the funding mechanism was not intended to drive course priorities, but to ensure that students took externally accredited courses. The rates paid for each course were intended to be a neutral reflection of the average cost of provision. The allocation of money among their courses was largely left to institutions.

The early days of the FEFC nevertheless demonstrated the capacity of a national body to design and impose a quasi-market that incentivized growth in student numbers and efficiency. It showed also the capacity of incorporated institutions to respond to those incentives. Efficiency, measured in terms of reduced unit costs, increased rapidly. Equity might be said to have increased, too, as a consequence of the higher level of student participation and the more equal allocation of resources across the country (Education Select Committee, 1998).

The latter days of the FEFC saw greater attention paid to curbing some of the excesses of a lightly regulated market. Colleges were not subject to restrictions on where they could recruit. Some grew rapidly through subcontracting delivery to third parties, a process known as franchising. Franchise partners were often able to deliver at very low cost, particularly where they offered a substitute for provision that had been previously paid for by an employer or by individuals. Where they were substantial, profitable franchise operations could be used to make up for inefficiencies in the core college operation. The ability to franchise with partners anywhere in the country made it difficult for any one college to stand out against the competitive race for unit growth, without being undercut by others perhaps located many miles away (Gravatt and Silver, 2000).

Provision for learners with learning difficulties and/or disabilities (LLDD) was funded outside the standard mechanism. Funding for additional learning support (ALS), as it was known, was allocated in response to individual claims. The system is widely credited with supporting a marked expansion in provision for disabled learners, but it also led to burdensome audit arrangements and some inconsistency (Learning and Skills Council, 2005).

The Learning and Skills Council

Unlike the FEFC and the Higher Education Funding Council for England (HEFCE), the Learning and Skills Council (LSC) was set up with powers for planning as well as funding. It rationalized the 72 Training and Enterprise Councils (TECs) as part of its remit to create a consolidated learning and skills sector. It started life with 47 local branches, each with a governing council, a large measure of control delegated to every one, and more than 5,000 staff. The LSC made significant changes to the funding tariff, but it also sharpened the focus on delivering central government priorities and managing provider allocations in detail. In the mid-2000s, for example, LSC staff described their process for 'managing the mix and balance of provision': seeking to promote courses that were accredited at the expense of those that were not; and those which met government targets at the expense of those that did not (Learning and Skills Council, 2006). This detailed central management of the system was made possible by further advances in information technology and it involved an unprecedented degree of intervention in the management of colleges. Combined with attempts to take on board the views of employment organizations and regional advisory bodies, the LSC's system became, in the words of a Parliamentary Select

Committee, 'impenetrable' (Innovation Universities Skills and Science Select Committee, 2009).

There was correspondingly less emphasis on improving the efficiency of the system, though this was also a result of higher public spending in the first few years of the LSC. Budgets were prioritized for those colleges or training organizations which could best increase learner numbers. Tightly defined funding rules were used as a brake whenever their activities moved out of control.

Efficiency became more of an issue after 2005. There was a new determination to increase the contribution of students and employers from 25 per cent of costs to 50 per cent. LSC's fee–income targets, and its pressure on reducing locally determined fee remission, were also used as a means to raise efficiency. While supporters argued that funding was being redirected appropriately towards priority groups, principally those not holding a qualification defined as a 'full Level 2' and young people not yet holding a 'full Level 3', opponents of this remedial approach responded that the effect was the loss of over a million places for adult learners and the grant of unnecessary financial subsidies to employers (Wolf, 2009 and Keep, 2014 make these arguments). The theory that government investment in the lower levels of education and training would persuade employers to spend more money on equipping their staff with higher skills never quite worked in practice.

Between 2005 and 2008, the LSC implemented a new funding system described as 'demand-led'. Though many have disputed the term, it perhaps accurately reflected a further reduction in the influence of colleges over what was delivered and another increase in the power of funders. The original ambition for a simple, easy-to-manage system, was undermined by changes that separated the arrangements for funding young people from those for adults and, within the adult budget, further distinguished between 'employer responsive' and 'individual responsive' provision. These features persist to the present day and many would argue they have undermined the role of FE as a predominantly adult vocational sector. The common measure became standard learner numbers (SLN) instead of units – to all intents and purposes a return to FTEs. The complex system of weighting to reflect the costs of different subjects, learners, and areas of the country was not amended, but the various weights were combined together with a factor reflecting success rates and presented at the individual college level as a 'provider factor'. The formula was even less transparent and it is possible that this, in itself, had an impact on college behaviour.

Throughout the LSC period, funding was a major lever of control. At different times, the LSC used its formulae to increase the numbers of people taking basic skills courses or apprenticeships. It introduced a national funding formula for school sixth forms and took slow steps towards harmonizing the money paid for students of the same age in schools and colleges. Between 2003 and 2006, the Department for Education and Skills (DfES) developed a new programme called 'Train to Gain', which was designed to tackle underinvestment in the skills of lower paid workers. LSC adapted its employer-responsive formula to manage the programme and spent almost £1 billion on it by 2010. Many observed that it involved substantial 'deadweight' – it paid employers for training they would have undertaken anyway. Typically, it comprised assessment of existing skills rather than teaching new ones (Wolf, 2009; Keep, 2014). Such criticism contributed to a shift in emphasis in 2010 when the LSC closed; new agencies started; and the Conservative–Liberal Democrat Coalition Government took office.

New funding approaches

The appointment of ministers committed philosophically to deregulation at a time of public spending cuts resulted in reductions in the size of the funding agencies. The priorities have been to cut costs, focus resources on government priorities, and simplify funding methods. From 2013, younger full-time students have been funded on a per capita basis – though with allowances for the extra costs for certain subjects, for disadvantaged learners and for those studying in London and the South East – following concerns that the funding system contained perverse incentives to maximize the number of qualifications taken (Wolf, 2011). Payment for successful outcomes was also removed, though the incentive to retain students for the full year was kept. The SFA, however, continues to fund adult provision on a per qualification basis. Meanwhile, funding innovation continued. A new system of income-contingent loans for adults took effect in 2013 to cut revenue spending. The reform extended the role of the Student Loan Company from HE into FE and the government has suggested that there may be another expansion of the loan system from 2016 to cover more students and more courses (Department of Business, Innovation and Skills, 2014a). Loans were briefly offered for advanced apprenticeships and then withdrawn five months later following minimal take-up. Undaunted by this reverse, the government continued to introduce new pilots involving new apprenticeship qualifications and funding models (Department of Business,

Innovation and Skills, 2014b). There was discussion throughout 2014 of the possibility of routing all government funding for adult further education either through employers or local government or through Local Enterprise Partnerships (LEPs). Many decisions remain to be made after the general election to be held in May 2015.

Twenty-one years of innovation have created an environment of constant change. Government has sought to drive up value and enforce its policies through adjustments to funding. Providers have become used to responding to small signals in complex rulebooks, in a process described by a government minister in 2010 as 'infantilising the system' (Hayes, 2010). The constant froth of reform has made it difficult to assess the movement of the underlying tides. Colleges benefited from significant increases in income between the late 1990s and late 2000s, which allowed them to increase full-time student numbers, particularly in the 16–18-year-old age group, and also to invest in their buildings, in better student support and in quality improvement. The financial crisis, recession, and a large government budget deficit saw the funding tide turn and college income contract. The future seems likely to involve still greater turbulence (Keep, 2014).

Inspection

Inspection began to play a major role in the operation of colleges only after their incorporation in 1993. Before then, colleges were subject to occasional inspection by Her Majesty's Inspectorate (HMI) and, in most LEAs, by local inspectors of education. For several reasons, however, the process had far less impact on college operations than it does today.

Regionally based HMI had infrequent contact with colleges and from time-to- time, carried out inspections of institutions or surveys of types of provision. Regional Staff Inspectors took the lead in helping plan the distribution of advanced courses. This was more of an administrative role than inspection itself. Individual HMIs were respected and their advice welcomed but inspection was infrequent; the process was less formal than it has become; reports were often seen as supportive or were ignored. Any intervention in schools and colleges was then seen as a matter for LEAs rather than for central government or its agents. LEAs varied in their practice but most had inspectors or advisers working alongside the education officers who administered local education systems. In most cases, the expertise of the LEA inspectorate centred on the school curriculum and few had an understanding of FE colleges. Often their role focused on staff selection and development, rather than on inspection.

The FEFC Inspectorate

As part of the incorporation of colleges the FEFC was given responsibility for assuring the quality of the courses it funded, as well as for calculating and arranging the distribution of money. FEFC sought to carry out this responsibility in two ways: by the development of performance indicators and by the creation of a new inspectorate.

The new FE Inspectorate used its fresh start to consult with the sector and secure widespread agreement for a new approach (FEFC, 1993b). The new system introduced:

- regular inspections of every college on a four-year cycle
- a fixed three-month period of notice for inspections
- a five-point numerical grading scale
- the extensive use of associate inspectors drawn from the sector
- an explicit and transparent inspection framework
- a process of systematic annual self-assessment
- detailed published inspection reports.

The new regime was seen as helpful by colleges. Some colleges did not fare well in the new nationally published reports, but the active involvement of many senior staff as part-time inspectors helped to establish a shared understanding of good practice across the sector. It also helped develop institutional expertise in making secure, evidence-based judgements, supported by an increasingly important self-assessment process. Inspection judgements were reinforced by elements of the funding system – colleges were not allowed to grow in areas of provision that had been identified as of poor quality – but the arrangements were essentially seen as supportive rather than confrontational.

The Training Standards Council

The Training Standards Council (TSC) was established in 1997 by the Department for Education and Employment (DfEE) working with the TEC National Council. Its remit was to help improve standards in work-based learning carried out by private training providers and employers. It commenced operation in 1998, when it published the first combined framework for inspection and self-assessment, *Raising the Standard*. It was led from the outset by a former senior inspector from the FEFC inspectorate – David Sherlock, one of the co-authors of this chapter and subsequently chief inspector of ALI – and it built on many of the features of the former body, in particular an explicit assessment framework; the use of a five-point numerical grading scale; an emphasis on self-assessment; and the extensive use of directly contracted and trained part-time inspectors with current sector experience.

TSC was a company limited by guarantee and operated at a still greater distance from government than the FEFC inspectorate, which had been part of a non-departmental public body (or quango). Its powers were not established by statute but by conditions attached to providers' contracts.

TSC introduced inspection into many organizations that were less familiar with teaching and learning than were colleges. For this reason, it placed greater emphasis on supporting the development of providers, as well as on judging their strengths and weaknesses. Evaluation reports suggest that TSC was successful in establishing good working relationships with providers (e.g. Stuart *et al.*, 2000) and that the arrangements described in *Raising the Standard* commanded broad assent (Training Standards Council, 2000).

The Adult Learning Inspectorate and Ofsted

The legislation that replaced FEFC with the LSC also placed colleges under the remit of two inspectorates. Ofsted took responsibility for inspecting provision for young people (under 19) while the Adult Learning Inspectorate (ALI) combined the responsibilities of TSC for work-based learning with the FEFC inspectorate's work with adults in FE colleges, as well as adult community learning from Ofsted. Colleges were inspected by joint teams, with the lead inspector determined by the proportion of young people to adults in the institution concerned.

The approach of the two inspectorates diverged, despite agreement on a Common Inspection Framework from 2001 (Adult Learning Inspectorate/ Ofsted, 2001). Ofsted focused primarily on making judgements of college performance, while ALI combined this with an increasing emphasis on its role in provider improvement; for example through publication of a monthly magazine *Talisman*, a good-practice website *Excalibur*, and establishment of a Provider Development Unit to help providers who were failing (see references in Training Standards Council, 1999). ALI divided this role from inspection by seconding those working in it from inspection for a fixed period. Under this regime, the success rates of learners in work-based learning, including apprenticeships, rose dramatically. In 2005 a revised inspection framework (Adult Learning Inspectorate/Ofsted, 2005) confirmed a move from a five-point to a four-point grading scale, intended to force inspectors (and colleges in self-assessment reports) to make clear judgements by removing a default middle grade. This new version of the Common Inspection Framework was adopted by Ofsted for its school inspections as well as for 16–18 FE, introducing criteria for judging quality that were truly 'common' across age ranges and educational settings for the first time in England.

Ofsted

In 2007, Ofsted took over the functions and most of the staff from ALI, as well as a new responsibility for regulating childcare and early years education from two other inspectorates. Colleges returned to having a single inspectorate. Government explained the change by talking of the advantages of one inspectorate covering every stage of education, applying common standards and a consistent approach, but the driving force behind the reform was a cross-government rationalization of regulators, undertaken in response to criticisms beyond FE about excessive bureaucracy (HM Treasury, 2005). Reform did not touch HE, which maintained its distinctive arrangements based on peer review. A secondary consideration was separation of the inspection function from the provision of quality improvement services, also reflecting wider trends in the management of public services. Improvement services for FE passed first to the Quality Improvement Agency (QIA), then to the Learning and Skills Improvement Service (LSIS), before settling with the current provider, the Education and Training Foundation (ETF).

The move to bring all FE inspections under Ofsted was controversial (see, for example, Education Select Committee, 2006). There were fears that Ofsted would be schools-focused; that it was over-reliant on subcontracted additional inspectors; and that it would make judgements without taking responsibility for improvement. Ofsted was also criticized as lacking independence from government.

Since 2007, Ofsted's approach to inspection has evolved. Instead of a regular inspection cycle, it has brought in a 'risk-based' approach, concentrating inspections on those institutions that desk-based analysis suggests might be cause for concern. Although designed to reduce the frequency of inspection of good colleges and training providers, this move raised the apparent proportion of poor inspection results in any single year and fuelled criticisms of FE from a new Ofsted chief inspector based on a presumed similarity of purpose between FE and schools (Ofsted, 2011). With new leadership in the Department for Education (DfE) calling for regulatory rigour, Ofsted changed the grade descriptor 'satisfactory' to 'requires improvement' and introduced a demanding timetable for re-inspection of those institutions so designated. The impact of inspection judgements on individual providers was heightened by Ofsted's introduction of a single numerical grade for the 'overall effectiveness' of colleges, which were often so large and heterogeneous as to make this designation questionable. The introduction of learner Safeguarding and providers' promotion of Equality and Diversity as 'limiting grades', able to override other aspects of educational quality in the formation of a judgement on overall effectiveness, emphasized the use of inspection, as well as funding, to enforce adherence to government policies. Ofsted now gives greater priority in assessing institutional performance to the quality of teaching and learning and has reduced the notice period for inspections to a few days, introducing the idea of 'no notice' visits.

Most recently, Ofsted has announced several important changes of emphasis. When the current contracts for the provision of part-time inspectors expire, the arrangements for their selection, training, and deployment will be brought back in-house. In another reversal of earlier practice, HMI will play an increasing role in supporting quality improvement. At the time of writing, it seems likely that a new revision of the Common Inspection Framework in 2015 will restore a position similar to that first reached in 2005, by bringing inspection of early years provision under the same criteria that are applied to schools and FE. There are concerns that this move, as well as a continued emphasis on benefit to the learner as the core of any judgement of quality, may cut across other elements of government policy favouring advantage to employers.

Performance indicators

In the years immediately prior to incorporation, the performance indicators in use in FE were primarily concerned with efficiency and were of most value at LEA or national level. The DfE Joint Efficiency Study of Non-Advanced FE in 1987 (Department for Employment and Skills, 1987) was a response to criticisms of poor value-for-money. It developed a shared understanding of a number of concepts used to manage resources. The study focused on the Staff–Student Ratio (SSR) and advocated wider use of that measure and its component ratios (Average Class Size, Average Lecturer Hours, and Average Student Hours). Government also funded the FEMIS programme which was run on newly installed desktop computers, to calculate these ratios. (The FEMIS system went through various owners until a later version was bought by Capita, which is now one of the main IT system providers to colleges.) While the enterprise had its enthusiasts at institutional level, most college leaders were more concerned to use the newly available computing power to keep track of their students.

In 1992, the government began to publish information on student achievement in the form of school and college league tables, ranking examination performance at institutional level. The rationale was to help students and their parents to choose where to study and to hold schools and colleges to account. League tables were popular with the media. It is not clear how far this information has been used by potential students to make choices. Nevertheless, data on comparative qualification performance increasingly influenced institutional practice.

From its early days, the FEFC published standardized benchmarking data for colleges (FEFC, 1994) in order to inform its oversight of the sector and to enable managers to compare their performance with that of similar institutions. The benchmarks comprised a mixture of efficiency and effectiveness indicators – achievement of recruitment targets, student number trends, average level of funding (ALF) per unit, plus 'student continuation' and 'qualification achievement'. Their calculation and dissemination was made possible for the first time by the increases in computer power available to central bodies.

Particular attention was directed during the mid-to-late 1990s on student retention as an area where progress could be made. Colleges would be able to make financial gains by reducing drop-out, but students would also benefit from taking a course they wished to complete. By the turn of the millennium, commercial companies were developing software that enabled colleges to analyse their own data on retention and success in more detail – products like ProAchieve, for example, gradually spread across the sector and became part of the standard toolkit of college managers.

In 2002, the government published a new strategy document, *Success for All* (Department for Employment and Skills, 2002), which had as one of its four strands the introduction of a framework for quality and improvement. The strategy introduced the notion of Minimum Levels of Performance (MLPs), described as 'floor targets'. These were calculated in terms of student success rates and were a response to concerns that success rates were sometimes below 50 per cent – the further education minister, Margaret Hodge, criticized colleges on several occasions in 2001 for achieving success rates of barely 50 per cent. Minimum levels of performance proved to be a powerful tool for changing behaviour among college managements in terms of the courses they chose to offer and how they organized themselves. They also led many to concentrate on work which most readily yielded good results, regardless of national priorities to enlarge provision in the most challenging subjects.

Success rates had become well established as a central performance measure in colleges and, towards the end of the decade, they were increasingly used by Ofsted to determine inspection success or failure. There were regular attempts to shift the focus away from raw success rates to other measures like value-added (VA) or distance travelled (DT), but these had limited success (Learning and Skills Council, 2006).

In 2007, the LSC published *A Framework for Excellence* (Learning and Skills Council, 2006), which set out how a 'balanced scorecard' of information would be developed to meet the needs of institutional managers, inspectors, and officials and, 'above all, users of the system – learners and employers'. The three components of the framework measured responsiveness to learners and employers; effectiveness based on success rates and Ofsted judgements; and financial health. It was presented as a joint document with Ofsted, with the authors declaring an aspiration that the framework would 'converge eventually' with the Common Inspection Framework in a single approach. As it has turned out, Ofsted's method has prevailed alone.

In the same year (2007), the LSC also published *Identifying and Managing Under-Performance* (Learning and Skills Council, 2007a), which built on earlier work on minimum standards. New ministers had set targets in the 2006 White Paper to 'eliminate inadequate and unsatisfactory provision across the FE system by 2008' (Department for Employment and Skills, 2006). Minimum Levels of Performance were to be defined in terms of financial health, Ofsted grades, and success rates, benchmarked against sector averages. Colleges failing against any of these criteria could be served with a 'notice to improve' or a range of other sanctions. Notices to improve had an immediate impact on those who received them. With a year to have them lifted, college managers closed courses, replaced staff, or advised students to take lower-level qualifications.

These various initiatives and the general approach to performance indicators were closely associated with the latter days of the LSC. They were primarily aimed at institutional managers, inspectors, and LSC officers concerned with 'provider performance management'. This emphasis reflected the ascendancy of central, regional, and sectoral planning. The use of statistical indicators to create informed 'consumers', who could shape FE through market forces, remained present in official thinking, but in a secondary role. With the change of government in 2010, the successor agencies promoted a different approach. 'FE Choices' was the name of a new website summarizing the performance of colleges and other providers. The idea, once again, was to drive improvement through better information for users (Department of Business, Innovation and Skills, 2010). Nevertheless, the indicators identified were familiar – success rates, destination data, and learner and employer satisfaction scores.

Although the learner and employer satisfaction surveys initiated in 2007 are still running at the time of writing, Ofsted launched its own 'Learner View' in 2012 (Ofsted, 2012). This is a website where students may record their comments on FE programmes they have undertaken. An 'Employer View' followed two years later. The Ofsted online approach is certainly much cheaper than the satisfaction surveys but is less statistically robust. The most recent development in relation to performance indicators for FE has been the publication by BIS (2014c) of experimental data on outcomes from college courses: destinations, progression, and earnings in subsequent employment. These indicators, which are currently only at a pilot stage, are envisaged as supplementing qualification success rates in giving a more complete picture of colleges' performance. The production of this information has only recently become possible. The technical ability (and political approval) to combine information from the huge datasets assembled by Her Majesty's Revenue and Customs (HMRC), the Department for Work and Pensions (DWP), and further and higher education administrations was not available only a few years ago.

Conclusions

Government ministers and officials have used a variety of levers to influence and control colleges in the two decades since they became independent incorporated institutions. This final section seeks answers to two questions that arise naturally from that narrative: why have the controls evolved and been used in the way that they have; and what have been the consequences? We have a strong sense that incorporation and the subsequent policy choices made by government have given colleges the freedom to fail but not the freedom to succeed.

Our survey of funding methods, inspection, and statistical performance management suggests that there have been three major factors that, at different times and to different degrees, have shaped the policy levers used to direct further education. The first is technological innovation. From the late 1980s, advances in information technology gave government policymakers the means to design and implement consistent national systems for the first time, as well as to gain a better insight into what might be happening on the ground. The application of a complex national funding formula to over 400 different colleges (now 339), and eventually to over 1,000 providers in various forms of ownership, would have been impossible a little more than a decade earlier. Technology also allowed colleges to compare course-by-course success rates against a variety of national benchmarks. The generation of reliable and up-to-date information on qualification success rates has also underpinned an increasingly assertive inspection regime and given a clear basis for defining the minimum acceptable standards of performance. The development of an accurate and comprehensive individual learner record (ILR) made this possible and is now being matched against the datasets held by HMRC and DWP. After years in which this has been discussed, government can now contemplate using information on changes to employment status and the earnings of former students as a means of judging the effectiveness of colleges.

Technology alone, however, cannot be the whole answer as to why policy levers have been used in this way to control colleges. The same technologies could have supported similar interventions in the HE sector but they did not. One possibility is that the more directive approach to FE derives in the main from its lesser capacity to resist government control. This, in turn, may reflect social status. There seems to be a direct relationship between the proportion of institutional funding linked to achieving outcomes and the status of the clients of those institutions. Outcome-based funding has never been used to pay universities or schools – school sixth-form funding was linked to school-specific success rates in the early 2010s but their funding for 11–16 has never been linked to the distance travelled by their students. It has been used modestly in further education and to a larger extent, historically, in work-based learning. Meanwhile training programmes for the unemployed have sometimes involved 100 per cent payment by results.

Alongside technological change, which has given the state an increased capacity for intervention, there has evolved a political philosophy which justifies it. Ideas around New Public Management have emphasized the desirability of separating the providers of services from those who purchase or commission them. Those running organizations are free to determine *how* to provide a service but not to determine *what* service to provide. It may be that the deliberate use of the term 'provider', initially as a way of describing schools, colleges, independent training organizations, and others in a simple and inclusive way, fuelled this philosophy by undermining the concept of schools and colleges as vital elements of civil society.

At the same time policymakers have often specified in great detail how individuals should spend their time when engaged in publicly funded education and training. This logic stands behind various attempts to hand 'purchasing power' to individuals (through Individual Learning

Accounts – ILAs) or employers (the current Richard proposals for apprenticeship reform) or the expansion of information sources intended to create intelligent consumers (FE Choices, Learner View, and Employer View). A recurring dilemma for governments has been how to empower individuals and employers, while preventing them from making the wrong choices. Occasional scandals around the misuse of ILAs or Train to Gain strengthen the hand of those who advocate caution (see Chapter 2).

The belief that purchasers (however they may be 'guided' by government), rather than providers, ought to determine priorities is reinforced by the technological changes considered earlier. Governments have access to more and more information suggesting that something, somewhere, might be wrong. For example, they have figures on the numbers of school leavers not in education, employment or training (NEETs); or the proportion of individuals lacking particular qualifications. They see data comparing educational performance in England with that in other countries. This welter of information creates an increasing pressure to act, but no commensurate increase in understanding of what might be the right action. One consequence seems to be the repeated cycles of policy failure, each one beginning with speedy identification of an issue; the rapid imposition of a poorly evidenced programme to tackle it; and then mounting evidence of unintended outcomes.

The specific policies enacted in FE have also followed policy fashion. In the early 1990s, as we have shown, the emphasis was on efficiency and reducing unit costs. Later in the decade there was a stronger focus on widening participation and social cohesion. More recently, there have been heightened priorities placed on safeguarding young or vulnerable people, promoting gender and racial equality and diversity and a narrower emphasis on workforce skills and supporting economic growth. Adult learning has, in turn, been both actively encouraged and effectively sidelined. Incorporation was not responsible for these shifting priorities but it provided the environment and the levers with which successive governments were able to initiate or terminate policy themes and actions in the colleges to pursue them.

A final factor might be termed tactical. There has often been a dialectical relationship between the evolution of national control systems and local actions taken in response. Markets involve supply and demand, while public sector quasi-markets involve incentives, responses, and compensating controls. Without wishing to exaggerate its impact, some institutions at certain times have invested considerable effort in gaming the system, whether to secure increased funding or to present the most favourable view of their performance. Often, as with the FE franchising bubble, there were significant or even crippling financial penalties for those who initially refused to participate on the grounds of principle.

In complex systems, it is often difficult to predict the outcomes of a policy change. Occasionally, politicians have been wilfully blind to professional advice. Moreover, by the time that it is clear at the centre that the outcomes of a policy have been perverse, a great deal of unwanted activity may have taken place, prompting a sudden swerve in direction. Changes in funding mechanisms produce new winners and losers, often in an unpredictable and unplanned way. New priorities in an inspection regime which increasingly requires compliance with the latest policy initiative (community cohesion a couple of years ago; British values today) may turn 'outstanding' institutions into ones that 'require improvement' seemingly overnight.

Managing the resulting instability has been a major preoccupation for institutional managers. A poor inspection grade or a financial deficit can spell the end of a professional career or a college. A particularly unfortunate consequence of this has been a tendency to prioritize the tactical skills needed for an institution to survive from day-to-day, rather than the strategic thinking demanded to take the sector forward in the national interest. The skills required to navigate the minefield of FE control systems differ from those needed to articulate a clear and compelling alternative vision for the future.

A key question for observers of FE must be why, despite genuine political support for moves towards a self-regulating sector, the process of growing autonomy has stalled on at least three occasions. It is arguably no further advanced today than it was twenty years ago. Many in the sector would agree with the former minister, John Hayes, that it is this recurring process of incentives and responses to them, which are subsequently seen as perverse, that has prevented FE from attaining the maturity envisaged for it in 1993 (Hayes, 2010).

The problem for governments is that, while they now have the means to drive through changes in FE and increasingly feel compelled to do so, they can neither predict the precise outcome of those changes nor fine-tune their interventions in time to avoid damaging consequences. The college experience ought to be a warning to those engaged in similar experiments in related areas of the public realm, such as HE and academies.

There are other, less dramatic, consequences of the way in which the levers of power in FE have developed. In the early years of incorporation, the focus on finance, personnel, and property challenges caused some colleges to neglect the curriculum. More recently, colleges have been criticized by Ofsted for making too little use of 16–18 study programme freedoms, perhaps because they are distracted by the importance of getting funding right or even by complying with Ofsted's own current priorities. It is arguable that the competitive environment set by the levers of control may also have resulted in over-investment. Many colleges have felt the need for new buildings to attract higher student numbers (see Chapter 6). Some colleges which took on high levels of debt in the process are now experiencing financial difficulties as revenue funding to service their loans falls. Other institutions have maintained the broadest possible choice of study programmes for competitive reasons, at the expense of retaining viable class sizes or of cutting teaching hours to the bare minimum. A malign combination of financial cuts, powerful and inconsistently applied policy levers, and tactical college management has led to a workforce with worse pay and conditions than that in our schools and universities (see Chapter 5). Colleges have responded to their circumstances by taking decisions that move them outside their immediate local community. There have been long-distance mergers, some national contracting, and the development of overseas work with the support of the UK government (Department of Business, Innovation and Skills, 2013). Despite the current rhetoric around localism, it still makes most sense for a college to seek to diversify its sources of income to protect against the instability of core funding.

It is sad to note that, while information technology has supported some changes in teaching and management practices, via virtual learning environments and e-mail, its primary use for the last twenty years has been for command and control. Its potential, meanwhile, to make FE both more responsive and more accessible to learners has been displaced or overshadowed by that preoccupation, and by its effects on provider behaviour. It may also be the case that heavy investment in e-learning capital is not consistent with rapid, unpredictable, and externally directed change.

This series of observations leads us to one overarching conclusion. The way in which policy levers have been used in FE has proved to be an effective method of ensuring compliance with government instructions and of delivering a rapid response to changes in policy. The outcomes for users of FE, however, have seldom been as planned or expected and occasionally were resoundingly negative. Furthermore, one clear consequence of a nationally managed system is that when problems emerge they are usually widespread. Ubiquity of problems leads, in a perverse way, to greater pressure for central intervention and an ever-repeating cycle.

The evidence for this conclusion is strong. It lies not only among the plethora of central initiatives, sometimes followed by disappointment or scandal and another policy change. It lies also in the fact that, after twenty years of increasingly high-stakes inspection, the proportion of colleges performing well (or badly) is about the same as it was at the outset. It lies in the fact that the criticisms of our vocational education system (whether justified or not) are about the same as they were before two decades of constant 'reform'. It seems most unlikely, therefore, that a continuation of current policies will make the system better. If controls stay the same as they have been, colleges will inevitably focus on avoiding failure, however that is defined from day to day, rather than building success. Perhaps a hands-off regime such as that of the universities with legally enforceable curricular freedom; a single funding agency with substantial sector representation and little government direction at quantum level; and a sector-owned quality peer review and improvement body, would be a better way forward. It is a formula that the universities have shown to be practicable and low-risk; there is nothing intrinsic about further education that precludes using the same approach.

References
Adult Learning Inspectorate (ALI)/ Ofsted (2001) *The Common Inspection Framework for Inspection of Post-16 Education and Training.* London: ALI/Ofsted.

— (2005) *The Common Inspection Framework for Inspection of Post-16 Education and Training from 2005.* London: ALI/Ofsted.

Department for Business, Innovation and Skills (BIS) (2010) *Skills for Sustainable Growth.* Online. www.gov.uk/government/uploads/system/uploads/attachment_data/file/32368/10-1274-skills-for-sustainable-growth-strategy.pdf (accessed 16 December 2014).

— (2013) *Internationl Education Strategy: Global growth and prosperity.* Online. www.gov.uk/government/publications/international-education-strategy-global-growth-and-prosperity (accessed 31 March 2015).

— (2014a) *Future Development of Further Education Loans.* Online. www.gov.uk/government/uploads/system/uploads/attachment_data/file/321921/bis-14-861-future-development-of-loans-in-further-education-consultation-v2.pdf (accessed 16 December 2014).

— (2014b) *The Future of Apprenticeships in England: Funding reform technical consultation.* Online. www.gov.uk/government/uploads/system/uploads/attachment_data/file/302235/bis-14-597-future-of-apprenticeships-in-england-funding-reform-technical-consultatation.pdf (accessed 16 December 2014).

— (2014c) *Outcome-based Success Rates, experimental data 2010/11.* Online. www.gov.uk/government/uploads/system/uploads/attachment_data/file/342727/bis-14-1004-adult-further-education-outcome-based-success-measures-experimental-data-v15.pdf (accessed 16 December 2014).

Department for Education and Skills (DfES) (1987) *Joint Efficiency Study of Non-Advanced Further Education.* London: DfES.

— (2002) *Success for All.* London: DfES.

— (2006) *Further Education White Paper, Raising Skills, Improving Life Chances.* London: DfES.

Education Select Committee (1998) *Further Education.* Online. www.publications. parliament.uk/pa/cm199899/cmselect/cmeduemp/56/5603.htm (accessed 16 December 2014).

— (2006) *Further Education* including minutes of evidence provided by Terry Melia, HMI, and ALI.

Hayes, J. (2010) Speech to AoC conference. Online. www.gov.uk/government/ speeches/association-of-colleges-annual-conference--2 (accessed 16 December 2014).

HM Government (2013) *International education, global growth and prosperity.* Online. www.gov.uk/government/uploads/system/uploads/attachment_data/ file/340600/bis-13-1081-international-education-global-growth-and-prosperity- revised.pdf (accessed 16 December 2014).

HM Treasury (2005) *Reducing Administrative Burdens, Effective Inspection and Enforcement.* London: HMT.

Innovation Universities Skills and Science Select Committee (2009) *Reskilling for Recovery, After Leitch.* Online. www.publications.parliament.uk/pa/cm/cmdius. htm (accessed 16 December 2014).

Further Education Funding Council (FEFC) (1992) *Funding Learning.* Coventry: FEFC.

— (1993a) *Recurrent Funding Methodology for 1994–95.* Coventry: FEFC.

— (1993b) *Assessing Achievement.* Coventry: FEFC.

— (1994) *Measuring Achievement: Performance indicators for further education.* Coventry: FEFC.

— (1997) *Learning Works, Widening participation in further education, report by Helena Kennedy QC.* Coventry: FEFC.

Gravatt, J., and Silver, R. (2000) 'Partnerships with the community'. In Smithers, A., and Robinson, P. (eds) *Further Education Re-formed.* London: Falmer Press, 111–23.

Keep, E. (2014) *What Does Skills Policy Look Like Now the Money has run Out?* Online. www.aoc.co.uk/sites/default/files/What_Does_Skills_Policy_Look_Like_ Now_the_Money_Has_Run_Out__0.pdf (accessed 16 December 2014).

Learning and Skills Council (LSC) (2005) *Through Inclusion to Excellence.* Coventry: LSC.

— (2006) *Managing the Mix and Balance of Provision.* Coventry: LSC.

— (2007a) *Framework for Excellence.* Coventry: LSC.

— (2007b) *Identifying and Managing Underperformance.* Coventry: LSC.

McClure, R. (2000) 'Recurrent funding'. In Smithers, A., and Robinson, P. (eds) *Further Education Re-formed.* London: Falmer Press 25–40.

National Audit Office (NAO) (2014) *Investigation into Financial Support for Students at Alternative Higher Education Providers.* Online. www.nao.org.uk/ wp-content/uploads/2014/12/Investigation-into-financial-support-for-students- at-alternative-higher-education-providers.pdf

Office for Standards in Education (Ofsted) (2011) *Chief Inspector's Annual Report.* London: Ofsted.

— (2012) *Learner View: Helping learners have a choice.* London: Ofsted.

Stuart, N., Lucas, D., and McKie, D. (2000) *Early Lessons from Training Standards Council Inspections*. Online. http://webarchive.nationalarchives.gov.uk/20130401151715/http://www.education.gov.uk/publications/eOrderingDownload/RB224.pdf (accessed 16 December 2014).

Training Standards Council (TSC) (1998) *Raising the Standard: Guidelines for self-assessment and inspection of work-based training*. Training Standards Council.

— (2000) *Annual Report of Training Standards Council 1998/99*. Online. http://dera.ioe.ac.uk/9882/1/Annual_report_of_the_Training_Standards_Council_1998-1999.pdf (accessed 16 December 2014).

Wolf, A. (2009) *An Adult Approach to Further Education*. Online. www.iea.org.uk/sites/default/files/publications/files/upldbook498pdf.pdf

— (2011) *Review of Vocational Education: The Wolf report*. Available at: www.gov.uk/government/uploads/system/uploads/attachment_data/file/180504/DFE-00031-2011.pdf (accessed 16 November 2014).

Chapter 9

Leadership and leaders of colleges
Tom Jupp

As Abraham Lincoln said, 'He who moulds public sentiment goes deeper than he who enacts statutes or pronounces decisions.' This chapter is based on the proposition that responding to and shaping the way staff and students see their work is the central task of college leadership.

This chapter has been much influenced by a series of 13 structured interviews and discussions with people who have many years' experience as principals and in other significant positions in the sector. Individual acknowledgements are made at the end of the chapter. A number of case studies and quotations are drawn from research into the first 20 years of City and Islington College (Jupp and Morris, 2013).

Leadership is both determined by and shapes the culture and context of a college. Everyone interviewed agreed that: 'There is a possibility that the only thing of real importance that leaders do is to create and manage culture ... the unique talent of leaders is their ability to work with culture' (Schein, 1987: 2).

There probably would not be the same agreement as to what 'culture' is, but clearly we are talking about things such as individual and collective behaviour, communication, and values, involving all the staff and students in order to get things done through tasks and targets and long-term vision. Culture is expressed in the phrase, 'The way we do things here.'

Context is also very important to leadership. At any given time, a college may be enjoying success or struggling with problems or often experiencing a mixture of both. Building on the discussion in Chapter 8, this chapter will illustrate how government policy and the leadership of inspection and funding agencies have been a potent force affecting leadership in colleges. There is also the emotional and psychological dimension of the context and culture of each college; what Ken Warman calls, 'the micro politics of personalities, including governors and the darker side of institutional functioning.'

Leadership is a contested concept. This chapter does not focus on theories of leadership and management – of which there are said to be more than 350 – or on checklists of leadership competencies. These theories and lists have value, particularly for individuals and individual colleges. Nor shall we look at Ofsted accounts of how colleges improve and succeed, written on the basis of inspection evidence and much studied in colleges (Ofsted, 2004; Ofsted, 2012). Books and gurus have also been influential. Three highly influential books in FE have been Senge, 1990; Goleman, 1998 and Collins, 2001. As Lynne Sedgmore put it, 'Leadership books are written from a particular perspective. But leadership is complex; it is relational, contextual, and dependent on the individuals who are exercising it.'

This chapter focuses on the changing culture and context of colleges and the emerging consensus that effective leadership requires clarity of educational mission, backed by appropriate values shared at every level in a college. We must also bear in mind the wider ideological dimension of leadership over these 21 years and how this has affected public services generally and colleges in particular. From the early 1980s, the concept of leadership by consensus and collaboration was regarded by many in government as a recipe for stagnation and corporatism. The professions were attacked for being focused on the interests of staff and not being 'customer-led'. The job of leadership was seen as changing all this with rigorous management accountable to external audit. By 2000, there was some decline in this thinking towards a more balanced view, but also to more centralized initiatives, targets, control, and planning (see Chapter 8). The concept of 'entrepreneurial leadership' has become more significant in recent years. And in the case of education, there has been increasing conviction by government that education needs to be driven by the market place and valued for the returns it produces in terms of employment (Leitch, 2006).

What is leadership and who provides it?

'In any organization, people can only work within the climate that is set. That's what leadership and management are about.' (Sir Derek Hutt, cited in the Times Educational Supplement, 2 January 2004: 10)

A successful college has to foster an ethos of professional relationships from top to bottom and has to transmit this culture to all new staff and students; continuity of successful culture is essential. Frank McLoughlin summed it up: 'It's the college values and core purpose – success for students – which defines what a professional person is in the college. Professionalism stands for high standards and teamwork both inside the college and with partners outside. Being professional does not mean top-down conformity. It means sharing a common value base and purpose within a system which is both, "loose and tight".'

Spreading leadership throughout the college is the hallmark of an effective principal and senior team. (Since 1993, heads of colleges have been chief executives and accounting officers for their colleges. The term 'principal' is used throughout this chapter. This is preferred over CEO because it emphasizses the professional nature of the job rather than the generic function.) The *evidence* of leadership will be found in the way staff at all levels see their jobs; how well supported they feel; whether they recognize their contribution to the college and feel recognized; whether they feel they are listened to.

> **A MEMBER OF THE SECURITY STAFF TALKS ABOUT HIS RESPONSIBILITIES**
>
> Arnie joined the college in 2004 after working in clubs. He came to England aged 17 and learned English from scratch.
>
> 'Student behaviour is much better than when I started. This is thanks to team effort, including the principal, the senior manager on this site, and all the staff working closely to back us up ... At the end of the year, half the students come and shake my hand. I feel I've done something. You get some grief at the beginning of the year – "kissing their teeth". When they enter I say "Good morning" not "Have you got your ID?" You have to be sensitive in the way you treat people. You explain the reason why. Everywhere I go locally I see ex-students. They say, "Hello security guard." I feel I've done something good. It's the same for all colleagues. We have a standard, a reputation.'

An ineffective principal fails to create a sense of common values and purpose across the whole college and this in turn allows the erosion of accountability and of ambition for students. It helps in understanding leadership to 'turn the coin over' and examine what creates 'followership'. Leaders talk in ways and create a vision which inspires people; they show empathy and understanding for staff; and they, in turn, earn the trust of staff.

Since the 1980s, the importance of leadership has often been emphasized in contrast to management: 'Managers do things right, whilst leaders do the right thing' (Holden, 2004). In 1993, the emphasis was upon senior teams managing their colleges more effectively. Then the emphasis shifted towards leadership. This sometimes favoured the notion of 'heroic' leadership; principals' jobs are to change everything so as to produce 'continuous change' and 'transformational change'. But a new management structure or a merger is only useful if it improves classroom quality or contributes to better strategic positioning for a college. If not, such changes absorb huge energy for little gain. Ian Pryce commented, 'Colleges have not been immune from the cult of the chief executive officer (CEO). The relative power of the principal compared with the governing body can allow principals to make big changes even if no obvious change is required.'

Effective principals must also be effective managers because without good management they cannot deliver and they will not know what is going on. As Geoff Hall put it, 'Leaders are expected to have a clear vision for their institution but .... they are also expected to have a firm grip on the tiller.' Above all, a principal's and senior team's management and organizational skills are essential to deliver a vision by establishing and monitoring appropriate systems to reach operational objectives. So, in this sense, leadership and management behaviours are inseparable.

Most principals understand that they are always 'in role' and that their behaviour sets a model for the institution. Sarah Robinson stated, 'I am very conscious of my role and position and that I must set standards. I wouldn't ask staff to do something I wouldn't do myself' (157 Group, 2014). If the principal is a bad time manager, how can he/she expect classroom punctuality by teachers? Setting an example is less well understood by all managers. But effective leadership requires everyone at every level to accept that they are always in role and that their behaviour affects the whole college. This is particularly true of the impact that teachers and support staff have on students. Staff in turn take their lead from their own managers. At incorporation, many middle managers found taking up a leadership role difficult, particularly when dealing with poorly performing staff. Many of these managers had to move from personal relationships to professional ones. As Wally Brown said, 'First-line managers have the most difficult job. It is difficult for them to build authority.' In many colleges, developing these staff as leaders as well as managers took some years and has been a focus for staff development.

It is achieving high standards and teamwork throughout the whole college that makes a successful college sustainable. The characteristics of the effective principal have not changed over the last 21 years. But the work of principals has changed significantly. First, they are managing larger organizations. Most general further education colleges (GFEs) are about 50 per cent larger than they were in 1993. This is because the volume of work with students has increased and the number of colleges has reduced from 463 to 336 through mergers (I am grateful to Julian Gravatt of the Association of Colleges for this information). Secondly, the environment for colleges has become higher risk, particularly in the last six years – because of significant policy changes and large reductions in funding – so external relations and the strategic positioning of colleges has become a more important and time-consuming task. Both these factors point to the importance of distributed forms of leadership.

Is the sector better led overall in 2014 than in 1993? Most long-standing participants would say definitely 'yes'. But they might add that there is a lack of outstanding leadership; it is more technocratic than visionary.

Incorporation, leadership, and managerialism

In autumn 1992, the government launched independence for colleges from local authorities with an Oscar-style event at Lancaster House for principals attended by the Prime Minister, John Major.

The Secretary of State told colleges the plan:

- reduce unit costs and work towards a uniform national level of funding – more money for some and less for others
- expand numbers of students by up to 25 per cent over three years and improve retention
- introduce new teaching contracts as a condition of funding to contribute to reducing costs and to reducing the power of the trades unions.

This was a major agenda for college leadership. But there was much more to come. Colleges were to be independent within a management and financial framework laid down by the new Further Education Funding Council (FEFC). The key to the new national system was the funding methodology based upon paying for the successful delivery of qualifications rather than periods of study (see Chapter 8). Behind this, there would be new systems of individual student records (ISR), and external auditing of these records. This was a revolution that required colleges to change most of their systems. Roger McClure later wrote: 'The funding methodology has taken on an almost mythical significance, being held responsible for nearly every woe real or imagined' (McClure, 2000: 37).

The FEFC also brought in the valuable management requirements for colleges to produce three-year strategic plans with three-year financial forecasts and to undergo systematic inspection on a four-year cycle. These new requirements were potentially empowering for college leadership.

What happened within the first couple of years of incorporation had a major impact for at least ten years and in some respects up to now. These changes profoundly affected the tasks and style of management and leadership. As Ian Pryce, new to the sector and working for the FEFC in 1993, explained, 'Principals were often keen on being "managerial" at the expense of providing "leadership"'. He considered that many principals lacked ambition for their students as well as the intellectual clout to engage with a long-term vision for their colleges.

To understand what happened, we have to recognize that there were two major weaknesses at the heart of the running of most colleges in 1993. Colleges had neither an accurate picture of what their students were achieving nor effective control of finances and the management of resources. Real accountability to students, to governors, and to funders is central to stewardship and leadership; it was largely missing.

Accountability for colleges had historically been on the basis of student enrolment. It is difficult to believe now, but well under half of enrolled students at most colleges ever successfully completed their courses. Many colleges only had incomplete and misleading student data. It took several years to build a culture of transparency and honesty of data as a fundamental requirement. There could be no consistent quality without transparent data.

THE BUSINESS SUPPORT SERVICES TASK

'Here was a college rooted in local authority control, thrust into an arena where it had to be run for the public good, but in a business-like way.'

'I found huge knowledge, loyalty, and commitment to students in an inner city environment, but no awareness of how to ensure management, communication, marketing, and finances were in order to support the educational purpose.'

Jack Morris, Chair of Governors City and Islington College

Finally, colleges had to introduce new contracts for teaching staff. This was one of the most difficult new tasks in many urban colleges, particularly given that they had no experience of managing human resources (HR). FEFC offered no guidance on HR, unlike finance, estates, and data. From the point of view of teaching staff, the whole agenda of change seemed remote and irrelevant – a waste of energy and money.

The changes were uncomfortable, involved huge amounts of work and often involved restructuring and redundancies. But in all colleges there were staff who wanted to see changes and would support them. A number of colleges rose to the leadership challenge by keeping the educational mission in clear focus when so much of the change was about processes and systems; by ensuring those in favour of change felt consulted and included; and by being willing to engage with those who felt largely negative and undervalued. As Susan Pember put it, 'You've got to like a good debate with teachers who like to challenge.'

Too many college managers had little experience of taking tough decisions and did not like arguments that publically challenged their views. It was convenient for them to retreat into a management role that focused on the imperatives of finance and numbers.

There was thus something of an educational leadership vacuum. Bill Stubbs and the senior FEFC staff were setting the agenda for colleges and had the authority to set the tone for leadership and vision for the sector. The style set was authoritarian and managerial and this encouraged principals to see their jobs in these terms. At an early FEFC conference, Stubbs spoke to principals before the minister arrived, warning them against any expressions of dissent or criticism. The tone was that of a school assembly addressed by the headmaster. Colleges that did not accept large cuts to their budgets were told to accept reality. FEFC considered the best colleges to be the ones with low costs who were eager to expand rapidly and take over more expensive ones.

Many people feel that at this point colleges started to become too 'compliant and deferential.' Geoff Hall suggested that there was no intellectual level of educational debate coming from colleges to challenge central leadership. There were too many principals who were 'doers and hewers' and wanted to just get on with things. At meetings of principals, there was little discussion of educational purposes and values.

There were substantial numbers of colleges that were flourishing in the new system – Clarendon College, Nottingham, for example. It was a 'can do' college run by command and control. The atmosphere of the college was one of opportunity and dynamism for staff. And by 1999, Clarendon had taken over three other colleges and the principal had been made a dame.

There was a great hotchpotch of leadership ideas in circulation in the early years of incorporation. Managerial language was much in fashion and educational language less so. The approach to leadership pushed by the top of the Education Department and the FEFC tended to be full of metaphors from manufacturing and retailing. We were reminded that we were now in a post-Fordist era and we should not provide everyone with a black car but with a customized vehicle!

There were two issues in the early years that produced great difficulties for college leadership – staff contracts and franchising. The way the contracts dispute with teaching staff was handled bred an atmosphere of negativity and confrontation in many colleges that stood in the way of other important changes for several years (see Chapter 5). Staff efficiency needed to improve in 1993, but a group of principals set up the Colleges Employers Forum (CEF) led by an industrial relations specialist who favoured confrontation and paying whatever cost was necessary to smash the union. The contracts dispute was a mess that, after many disputes, gradually fizzled out as colleges found the only way forward was to negotiate locally and to fragment. The CEF also encouraged colleges to adopt other HR strategies that were detrimental. For example, they encouraged the employment of part-time teachers through agencies. This greatly damaged the role of part-timers who were often a source of up-to-date professional/vocational expertise. Teaching was being treated as a commodity to be obtained as cheaply as possible. It is one thing to outsource security, it is quite another to outsource teaching, which is a college's core business.

The other important issue was franchising. This was conceived as an arrangement under which colleges could fund provision in other locations through small and community-based providers: a sound concept. Colleges with large allocations for growth spotted that they could fund large scale programmes, take a substantial cut for doing very little, and thus avoid financial difficulties. Franchising ballooned, targets were hit and exceeded, and eventually the Treasury got nervous. Other colleges had to watch their budgets being cut and potential full-time students were denied opportunities while the money was used to pay Tesco for providing National Vocational Qualification Level 1 to shelf-filling staff. Guardino Rospigliosi summed it up: 'Franchising offers ... an ersatz activity which displaces the beneficial experience of mainstream further education' (Rospigliosi, 2000: 152). FEFC publically endorsed large-scale franchising.

Staff contracts and franchising damaged trust in the leadership of colleges in the long run, particularly with the new Labour Government in 1997, possibly encouraging the more centralized approach that was brought in through the Learning and Skills Council (LSC). These issues showed a lack of strategic purpose to benefit young people and adults and a lack of ethical principles in the use of public money. As staff said, and many principals believed, finance overwhelmingly mattered and far too often led.

Was it inevitable that contracts and franchising were handled like this? Yes, in the sense that a majority of principals supported what happened and controlled the college associations. No, in the sense that a number of colleges took independent lines on both issues and were no less successful as colleges. When open-ended franchising was stopped, some colleges were to pay a high price. It was time for a change from the policy of 'stack 'em high' regardless of who 'they' were. By 1996/7 the mood music was changing: there were more colleges calling for a stronger vision and purpose in further education and the managerial ideology was declining.

Leadership for the teaching and learning college

In 1996/7, changes started that were to affect profoundly the context and priorities for leadership of the sector. The FEFC published *Inclusive Learning* (Tomlinson, 1996) with an emphasis on pedagogy. Next came *Learning Works* (Kennedy, 1997), which argued that a key aspect of the work of colleges should be to widen participation for the disadvantaged, and colleges should be rewarded for doing so. And the latter report set the long-term aspiration of every young person and adult without a Level 3 qualification having an entitlement to government funding to study for one. All this chimed with the new government's inclinations. The FEFC inspectorate was changing its emphasis towards student results and funding supplements were introduced for students from disadvantaged areas. David Melville took over leadership of the FEFC in autumn 1996 with a more consultative style and an emphasis on independence for colleges.

New priorities for leadership

The focus upon quality was underway. Colleges embarked on a journey in which more and more emphasis has been given to ambition for students and to outstanding teaching and learning to achieve this. There have been plenty of problems on the way for college leadership: too much emphasis on statistical results narrowing educational aspirations for students; too much interference from LSC officials who made bureaucracy seem more important than teaching and learning. The biggest external influence has been the Ofsted Common Inspection Framework (Ofsted, 2014a), which has gradually moved from mainly focusing on results to focusing also on the quality of teaching and learning as a limiting grade. This shift was anticipated in the Schools' White Paper 2010: 'All the evidence ... shows the most important factor in determining how well students do is the quality of teachers and teaching (Department for Education, 2010: 9).

There is a degree of consensus that the leadership of learning involves four key areas of practice:

- Investing time and resources to promote the professional development of staff.
- Having a close involvement in the management of the teaching programme.

- Setting clear directions for the organization, including the centrality of teaching and learning.
- Establishing a culture that respects the professionalism of teachers and empowers them to innovate.

(157 Group and CfBT Education Trust, 2011: 30)

The Commission on Adult Vocational Teaching and Learning (CAVTL) reported in 2013, mapping new processes and practices to raise quality and engage more effectively with employment (CAVTL, 2013). Also in 2013, and partly arising from work for CAVTL, the 157 Group published a report on pedagogic leadership of vocational education addressing the paradox that 'pedagogy is both felt to be a concept tainted by academia in the real world of vocational learning *and* considered by vocational leaders to be too unsubtle for their contexts' (157 Group and City & Guilds, 2013: 12). Leaders, it was suggested, need to engage more fully and invest in the vocational classroom; too many find it difficult to engage with specialized vocational areas outside their own experience. In 2014, the government announced funding for a research centre for vocational education.

Mike Sheehan has been an advocate for 'the rediscovery of teaching and learning' by college leadership. He believes many senior managers need to refocus their jobs. He argues that successful leadership is about striking the right balance between four aspects of the jobs: leading learning, standards, and student support; employability and educating the whole person; leading on business services; and undertaking external strategic leadership.

By the early 2000s, senior management in many colleges provided more professional development for middle managers, who hold such a crucial role in the leadership of teaching and learning. Middle leaders need to feel that they have collective ownership of the culture of the college, and that, as middle managers, they are understood by the college and listened to. This must be genuinely reflected in college practice. For example, one college actively involved all its managers in defining a management behaviour framework for themselves over a period of a year. Subsequently, the framework was tied in with every aspect of staff selection procedures, work planning, support, and supervision and appraisal. And extensive learning materials were developed on the college staff intranet, covering every aspect of the behaviour framework.

The role of the Centre for Excellence in Leadership (CEL)

The most important initiative in sector-wide leadership development came in 2003: the Centre for Excellence in Leadership (CEL) was established as part of the New Public Service Management initiative, which set up 11 Leadership Academies. CEL developed a comprehensive programme, including coaching, in-house organizational development, and peer review with other colleges, as well as courses at every level of leadership and preparation for leadership. The CEL approach encouraged collective and distributive leadership and was underpinned by the conviction that good leadership requires a person to know her/himself.

CEL also addressed diversity in leadership and worked to improve the representation of women and people from black and ethnic minority groups in senior posts. There has been a substantial increase in the number of women principals since 1993. In 1999, 19 per cent of principals were women and this figure had risen to 44 per cent by 2014. (These figures on diversity of principals were provided by the Association of Colleges from their senior pay review. Figures before 1999 are not available.) Progress with the appointment of black and minority ethnic senior leaders has been much less successful. The LSC took up this issue in 2002 with the Black Leadership Initiative (Walker and Fletcher, 2013). CEL promoted a range of initiatives, but in 2014, only 12 principals (between 3 and 4 per cent) came from black and minority ethinic backgrounds. This contrasts sharply with the rising percentage among learners and staff.

Failure to sustain success

Several people have suggested that the test of a successful college is that it remains consistently good over a number of years and over several principals. Only about a dozen colleges have passed this test, according to Geoff Hall. There have been a number of cases of successful colleges declining dramatically, particularly after a new principal arrives.

If college success depends on leadership establishing an effective and shared culture, then the transmission of this culture to new staff, including senior staff, is critically important. It can feel difficult for a new principal taking over at a successful college. He/she may introduce changes as a means of establishing him or herself. What Wally Brown described as a 'year zero mindset': 'I don't want to hear about the past. We start here.'

BARNFIELD COLLEGE: A STORY OF RADICAL DECLINE

The college built up an impressive range of vocational courses for young people and adults. The college's mission fitted well with the area and complemented the successful Luton Sixth Form College.

In June 2003, Ofsted judged the college provision as very good and the leadership and management as outstanding. The successful principal of the college retired shortly before the next inspection in 2007 when the college was judged outstanding with, 'Inspirational leadership and ... a clear strategic direction.' But in April 2012, Ofsted stated, 'All aspects of provision ... require improvement.'

By 2012, the management, leadership, and organization of the college had completely changed. The Barnfield Federation ran an Academy Chain consisting of six secondary schools, four primary schools, and a nursery. All these schools and the college itself were linked in the federation by complex management, governance, and financial relationships. The secondary schools were regarded as highly successful, but the college was a different story. College turnover by 2012/13 had declined from £35 million to £26 million and the college ran a deficit of £7.3 million. In the same year, the CEO of the federation, previously college principal and still the accounting officer for the college, received a knighthood.

After complaints in 2013, the Education Funding Agency and the Skills Funding Agency both set up investigations. The reports published in 2014 found 15 breaches of regulations, including governor conflicts of interest, lack of procedures, double funding of students, and malpractice on success rates.

Leadership questions:

- Was the college pursuing a new strategy inappropriate for the area served and why had the governors agreed it?
- Had the changes of management and other personnel resulted in a loss of the college's successful culture?
- Had senior management invested too much time and funds in the academies?

- Was there a lack of delegation to the college within the overall federation and had the CEO effectively lost interest in the college while achieving success with the schools?
- Did the governors know what was going on?

Leadership difficulties can also arise when the strategic position of a college becomes difficult to sustain, particularly colleges with large amounts of adult work in recent years. On the other hand, colleges that have always had a substantial amount of full-time, Level 3 provision and a majority of full-time 16–19-year-old students or have repositioned themselves in this way are now better placed. Colleges more dependent on vocational and adult work have experienced a maelstrom of changes. The leadership of these colleges has had to strike a principled balance between being opportunist and the long-term task of repositioning their colleges within the ecology of local provision, including through merger. Sometimes the options have been limited and in other cases the wrong choices, or no choices, have been made.

The formation of leadership

There is no evidence that suggests successful principals come from any particular background. Although there are several examples of successful principals who have come from outside colleges and outside education, the majority are always likely to come from within. So the arrangements for the professional development that prepares future leaders are important. But when we look at an actual example, we see there are so many other things in people's backgrounds, experience, their models of leadership, and their personalities that contribute.

THE FORMATION OF A PRINCIPAL: A CASE STUDY

Helen taught humanities for several years in inner-city secondary schools before she worked in two local colleges: 'I was a radical feminist who was passionate about education for the less privileged.'

At incorporation, she was on secondment as a 14–19-year adviser. She came back to her newly merged college as a curriculum manager. She supported the focus on improving student outcomes and changing staff cultures. 'I never accepted it was OK for staff to turn up late or for students to give in tatty work.' Equally she always accepted that student numbers had to be viable. Helen was given a free hand by a supportive Head of School and successfully sorted out weak areas.

Helen moved to become a Head of School in a large college with an outstanding record. The principal spent a great deal of time out of the college and 'created a reign of fear and terror when she was around.' Helen considered the student results were poor. After two terms, she left.

She moved to a large and successful tertiary style college as new Head of E-Learning and ICT. 'I found it very isolating and learned a lot about the culture of "them and us" between teaching and support staff. I understood the role of support staff unlike before.' At this time, she started an MA in management. It enabled her to stand back and understand more about how organizations work.

Helen was soon promoted to the senior management team as Director of Learner Services. 'I was working in one college, going one place, with a principal totally committed and many managers at all levels who had come up through the college and really knew the place. And there were lots of good teachers.' The best professional development Helen remembers was in-house. Later, she attended the Aspiring Principals' course.

After five years as a college director, Helen moved to another large college to become a Vice-Principal - Curriculum and Learners. The next inspection found serious weaknesses. The ethos of the college was trusting of staff - 'difficult people had been managed around rather than dealt with'. Helen stopped 'trusting' people and introduced much greater professional accountability. 'My values and concepts hadn't changed, but I learned to "drive" performance management. People had to be closely supported to achieve targets. Programmes that couldn't perform were closed.'

The results were successful and today the college achieves excellent results. Helen took over as interim principal going into the next inspection. The college was judged 'good'. 'I couldn't have possibly done it without the support of the whole college. Everyone believed we were entitled to a good result. It was a huge team effort. But I still aspire to "outstanding" ...'

Helen's career has been driven by her educational values. She only came to recognize her potential for senior leadership as a result of fifteen years' experience in both curriculum and cross-college leadership roles.

Professional development did not stand out in her reflections. She learned from her own managers and Helen is driven by professionalism and sheer determination to achieve.

Current and future leadership challenges

The funding landscape

College leaders have experienced substantial financial cuts following the recession of 2008 and from the policy of cutting adult provision to pay for 16–19-year old provision. These financial reductions will continue into the foreseeable future. So college leaders face a double challenge of both reducing internal costs and strategically repositioning a college away from adult provision. Even the senior civil servant responsible has been reported as saying that the sector will face financial difficulties for years (*FE Week*, 1 December 2014). Gary Warke expressed the view that, 'FE will never be the same again. We have to look to the future.'

Provision for post-19-year olds and certainly for post-25-year olds will no longer be primarily publically funded. Ian Pryce asked, 'Just because public funding is withdrawn doesn't mean the demand is not there anymore. We can find new ways. Why do we talk about full-cost provision as if it is something different and marginal?' This poses new types of leadership challenges in terms of judging risk and commercial marketing.

There are dangers for leadership in this context of ongoing financial pressures. Principals may feel under pressure to reduce management delegation, professional development, and new curriculum developments. But the bottom line is not money; it is student success. Experience in the 1990s demonstrates the dangers of confusing money and mission.

Governance

While monitoring of sound finance is vital, governors also have to ensure that leaders, under the severe pressure of financial difficulties, do not take their eyes off the educational vision and mission. Government concern with the adequacy of governance has been reflected in the research commissioned from AoC in 2013, undertaken by Susan Pember, and the recently published new code of practice (AoC, 2014). Too many governing bodies are thought to lack 'grip' on their colleges, particularly in respect of college strategy and holding leadership to account (see Chapter 7). Some principals consider that leadership from governors will inevitably be inadequate because people cannot be recruited with the knowledge and the commitment to do the job adequately. Others hold the view that many college leadership teams invest too little in empowering governors to undertake this important public service.

Strategic positioning and collaboration

External leadership and strategic positioning with local and regional partnerships is of great importance for the future of colleges (see Chapter 10). The financial position is destabilizing, as is the wasteful creation of new school sixth forms and training providers. At the same time, college leaders should be confident that they have much to build upon; colleges are the main providers of full-time education and training for 16–18-year olds (Ofsted, 2014b) as well as possessing unique strengths with adults and with higher vocational qualifications. A college has first to maintain itself as a centre/series of centres of local demand and community links with students and employers. Some colleges have paid dear in the past for over committing to government initiatives, for example, through franchising. Strategic leadership requires both qualities of vision and foresight and the capacity to gain the confidence of other institutions. It is worth remembering that an extended bulge of 16-year olds will reach colleges after 2020.

Over the last ten years, colleges have developed their strategic positions in a variety of ways (see Chapter 6). Some have provided opportunities for 14–16-year olds and are now becoming 14–16 college pathfinders. Others have sponsored and supported new schools: academies, university technical colleges (UTCs), studio schools, and free schools.

Supporting schools builds local leadership and influence and may help support college corporate services, but it also uses senior time and can carry dangers, as we saw with Barnfield College. For this reason, some colleges are pulling back and wanting to strengthen their core business.

BEDFORD COLLEGE: MISSION-LED REPOSITIONING AND CONSISTENT GROWTH OVER TEN YEARS

The college aims to be a centre of excellence and leadership for skills and vocational education for the communities served, becoming 'stitched into the fabric of Bedford.' This has been the criterion against which all decisions on development have been taken.

The college first improved its existing vocational portfolio and then opened new niche vocational areas with regional potential. Apprenticeships were of poor quality and seen as high risk. The college again invested heavily and now offers high-quality apprenticeships.

Bedford College took over the FE work of Shuttleworth Agricultural College, which kept its distinctive culture and brand, with Bedford providing a range of strong corporate services, including quality assurance and staff development. More recently, existing A level provision was closed and a free-standing Bedford Sixth Form was set up, again with a distinctive student culture and brand, which is proving popular.

The college has sponsored an academy and is rescuing a UTC. In 2015, it will sponsor a technical academy for 13–19-year olds – an upper free school.

Bedford College has also led a college group in the South East Midlands for its Local Enterprise Partnership (LEP).

Partnerships have been important to the development of the college both in terms of helping it to deliver courses for 14–16-year olds and to provide strong progression pathways into its provision from local schools.

Challenges for teaching and learning

Colleges are the major players in addressing the needs of the 40 per cent of young people at 16 who have not done well in the school system. Bold college leadership has to seize ownership of curriculum, assessment, and quality debates and avoid the unintended consequences of targets. Colleges themselves must invest substantial staff and resources in a more developed alternative pedagogy of blending work skills and soft employability skills, including mathematics and English and creating 'lines of sight' to work. They must capture and hold this agenda and not allow Ofsted to set the agenda. Solutions require new partnerships and particularly more innovation with IT. Leadership of ideas is required, such as that emerging in relation to vocational teaching and learning as a result of CAVTL. Success may lead to colleges being able to customize qualifications in the future and even to awarding qualifications themselves.

Mergers, expansion, and leadership structures

Colleges have become fewer and bigger over the last 21 years. The signs are that financial and marketplace recruitment pressures will continue to result in college mergers in the coming few years. The new FE Commissioner recommended three college mergers in 2013/14 out of only 11 interventions (Department of Business, Innovation and Skills, 2014). And 9 of these interventions were caused by major financial difficulties. Larger colleges have developed distributed leadership from the first round of mergers in the early days of incorporation. More recently, colleges have designated themselves groups, for example the Hull Group of Colleges. The group structure is a decentralized model for college mergers and expansions into training companies, where distinct brands and cultures need to be maintained. These arrangements are well proven for large colleges as providing decentralization and delegation in the context of strong performance management and distinct local identities.

There are many factors that make for a successful merger (Centre for Education and Industry, University of Warwick, 2003) and one is strong leadership. Particular skills of leadership are required to change, blend, and support different cultures as well as introduce efficient new business systems. Mergers are usually takeovers and require leadership to build internal confidence in turbulent and emotional times. At the same time, the natural tendency to become too inward looking during the years of merger must be avoided.

A new structure has emerged in some large college organizations of having a CEO in overall charge and a principal responsible for the internal running of the college. This model seeks to address the competing demands in large colleges for external and internal leadership; and the balance between leadership of the business side and leadership of teaching and learning. Could this arrangement destroy the right balance between the two sides of college leadership? The structure may also encourage the CEO to spend too much time away from the college and become engrossed in projects and ideas that do not fit college reality; a danger which has been demonstrated over the years.

Government intervention

Inspection has proved a great support and incentive for improvement since incorporation. And recently Ofsted has raised a number of important policy questions, such as the nature of careers education (Ofsted, 2014b). But Ofsted is widely seen in colleges as punitive, regularly shifting focus, and less than comprehensive in the way it judges colleges. Have the FE Commissioners for GFEs and SFCs been created to balance the current limitations of Ofsted inspection, particularly in relation to finance and governance?

Is government too preoccupied with audit and intervention modelled on business and finance? Data are considered adequate to monitor performance, but do not tell the whole story. Less formal ways of monitoring colleges regionally are needed, which would result in early identification of problems and save a great deal of time and money. The FEFC had regional inspectors and accountants who kept colleges under unpublished review. The approach was helpful to colleges and to the FEFC. The present systems seem designed to minimize the risk of embarrassment for government rather than providing an effective way to avoid failures before they happen to the detriment of learners. Under present procedures, failure can be presented as the sole responsibility of the colleges; government has power without responsibility.

Reflections in 2014

So what are the lessons for leadership from the last 21 years? The essential ingredients have not changed: appropriate educational mission and outward-looking strategy, shared leadership at all levels, open communication and respect for all staff, efficient management and uncompromising professionalism and determination for the college to succeed. Today there is certainly more understanding of what is involved in college leadership in its own terms than there was in 1993, and there have been demonstrable improvements in much leadership and management.

Many senior staff now share a language about leadership. But as Richard Atkins pointed out, 'Some people only talk it, but don't walk it. Changing the culture is a slow process.' A successful culture can be quickly destabilized and the loss of effective leadership follows. In 2013/14 Ofsted inspected 112 colleges – 62 per cent of GFEs and 67 per cent of SFCs were judged good or outstanding (Ofsted, 2014). Leading a large college – and most colleges are large – is a difficult and complex job.

There are still big opportunities for colleges, but these are closely balanced by threats and risks. Leaders are responsible for the correct strategic positioning of the college and part of this requires investment in research and innovation around teaching and learning. In difficult circumstances, a college leadership also needs to maintain independent thinking and innovations based on that college's own mission. As always, the future requires leadership capable of inspiring a sense of purpose and responsibility, and 'followership' amongst all staff combined with a willingness to innovate and change. There must be values underpinning the vision informed by public ethics. Success itself is also a significant factor in making a college dynamic and self-critical and holding everyone accountable.

Acknowledgements

The views expressed in this chapter are my own and, unless otherwise attributed, I am responsible for content and inaccuracies. But this chapter could not have been written without help from many individuals, who have been most generous of their time and ideas. They have between them over 110 years of successfully leading colleges. First, I must acknowledge my debt to Frank McLoughlin, City and Islington College, with whom I have discussed these matters for the past 21 years and who encouraged me in writing this chapter with ideas and feedback. I am also most grateful to Ian Pryce, Bedford College, and Ken Warman, Brooke House Sixth Form College (BSix), for their ideas and help with the chapter. I conducted a series of structured interviews around college leadership with Richard Atkins (Exeter College and President of the Association of Colleges, 2014), Wally Brown (formerly City of Liverpool College), Geoff Hall (formerly of the FEFC and New College Nottingham), Jane O'Neil (formerly College of Haringey, Enfield and North East London), Susan Pember (formerly Canterbury College and the DfE), Lynne Sedgmore (formerly Guildford College, CEL and the 157 Group), Mike Sheehan (Wigan and Leigh College), Geoff Stanton (UCL Institute of Education), Gary Warke (Hull College Group), and Kathryn James (Education and Training Foundation). I must also acknowledge my debt to Andrew Morris with whom I researched, interviewed 69 staff and students, and wrote *City and Islington College: The first twenty years 1993–2013*. We learned a great deal together, some of which is reflected in this chapter.

References

157 Group (2014) *Leadership conversation – video think pieces*. Online. www.157group.co.uk/practice (accessed 9 September 2014).

157 Group and CfBT Education Trust (2011) *Leading Learning in Further Education – Thinkpiece*. Online. www.157group.co.uk/practice (accessed 9 September 2014).

157 Group and City & Guilds (2013) *Pedagogic Leadership: Creating cultures and practices for outstanding vocational education*. Bill Lucas and Guy Claxton. Online. www.157group.co.uk/practice (accessed 9 September 2014).

Association of Colleges (AoC) (2014) *English Colleges' Code of Good Governance: Consultation draft*. Online. www.aoc.co.uk/publications/consultation-the-english-colleges-code-good-governance (accessed 15 December).

Centre for Education and Industry (CEI) University of Warwick (2003) *An Evaluation of Mergers in the Further Education Sector: 1996–2000 Research Report 459*. London: Department of Education and Skills.

Collins, J.C. (2001) *Good to Great: Why some companies make the leap ... and others don't*. London: Collins.

Commission on Adult Vocational Teaching and Learning (CAVTL) (2013) *It's about work ... Excellent adult vocational adult teaching and learning*. Online. www.excellencegateway.org.uk/cavtl (accessed 27 December 2014).

Department for Business, Innovation and Skills (BIS) (2014) *Further Education Commissioner Annual Report 2013/14*. Online. www.gov.uk/government/uploads/system/uploads/attachment_data/file/375383/bis-14-1209-further-education-commissioner-annual-report.pdf (accessed 17 December 2014).

Department for Education (DfE) (2010) *The Importance of Teaching: The schools White Paper 2010 Cm7980*. London: HMSO.

FE Week (2014) 'New SFA Chief Peter Lauener reveals college finance concerns'. 15 December, 6 Online. www.feweek.co.uk (accessed 27 December 2014).

Goleman, D. (1998) *Working with Emotional Intelligence*. London: Bloomsbury.

Holden, R. (2004) *What is Leadership? Leadership South West Research Report 1* University of Exeter Centre for Leadership Studies Online. www.leadershipsouthwest.com (accessed 12 December 2014).

Jupp, T., and Morris, A. (2013) *City and Islington College – The first twenty years 1993 to 2013*. London: City and Islington College.

Kennedy, H. (1997) *Learning Works: Widening participation in further education*. Coventry: FEFC.

Leitch, S. (2006) *Prosperity for All in the Global Economy*. Online. http://webarchive.nationalarchives.gov.uk/20130129110402/http://www.hm-treasury.gov.uk/leitch (accessed 31 March 2015).

McClure, R. (2000) *Recurrent Funding*. In Smithers, A., and Robinson, P. (eds) *Further Education Re-formed*. London: Falmer Press, 37–59.

Ofsted (2004) *Why Colleges Succeed* reference HMI2409 Online. http://dera.ioe.ac.uk/5184/1/Why%20colleges%20succeed%20%28PDF%20format%29.pdf (accessed 31 March 2015).

— (2012) *How Colleges Improve* reference 120166 Online. www.aoc.co.uk/sites/default/files/How%20Colleges%20Improve%202012.pdf (accessed 31 March 2015).

— (2014a) *Common Inspection Framework for Further Education and Skills* Online. www.ofsted.gov.uk/resources120062 (accessed 19 December 2014).

— (2014b) Annual Report 2013/14 further education and skills report London Online www.gov.uk/government/publications/ofsted-annual-report-201314-further-education-and-skills-report (accessed 31 March 2015).

Rospigliosi, G. (2000) *Franchising*. In Smithers, A., and Robinson, P. (eds) *Further Education Re-formed*. London: Falmer Press, 152–9.

Schein, E. (1987) *Organizational Culture and Leadership*. San Francisco: Jossey-Bass.

Senge, P. (1990) *The Fifth Discipline: The art and practice of the learning organization*. New York: Century Business Books.

Tomlinson, J. (1996) *Inclusive Learning: The report of the Learning Difficulties and Disabilities Committee of the FEFC*. London: HMSO.

Walker, E., and Fletcher, M. (2013) *The Black Leadership Initiative: The first ten years*. Online. http://webarchive.nationalarchives.gov.uk/20130802100617/http:/lsis.org.uk/sites/www.lsis.org.uk/files/LSIS-TBLI-Full-Report.pdf (accessed 31 March 2015).

Chapter 10

The future for FE colleges in England: The case for a new post-incorporation model

Ann Hodgson and Ken Spours

Introduction

In this final chapter we will suggest that the incorporation logic that has guided general further education colleges (GFEs) in England for the past twenty years has now reached a crossroads. This is due to a variety of circumstances, including the system legacy of incorporation; the socio-economic changes that have had a major impact on the UK (and world) economy; and the effects of the Conservative–Liberal Democrat Coalition Government's neo-liberal approach to education, particularly its focus on schools and the academic track and its austerity approach to the economy.

We will argue that it is time to start thinking in post-incorporation terms, which go beyond the logic of top-down managerialism and marketization that all shades of government have, in their different ways, pursued since the early 1990s. This post-incorporation thinking does not, however, mark a return to the bureaucratic and highly variable local authority approach of the past. Rather, it seeks to chart a third course in which GFEs play a decisive and leading role in a new, more democratically accountable regional and local landscape that is part of a wider rebalancing of policy and governance relationships between national and local power and policymaking.

In their contribution to what might be called 'local/regional vocational education and training (VET) and lifelong ecosystems' GFEs would move towards a stronger technical and vocational leadership role, be more focused on learners at 19+, and better integrated into a more unified tertiary system that includes vocational higher education. At the same time, we do not see GFEs abandoning their social inclusion role. Rather, they should be working with other institutions, such as sixth form colleges and school sixth forms that would need to become more comprehensive and inclusive, so that social inclusion becomes a shared area of responsibility and not just the preserve of GFEs and Independent Learning Providers

(ILPs). Nor do we see a contradiction between vocational specialization and lifelong learning. These roles too may be more shared with other providers in the local landscape, but with GFEs, because of their size and vocational expertise, playing a leading role.

What we thus envisage is a new model of FE – a 'public social partnership' approach that contrasts with the privatized and marketized 'social enterprise' model that the Coalition seeks. In November 2014 Nick Boles, Minister of State for Skills and Equalities, referred to GFEs as 'social enterprises' in his letter to the Chairs of FE College Corporations and FE College Principals. Although in the same letter he also noted the 14 interventions into GFEs made by the government-appointed FE Commissioner in the year 2013/14 (Boles, 2014). We think that this strongly area-based, vocational, and collaborative approach can build on the best that GFEs have to offer and provide the environment within which they can use their responsive and entrepreneurial capacities to make a unique contribution to local and regional skills ecosystems. (For further discussion of regional skills ecosystems see Finegold, 1999; Buchanan *et al.*, 2001; Hodgson and Spours, 2013a; Hodgson and Spours 2013b.)

These arguments begin to address the questions arising from previous chapters by making an assessment of the gains and limitations of incorporation; responding to the continued identity crisis for GFEs; envisaging a future that builds on what they do best – fostering vocational knowledge and skill; shaping localities; providing opportunities to learn throughout the life-course – and devising a new system of governance that, unlike incorporation, applies to all providers and not just to the FE sector.

GFEs over the past two decades: Reflections on earlier chapters

Chapter 1 noted the importance of raising the profile of the further education sector because of its relative invisibility in the education and training system, despite the very large number of learners who study in GFEs, sixth form colleges (SFCs), and independent learning providers (ILPs) and the crucial role that it plays in VET and lifelong learning. Because of the size and diversity of the sector we focused primarily on GFEs in England. Subsequent chapters have discussed various aspects of the work of GFEs as a way of understanding and appraising their role and purpose within the English education and training system and have, in different ways, evaluated the impact of incorporation on colleges within the wider economic and political landscape over the last 21 years. Drawing on these, we reflect on two themes as a starting point for a wider discussion about the future of GFEs in England.

The effects of incorporation

Given the landmark change in the governance and funding of FE colleges in 1992, previous chapters have highlighted the paradox between institutional freedom and autonomy, on the one hand, and constant central government intervention and steering on the other. While this has taken different forms under the Further Education Funding Council (FEFC), the Learning and Skills Council (LSC), and the Coalition Government, as Chapter 8 points out there has never been a period when colleges entirely set their own agendas. However, it could be argued that since incorporation colleges have been much more aware of their role as major providers in a locality or region with the need to recruit students, to compete, to be adaptable and innovative, and to grow at reduced unit cost. They have also learned to respond to constant national policy and funding steers.

Earlier chapters are divided about whether, following incorporation, GFEs in England constituted a distinct national sector. Whatever position is taken on this, it is undoubtedly the case that these institutions play a role that no other provider does and have increasingly taken on features of a distinctive sector through using their professional associations – for example, the Association of Colleges (AoC) and the 157 Group – to raise their profile as an important national player and to lobby policymakers. At the same time, GFEs have been subjected to considerable policy turbulence. This is partially perceived as having been possible because of their lower status when compared with schools and universities. However, it is also the result of the way that individual GFEs have developed in often unforeseen ways since incorporation and have frightened policymakers into periodically reining them back through powerful central steering mechanisms, even if the dominant rhetoric has been one of freedom and autonomy. GFEs' continuing dependence on national funding, despite a growing trend to look to alternative sources, has nevertheless kept them dancing to the tune of their political masters and has had a particularly powerful effect on the composition of their learners – for example, the rise in the number of young people they serve and the reduction in adult enrolments (see Chapter 3).

Despite this, over the past 20 years, there have been considerable achievements – post-16 participation, retention, and success rates have risen; GFE buildings have been transformed; regular national and international Skills Competitions have provided exciting platforms to showcase the excellent work that GFEs and other FE providers support;

GFEs have become much more adept at carrying out self-assessment and devising their own quality assurance systems; and many colleges now have an international as well as a national, regional, and local profile. But there have also been downsides. As Chapter 5 points out, staff morale remains fragile and conditions of service for staff in GFEs remain worse than for those in schools or universities. This concern about professional status, together with notable instances of poor management style and 'gaming' behaviour (see Chapters 8 and 9), has tarnished the reputation of the sector. Furthermore, there has been a continuing reduction in student course hours in GFEs, which cannot be fully compensated for by new technologies, and clear winners and losers in the competition for learners, with some colleges thriving and others closing or facing merger. It could be argued, moreover, that in some instances funding steers have led GFEs to put financial viability above the needs of their students, employers, or their relationship with their local communities.

Some of this can be put down to the freedoms that incorporation brought with it and may well not have happened in the same way without incorporation, but wider social, political, and economic factors have also had a major part to play and it is to these that we now turn.

The powerful influence of wider social, economic, and political factors

It is widely recognized that the development of all public services has been affected by what is commonly termed the New Public Management (NPM) that is associated with a neo-liberal approach to policy (Newman, 2000; Ainley, 2004). Going back nearly thirty years, NPM refers to changes in the nature of governance of the public sector, which has focused on the idea of the 'purchaser/provider split' and the use of particular forms of accountability and policy levers – for example performance measures, inspection, funding – that go hand-in-hand with the idea of a marketplace for public services. While in theory this was intended to enhance quality at lower levels of cost, avoid bureaucracy, give greater autonomy to public service providers, and more power to the users (customers) of these services, in practice in England it has resulted in a growth of central policy steering and a reduction in the role for democratically elected local government without the benefits of a greater voice for the users or a reduction in bureaucratic processes (Coffield *et al.*, 2007). This approach to governance can be seen across not only education, but also the health service and parts of the welfare system.

However, it could be argued that NPM was experienced by GFEs in an extreme form because of the financial pressures on them in the early 1990s, together with their less prominent political profile as providers for 'other peoples' children'. GFEs were subjected to a level of experimentation that would have been inconceivable in schools and universities. The NPM period heralded by incorporation was not an entirely even experience due to changes in government and in policy emphasis. As earlier chapters have noted, there was a brief period under the LSC where a greater emphasis was placed on local planning, coordination, and area-wide inspections, but this proved to be a fleeting interlude amid a general move towards marketization and central steering.

Behind these governance developments lay wider economic and social trends that impacted on education and training generally, but had a strong effect on GFEs. Fluctuations in the labour market and the long-term decline in 'youth jobs' (Ainley and Allen, 2013) hit GFEs particularly hard because they had to substitute for jobs and apprenticeships. Moreover in times of austerity, schooling and even higher education take precedence over further education in terms of their claim on public expenditure even though GFEs do not on the whole cater for the type of students who are fully capable of self-funding.

It is impossible also to understand the position of GFEs without taking into consideration the dominance of academic over vocational education in the perception of politicians and the wider public. Broadly speaking, the middle classes do not send their children to GFEs and vocational education still struggles for recognition and esteem.

These wider political, governance, economic, and social factors impact on GFEs particularly strongly because of their location between phases of education, between better-known education institutions and between the education system and the labour market. One way of understanding this position of GFEs is to see them as located on a 'negative nexus' and subject to the combined effects of powerful factors that trap them in a 'low recognition/low status/unclear identity' syndrome. Along with those already discussed above, these factors include the evolution and crisis of the economy over the past two decades with its negative effects on the youth labour market; the subsequent rise in post-16 participation and the need to cater for a wider range of learners (see Chapter 3); the increasing marketization of the education system and the effects of competition from school sixth forms (see Chapter 8); together with constant reform of the qualifications system that largely determines the FE curriculum (see Chapter 4). Moreover, GFEs have become responsible for those students that other institutions do not want, but often without the necessary recognition for their efforts or the funding to cater adequately for them. At the same time, they often struggle to provide the strongly vocational programmes and experiences that many learners are seeking from GFEs because they do not have sufficient employer involvement or access to youth jobs.

Despite the sterling, innovative, and often difficult work that GFEs do, sitting on the 'negative nexus' is not comfortable. It was made somewhat less uncomfortable by some serious investment under the previous Labour Government, at least until the economic crash in 2008. However, the consequences of occupying this nexus have deteriorated under the Conservative–Liberal Democrat Coalition Government. Over the last five years, GFEs have been subjected to further policy change, including the shift towards academies and academic learning, further privatization of the education system, greater deregulation in terms of professional qualifications, and, crucially, financial cuts as a result of austerity policies. Vince Cable's revelation that officials from the Department for Business, Innovation and Skills proposed that FE colleges be abolished to save money and no one would notice shows just how peripheral GFEs have become to this government (Wheeler, 2014).

Because of this combination of wider factors and recent policy shifts, not least the Raising of the Participation Age to 18 by 2015, GFEs could now be considered to be at a crossroads where radical rethinking is required in order to ensure that their potential for positive social, economic, and educational purposes can be harnessed. In the remainder of this chapter we will discuss the dimensions of what we term a 'post-incorporation landscape' that is designed to take GFEs out of the 'low recognition/low status/unclear identity' syndrome and to turn their unique position on the nexus between education and employment into a benefit rather than a deficit.

Ten dimensions of a post-incorporation landscape

In the light of this assessment, how might we see the future for GFEs and what needs to change to allow them to achieve their unique and rightful place within the English education and training system? Below we propose ten interconnected dimensions of thinking and reform, some of which are partially underway but need further development and others of which require more fundamental change.

1. The case for a post-incorporation model

The first battle is to make a convincing case for a post-incorporation model that recognizes the limitations of both top-down political managerialism and marketization, which in combination have produced an unstable and unsustainable landscape for GFEs in England. As each of the earlier chapters in this book demonstrates, the gains associated with these approaches may have run their course, much has also been lost and we now need to think and talk in new terms. This then raises questions about what any new model might comprise, what governance arrangements need to be put in place, and, crucially for our discussion here, what role GFEs would play in this new landscape.

2. Colleges as local and regional economic and vocational hubs

Along with other chapters in this book, and in line with earlier work in this area (Hodgson and Spours, 2013a; Hodgson and Spours, 2013b), we believe that GFEs have a pivotal role to play at the local and regional levels. This means envisaging them less as a distinct national sector, comprising a number of individual institutions, and more as the hub in a local/regional VET and lifelong learning ecosystem. Within this conception they would be able to return to their traditional roots and to exploit fully their expertise and facilities as specialists in technical, vocational, and adult learning. In order for GFEs to play this part, however, there would need to be changes in the roles of other 14–19 providers. The number of school sixth forms (particularly those with small numbers of learners) would need to be reduced, with those that survive making general education programmes available at all levels, rather than simply at Level 3. These institutions would be complemented by, and feed into, more comprehensive sixth form/tertiary colleges for younger learners that focused primarily on general and applied learning. As now, ILPs would continue to offer a rich variety of niche programmes for specific groups of learners, mainly in the areas of work-based learning and basic skills provision. Higher education institutions would also play an important part in this local/regional conception alongside their role as national and international providers. Together these five sets of providers would need to see themselves as part of collaborative local and regional groupings, whichever scale is more appropriate to the geographical area. This does not suggest a 'one-size fits all' approach in each locality/region – each area would need to determine what configuration of providers most effectively served the needs of the local community and local/regional labour market, depending on demographics, geography, and transport links as well as historical and cultural factors. However, there would be greater clarity about the main roles of each of the five provider groups, with the potential for better public understanding of their purposes and functions, a clearer channel of communication between education and the workplace and less wasteful duplication of provision.

It is possible to see the beginnings of this approach in Scotland, Wales, and Northern Ireland, where GFEs have been merged into regional groupings and focus more on adults and technical specialization, right through to the highest levels, rather than on younger learners and second chance general education – see Chapter 1.

What we are suggesting, therefore, is that GFEs in England also begin to take on a leading role in a reconfigured local and regional post-incorporation landscape.

3. A new devolution context for England

The Scottish referendum on whether to remain as part of the UK or to become an independent country has brought notions of devolution very much to the fore over the past year. While ideas about devolving more powers to regions and localities have been bubbling away under the surface on both sides of the political divide (Heseltine, 2012; Adonis, 2014), suddenly there is a greater impetus for devolution, not just to the constituent countries of the UK, but also to regions. London has seen itself as a distinctive region for some time, of course, and has its own elected mayor and regional governance structure. In November 2014, however, the Chancellor, George Osborne, announced a formal agreement between the government and the Greater Manchester Combined Authority (GMCA) to create a directly elected mayor for the city and also to devolve responsibility for a number of areas of policy, including adult skills, to the GMCA (see gov.uk, 2014).

It is important, therefore, that GFEs catch the tide of devolution to regions and localities so that they can fully embrace their identity and function as hubs of VET and lifelong learning and manage this role both in relation to the other providers in their community and to local/regional employers.

4. A new role for national government – The end of policy micromanagement

In addition to its support for devolution to regions and localities, national government also needs to play its part in encouraging collaborative behaviour at the local and regional levels. This means moving away from top-down policy levers that focus on competition between providers for students and funding; high profile performance measures that highlight institutional ranking; punitive inspections that encourage conformity rather than innovation; and the constant introduction of new types of providers into the system to stimulate the market (see Chapter 8). Rather, there needs to be a more facilitative national policy framework that sets national standards, priorities, and objectives, but encourages a climate of longer-term planning, area-wide funding and jointly owned performance measures related to progression and learner destinations. Alongside its quality assurance role, the inspectorate should be promoting collaborative practices that support effective and exciting area-based provision, closer working arrangements between education providers and employers and professional learning through subject and sectoral communities of practice coming together to discuss curriculum development and to improve teaching, learning and assessment. In our view it is this type of climate that would provide the space for gradual change, stability, and support for local system building while continuing to encourage the innovation and entrepreneurialism that has been one of the major strengths of the FE sector.

We would suggest that, as in Scotland, further and higher education are brought together in a joint national funding council, but that resources are then devolved to the regional and local levels to be distributed by a body that represents all local and regional social and economic partners and education providers. Local Enterprise Partnerships (LEPs) and Local Authorities (LAs) are the only existing organizations that might fulfil this role, but the former still have patchy geographical coverage and are not yet representative of all relevant stakeholders and the latter do not have the capacity or reach to undertake this task effectively. As we discuss in more detail below, there is thus a case for the formation of a new body that would be responsible for overseeing further education provision in the locality or sub-region.

5. New forms of accountability – A more democratic approach

The question of to whom GFEs in England are accountable is one that has resonated throughout the chapters of this book and is discussed in some depth in Chapters 7 and 8. Are GFEs simply accountable to their staff, current learner community, and governors? Or should they also be accountable to their local communities, including potential future learners, employers, and other education providers in the locality, as well as to their regional and national professional associations?

Under incorporation it is the governors of the corporation of each GFE who have ultimate responsibility for the strategic direction and finances of the college, with the principal and senior management team reporting regularly to their board on how they are managing the day-to-day business of the organization. Chapter 7 discusses the major weakness in these arrangements – the difficulty of recruiting sufficient governors that represent and reflect the locality, but who also have the skills to both support and challenge the senior management team and the time to take on what has become an onerous and often bureaucratic task.

There is also a question of how democratically colleges work internally in terms of their staff and students. In some GFEs staff and students are actively involved in the key decision-making processes of the organization through bodies such as Student Councils and Staff Forums and participate fully in quality assurance processes, such as regular student and staff surveys, and observation of teaching and learning. However, this is not universally the case.

But even were the governors to be broadly representative of the local community, and colleges' internal democratic processes working transparently and effectively, this does not address the role of the GFE within its 'local learning ecology' or the nature of local democratic accountability. In the more devolved post-incorporation model we have begun to discuss above, there is a need for accountability at a wide level across the locality/region. The Compass Enquiry paper on further education and lifelong learning (Edwards and Yarnit, 2014) has identified a number of issues that would require greater coordination and collaboration across a local area:

- organizing provision for 14–19-year olds, including students with learning disabilities, as they move between institutions or leave education altogether
- reducing the number of young people not in employment, education, or training (NEETs)
- matching skills provision to local labour market demand
- ensuring ancillary services, such as local transport or the provision of regularly updated directories of provision support rather than undermine the take up of opportunities.

It has also been suggested that there should be a split within local government between educational management and oversight. The former, which would include planning and delivery to a locally devised strategic plan, would be undertaken by LA officers in collaboration with local education providers and voluntary and community organizations. The oversight function would be undertaken by a Local Education Board (LEB), comprising elected members and representatives of key stakeholders, which would review progress on the local strategic plan and make recommendations for changes where appropriate. In their proposals the Compass Enquiry envisages the LEB, which might represent one large, or a cluster of smaller, LAs, working with the LEP on issues related to economic development and employment. LEBs in turn would be accountable to Ofsted via area-wide reviews.

We broadly concur with these proposals, although we are agnostic about the name LEB and, as indicated above, we still have concerns about the reach and representativeness of LEPs in their current conception (a concern shared by Ofsted – see Ofsted, 2014: 17). What is important, however, is to involve employers more actively in strategic planning at the local level not only because of their vital role in providing jobs and apprenticeships, but also because of the potential for the formation of deeper partnerships between employers and GFEs that will create both innovative and relevant vocational programmes and new developments in workplace organization and practices. It is in this area – what has been referred to by the Commission on Adult Vocational Teaching and Learning (CAVTL) as the 'two-way street' (CAVTL, 2013) – that we see an important leadership role for GFEs working also in partnership with local HE providers in relation to higher level vocational provision.

6. New forms of collaborative professionalism

The post-incorporation model will also make new demands of those working in GFEs, just as incorporation has done (see Chapters 5 and 9). As we have argued elsewhere (Hodgson and Spours, 2013c), while 'dual professionalism' has undoubtedly been a useful way of conceptualizing the role of the GFE teacher as both expert in her/his vocational area and in teaching and learning, we do not think this is enough for the model that we have described above. Collaborating with other providers and wider social partners in the locality requires a broader set of skills and knowledge, so we have proposed the concept of 'triple professionalism'. This, we have suggested, requires a more political mode of engagement and an ability to work on connected scales – institutional, local, regional, national, and international. The recently published *Professional Standards for Teachers and Trainers in Education and Training – England* (Education and Training Foundation, 2014) is a good starting point with its emphasis on reflective practice, updating vocational and pedagogical knowledge, and using research to improve practice, but it does not emphasize strongly enough the need for the active collaboration and democratic engagement that is required for the post-incorporation model we are proposing.

In this model, practitioners would not only be taking charge of their own professional learning to build on the knowledge and skills gained through initial teacher education, but would also ensure that they engaged with professional networks and communities of practice that were outside their own organization. Alongside the importance of keeping abreast of national and international research and development in their subject area, which many practitioners already do, there would be a need to work more actively in partnership with others in the local community. Coming into contact with professionals working with similar learners but in different institutional contexts or services and using a different approach would not only enhance their own professional learning, but would also begin to break down barriers between providers within the local community and create a stronger sense of shared common purpose. Similarly, partnering local employers on joint research, reciprocal work shadowing, or locally based projects would increase mutual understanding and forge the kind of relationships that would ultimately benefit learners, employers, and the local community. This, we suggest, requires a third dimension of professionalism, hence our argument for 'triple' rather than 'dual professionals'.

However, this view of the role of professionals within GFE requires recognition by principals and senior managers of the need for teachers and others who support learners to be given the resources, time, and space to benefit from the professional learning opportunities that accompany working across different scalings and with different partners (See IfL/157 Group/IOE, 2014). This means seeing the college as both a workplace and a learning organization and creating the 'expansive learning environments' that Alison Fuller and Lorna Unwin describe (Fuller and Unwin, 2004). It also calls for a new form of leadership that emphasizes the viability of individual institutions alongside the health of the local learning system. This form of 'system leadership' will require additional capacities of college leaders (see Chapter 9).

At the national level, the Commission on Adult Vocational Teaching and Learning's (CAVTL) proposal for a national Vocational Education and Training Centre to take responsibility for the research and development of vocational education and training (VET) has been seen as a way of raising the profile of VET, ensuring a stronger connection between practice and theory and providing a hub for 'the development and sharing of effective vocational teaching, learning and leadership practice' (McLoughlin, 2014: 15).

7. New roles for other education providers in a more unified tertiary system

But it is not only GFEs who need to reconsider the way they operate. Without changes in the way that others work at the local level, GFEs will not be able to fulfil their role as specialists in vocational, technical, and adult education. If they are constantly having to play a remedial role in relation to young people because school sixth forms and sixth form colleges are not willing or able to support all those young people interested in pursuing general education, whatever their level of attainment, GFEs will not have the capacity to play a full part in the economic development of their area. Similarly, if higher education institutions are not prepared to work with GFEs and employers jointly to develop clear, locally accessible, higher level vocational and technical routes to and within employment, much as there were under the polytechnic system, then again GFEs will be unable to fulfil their potential as cutting-edge technical specialists.

In the post-incorporation model, therefore, in order for GFEs to come of age, all the other key players in the local learning ecology also need to grow up and make their collective contribution to the more unified tertiary system we are proposing. This would allow specialist equipment, facilities, and staff to be concentrated in one regional or local hub, which would not only be more cost effective but would also signal more clearly to potential students and employers where they might invest their time and money. Chapter 6, discussing the architecture of GFEs, demonstrates what can be done with imagination and resources to make VET more attractive as an option for young people and benefit the whole community at the same time.

8. Increased investment in lifelong learning

As several contributors to this book have argued (notably in Chapter 2), lifelong learning is a phrase that had its real heyday in the 1990s and early 2000s. However, while the phrase may have gone out of fashion, the concept is as important today as it was then. In fact, given the reduction in the number of adults participating in GFEs, our ageing population, and recent findings about the low levels of adult skills in England when compared with other countries (OECD, 2013), further thinking about lifelong learning is timely. As Schuller and Watson remind us in their seminal report on the Inquiry into Lifelong Learning, 'the right to learn throughout life is a human right' (Schuller and Watson, 2009: 2). They go on to suggest that public resources should be balanced more fairly over the life-course, that there should be a clear set of learning entitlements, and that more responsibility and power for this area of work should be devolved to the local level. All of this strongly resonates with the ideas already discussed about a post-incorporation model. While GFEs would not be the only institutions responsible for the provision of lifelong learning, they would be major players.

Moreover, if opportunities for lifelong learning at different stages from cradle to grave were made more transparent through LEBs and LEPs producing local progression maps, and providers were clearer about their mission and role, some of the current concerns about the lack of Careers Education Information Advice and Guidance (CEIAG) (e.g. Ofsted, 2013) could be addressed. By having a simpler and more transparent education and training system with an entitlement to lifelong learning, young people, adults, and employers would be clearer about where to go for what at the local level.

9. An enhanced curriculum and qualifications framework

Of course, it is not as straightforward as this. There are other barriers in the way of a simplified and progression-focused lifelong learning system. One major barrier is the complex qualifications system that faces young people when they are moving beyond compulsory education and making choices about their future education and career pathway, as well as adults as they look to upgrade their skills. This is particularly the case where vocational qualifications are concerned. Firstly, there are a very large number. At the 'It's About Work ...' National VET Conference in November 2014 when launching the OECD's report, *Skills Beyond School* (OECD, 2014), Simon Field noted that when it comes to vocational qualifications, 'some countries have too many, some have far too many and others have far, far too many'. England was in the final category, he suggested, and needed to do something to reduce the number of awards on offer. Secondly, and perhaps of more importance, in very many cases the currency and progression possibilities associated with each qualification are unclear (Wolf, 2011). This makes it difficult for all parties – providers, potential learners, and employers – to decide on which might be the best option.

So, while reducing the number of qualifications on offer, as the current government has been attempting to do, might be a useful first step, it is not the full answer. The Chair of CAVTL, Frank McLoughlin (2014), offered two helpful suggestions for addressing the issue of transparency and credibility of qualifications – that they should be co-designed and co-delivered by education providers and employers; and that they should contain a national core but also a locally tailored element that serves the needs of the local/regional labour market. As Chapter 4 has highlighted, this would both put GFEs and employers back in the driving seat, with a shared agenda for action in their local area, and also give learners a much clearer idea of what progression routes were on offer locally.

The CAVTL also suggested four curriculum features that should characterize all vocational qualifications (McLouglin, 2014: 13; original emphasis):

- 'the development of *knowledge*
- combined with the development of *skills/practice*

- with opportunities for *practical problem solving* and *critical reflection* on experience
- within a *community of practice* that supports the *development of professional identity.*

These features suggest the need for a major element of work-based learning in vocational qualifications, something that the OECD (2014) and the UK Commission on Education and Skills (UKCES, 2013) have also both stressed. Other characteristics that the OECD report, which reviews vocational education across 20 countries, indicates are important for successful vocational qualifications are robust assessment; an outcomes-based design; a core of literacy and numeracy; and better articulation between higher level vocational awards and higher education systems.

While all of these features are undoubtedly important, we would suggest a number of provisos in the English context. Based on this country's experience of National Vocational Qualifications (NVQs), outcomes-based designs need to be underpinned by a strong general education component and the opportunity for critical reflection. Robust assessment should not be translated purely as the need for external examination, whether written or oral, but should also allow for different modes (e.g. observation in the workplace, e-assessments, project-based work) in order to ensure validity as well as reliability. Moreover, there is a need for both education provider validation and a strong locally based quality assurance process that sees its function not only as assessing student work, but also as a means of stimulating employer–provider dialogue and understanding, and the building of the type of active professional communities of practice described earlier. Finally, the links between higher vocational qualifications and the higher education system in England already exist to some extent with Foundation Degrees and GFE–university partnerships. However, what has been lost are the clarity and strong sense of local/regional identity that existed under the polytechnic system and with Higher National Certificates and Diplomas.

These common features of the vocational curriculum and qualifications framework also need further calibration to meet the specific needs of adults for continuing vocational education and training (CVET) and for young people in terms of initial vocational education and training (IVET).

Qualifications designed for CVET require an emphasis on flexibility in both design and delivery – they need to be available part-time, as short courses, in a modular mode, as distance learning and with opportunities for accreditation of prior learning.

Those for IVET, on the other hand, need to ensure an initial educational foundation for young people upon which they can build. It is therefore important to include a strong component of general education and twenty-first century competences, such as problem solving, research skills, communication and mathematical skills, and team working. Here we have in mind the development of a unified National Baccalaureate at Levels 2 and 3 with a strong vocational variant that would provide a bridge to both work and vocational higher education and that would be taken at 18 or 19 but could be completed in the workplace. The term National Baccalaureate has been used by the Independent Skills Taskforce (2014) in its third report, *Qualifications Matter: Improving the curriculum and assessment for all.* The National Baccalaureate vocational variant could be seen as a signature qualification for English GFEs and would build on full BTEC awards, ideas currently being developed around the TechBac (see City & Guilds, 2014) and the new version of the Welsh Bac (see Welsh Baccalaureate, 2015).

In order to preserve the high quality and distinctiveness of both the National Baccalaureate and Apprenticeship programmes, it would be necessary, as McLoughlin argues (McLoughlin, 2014: 16), to develop broad-based and motivational pre-vocational awards to ensure that young people (and some adults) were effectively prepared before being ready to access the prestigious National Baccalaureate or Apprenticeship programmes.

10. Integrating employers into the VET system

Apprenticeship is seen by all countries as the VET gold standard and there is cross-party support in this country for its extension. Currently, however, according to UKCES (2014) only 10 per cent of UK employers offer apprenticeships and the majority of these are still at Level 2 with a much smaller number at Level 3 and above and only 30 per cent of workplaces offering work experience.

The task is therefore to increase the incentives for employers to offer apprenticeships and to play a more active role in VET programmes more generally. The recent OECD reports (OECD, 2010; OECD, 2014) on this topic suggest the importance of a social partnership approach involving employers, trades unions, and government in the design of apprenticeship frameworks and vocational qualifications as well as the need to demonstrate a 'business case logic'. The drive for a social partnership approach is unlikely to come from the current national government in England, but could be facilitated at the regional and local levels where it suggests a major leadership role for GFEs.

CAVTL has used a somewhat different language in its proposals for re-energizing the VET system: it refers to the 'two-way street' approach. By this it means GFEs and other VET providers not only seeing their role as providing off-the-job training, but also offering business support for employers in terms of professional development and changes to working practices.

On 13 November 2014 in a speech on Building Professional and Technical Skills Across the UK to the 'It's about work' National VET Conference in Birmingham, Michael Davis, Chief Executive of UKCES stated that according to his organization's employer surveys, when it comes to purchasing training, employers spend more money on private providers than they do on GFEs, and that for many employers the relevance of the training is more important than the cost. If GFEs are to increase their market share in this area, according to UKCES it means being clearer about their vocational mission and conveying this more carefully to employers as well as actively seeking to co-design and co-develop programmes with their clients. If this is done effectively, employers are more likely to see GFEs as their natural allies in local and regional economic development and regeneration.

Conclusion – The transition to a post-incorporation era

What is being proposed is a new post-incorporation era in which GFEs form the hub of a strong and transparent local and regional VET and lifelong learning ecosystem. Elements of this future already exist where GFEs focus on their localities and communities, collaborate with other education providers and employers, and have a good working relationship with local government. But this is not universally the case. The locally oriented GFE college still faces strong headwinds from funding regimes and national policy levers that can deflect it from its mission. It can also meet with indifference or even hostility from other providers that may be struggling to remain economically viable in what continues to be a strongly competitive environment.

So while it is important to discuss openly the need for a new era with more altruistic and collaborative institutions, there is also an important role for national government in encouraging a behaviour shift in all providers, including academies. And this will have to take place at a time when there is not a great deal of money to go round to incentivize partners to come to the table. What the new model requires, therefore, is change at all levels of governance – national, regional, local, and institutional – and by both providers and employers to bring a greater clarity of roles for education institutions and wider social partners in a more collaborative and economically connected local learning system. This governance framework has the potential to provide the environment within which innovative curriculum and pedagogic reform, deeper professional learning, new research and development, lifelong learning, and effective workplace practices could begin to flourish.

This rationalist scenario is not without its controversies, not least in relation to the issue of institutional autonomy. However, the future we envisage for colleges involves more not less freedom, helped by the distinction between 'freedom from' and 'freedom to' (Pratchett, 2004). Although incorporation promised freedom from outside interference, this has proved hard to realize because of constant national policy steering. Freedom to, on the other hand, appreciates institutional autonomy but places greater priority on the ability to work with others to bring about positive change for the locality. What we have discussed above is a new governance climate in which GFEs will experience greater stability and freedom in relation to funding, inspection, and performance management, but with new obligations to seek agreement with local partners.

Given the state of the economy and public finances, this new environment will undoubtedly be difficult. There will have to be rationalization of institutions and provision, not least because of demography, but these decisions are better made collaboratively and at the local level rather than being imposed from above or avoided altogether. The alternative would be more competition, more fragmentation, and greater inefficiencies in which the most vulnerable learners will inevitably lose out.

We began this book by reflecting on the relative 'invisibility' of the FE sector. In comparison with schools and universities, it is unlikely that national politicians or the national media will promote the profile of colleges. As this chapter has argued, their future visibility may lie less with being a discrete national sector and more with their role as hubs in the building of vibrant regional and sub-regional high skills ecosystems. It is local/regional employers and learners that have become successful vocational specialists who will help to raise the status of colleges in this new setting.

References

Adonis, A. (2014) *Mending the Fractured Economy: Smarter state, better jobs*. Online. www.yourbritain.org.uk/uploads/editor/files/Adonis_Review.pdf

Ainley, P. (2004) 'The new "market-state' and education"; *Journal of Education Policy*, 19 (4), 497–514.

Ainley, P., and Allen, M. (2013) 'Running up a down escalator in the middle of a class structure gone pear-shaped'. *Sociological Research Online*, 18 (1), Online. www.socresonline.org.uk/18/1/8.html (accessed 18 November 2014).

Boles, N. (2014) Letter to all Chairs of FE College Corporations, College Principals. 10 November. Online. www.gov.uk/government/uploads/system/uploads/attachment_data/file/373733/bis-14-1201-update-on-further-education-reform-nick-boles-letter-to-fe-and-sixth-form-college-chairs-10-november-2014.pdf (accessed 31 March 2015).

Buchanan, J., Schofield, K., Briggs, C., Considine, G., Hajer, P., Hawke, G., Kitay, J., Meagher, G., Macintyre, J., Mournier, A., and Ryan, S. (2001) *Beyond Flexibility: Skills and work in the future*. Sydney: NSW Board of Vocational Education and Training.

City & Guilds (2014) 'TechBac'. Online. http://techbac.com/ (accessed 31 March 2015).

Commission on Adult Vocational Teaching and Learning (CAVTL) (2013) *It's about work ... Excellent adult vocational teaching and learning*. Online. www.aoc.co.uk/sites/default/files/Its%20About%20Work.pdf (accessed 20 November 2014).

Coffield, F., Steer, R., Allen, R., Vignoles, A., Moss, G., and Vincent, C. (2007) *Public Sector Reform: Principles for improving the education system*. London: IOE Publications.

Education and Training Foundation (2014) *Professional Standards for Teachers and Trainers in Education and Training – England*. Online. www.et-foundation.co.uk/wp-content/uploads/2014/05/4991-Prof-standards-A4_4-2.pdf (accessed 31 March 2015).

Edwards, J., and Yarnit, M. (2014) Lifelong Learning and Further Education - Steps towards the good society: Proposals from Compass. Online. http://pascalobservatory.org/pascalnow/pascal-activities/news/lifelong-learning-and-further-education-steps-towards-good-society- (accessed 31 March 2015).

Finegold, D. (1999) 'Creating self-sustaining, high-skill ecosystems'. *Oxford Review of Economic Policy*, 15 (1), 60–81.

Fuller, A., and Unwin, L. (2004) 'Expansive learning environments: Integrating personal and organisational development'. In Rainbird, H., Fuller, A., and Munro, A. (eds) *Workplace Learning in Context*. London: Routledge, 107–18.

Gov.uk (2014) 'Manchester to get directly elected Mayor'. Online. www.gov.uk/government/news/manchester-to-get-directly-elected-mayor (accessed 31 March 2014).

Hodgson, A., and Spours, K. (2013a) 'An ecological analysis of the dynamics of localities: A 14+ low opportunity progression equilibrium in action'. *Journal of Education and Work*, 28 (1). Online. http://dx.doi.org/10.1080/13639080.2013.805187 (accessed 20 November 2014, requires subscription).

— (2013b) Tackling the crisis facing young people: Building 'high opportunity progression eco-systems', Oxford Review of Education, 39 (2), 211–28. Online. http://dx.doi.org/10.1080/03054985.2013.787923 (accessed 27 November 2014, requires subscription).

— (2013c) 'Why IfL should promote "triple professionalism"'. *InTuition*, Issue 13 16–18. Online. www.ifl.ac.uk/media/114820/InTuition13.pdf (accessed 20 November 2014).

Heseltine, M. (2012) *No Stone Unturned in the Pursuit of Growth*. Online. www.gov.uk/government/uploads/system/uploads/attachment_data/file/34648/12-1213-no-stone-unturned-in-pursuit-of-growth.pdf (accessed 20 November 2014).

Independent Skills Taskforce (2014) *Qualifications Matter: Improving the curriculum and assessment for all: The third report of the Independent Skills Taskforce*. Online. www.yourbritain.org.uk/uploads/editor/files/Skills_Taskforce_3rd_report.pdf (accessed 31 March 2015).

Institute for Learning (IfL)/157 Group/Institute of Education (IOE) (2014) *Professionalism in Further Education*. Online. www.ifl.ac.uk/media/1263118/Professionalism-in-further-education.pdf (accessed 20 November 2014).

McLoughlin, F. (2014) CAVTL: One Year On Review. Online. www.excellencegateway.org.uk/node/27691 (accessed 20 November 2014).

Newman, J. (2000) 'Beyond the new public management? Modernising public services'. In Clarke, J., Gewirtz, S., and McLaughlin. E. (eds) *New Managerialism, New Welfare?* London: Sage, 45–61.

OECD (2010) Learning for jobs, OECD reviews of vocational education and training, Paris: OECD.

— (2013) *OECD Skills Outlook 2013: First Results from the Survey of Adult Skills*. Paris: OECD.

— (2014) *Skills beyond schools: Synthesis report, OECD reviews of vocational education and training*. Paris: OECD Publishing.

Ofsted (2013) *Going in the right direction? Careers guidance in schools from September 2012*. Online. www.thecdi.net/write/News/News%20via%20Email%20Uploads/Going_in_the_right_direction_(Ofsted_Report).pdf (accessed 20 November 2014).

— (2014) *Report of Her Majesty's Chief Inspector – Further Education and Skills*. Online. www.gov.uk/government/uploads/system/uploads/attachment_data/file/384709/Ofsted_Annual_Report_201314_FE_and_Skills.pdf (accessed 16 December 2014).

Pratchett, L. (2004) 'Local Autonomy, Local Democracy and the "New Localism"'. *Political Studies*, 52 (2), 358–75.

Robson, J. (1998) 'A profession in crisis: Status, culture and identity in the further education college'. *Journal of Vocational Education and Training*, 50 (4), 585–607.

Schuller, T., and Watson., D (2009). Learning through Life: Inquiry into the future for lifelong learning. Leicester: NIACE.

UK Commission on Education and Skills (UKCES) (2013) *Review of Adult Vocational Qualifications in England (led by Nigel Whitehead)* Online. www.gov.uk/government/uploads/system/uploads/attachment_data/file/303906/review-of-adult-vocational-qualifications-in-england-final.pdf (accessed 20 November 2014).

UKCES (2014) *Growth through People*. Online. www.gov.uk/government/uploads/system/uploads/attachment_data/file/378810/14.11.26._GTP_V18.3_FINAL_FOR_WEB.pdf (accessed 27 November 2014).

Welsh Baccalaureate (2015) 'Welcome to the Welsh Baccalaureate website'. Online. www.welshbaccalaureate.org.uk/Welsh-Baccalaureate-Home-Page (accessed 25 March 2015).

Wheeler, B. (2014) 'Officials wanted to axe FE colleges – Vince Cable'. Online. www.bbc.co.uk/news/uk-politics-29496475 (accessed 20 November 2014).

Wolf, A. (2011) *Review of Vocational Qualifications: The Wolf Report.* Online. www.gov.uk/government/uploads/system/uploads/attachment_data/file/180504/ DFE-00031-2011.pdf (accessed 20 November 2014).

Index

Index